Donating to the
Library

# THE DIVIDEND GROWTH INVESTMENT STRATEGY

# THE DIVIDEND GROWTH INVESTMENT STRATEGY

## *How to Keep Your Retirement Income Doubling Every Five Years*

**RoxAnn Klugman, J.D., L.L.M.**

*Founder, Retirement and Estate Planning Services*

CITADEL PRESS
Kensington Publishing Corp.
www.kensingtonbooks.com

CITADEL PRESS books are published by

Kensington Publishing Corp.
850 Third Avenue
New York, NY 10022

All Kensington titles, imprints, and distributed lines are available at special quantity discounts for bulk purchases for sales promotions, premiums, fund raising, educational, or institutional use. Special book excerpts or customized printings can also be created to fit specific needs. For details, write or phone the office of the Kensington special sales manager: Kensington Publishing Corp., 850 Third Avenue, New York, NY 10022, attn: Special Sales Department, phone 1-800-221-2647.

Citadel Press and its logo are trademarks of Kensington Publishing Corp.

First Citadel printing: July 2001

10  9  8  7  6  5  4  3  2  1

Printed in the United States of America

Library of Congress Control Number 2001094647

ISBN 0-8065-2182-1

# CONTENTS

# PREFACE

I wrote this book based on Albert Einstein's theory of economics. Einstein's theory of economics? You always thought that he was a physicist. What does $E = mc^2$ have to do with wealth creation? If you are looking toward retirement, you are probably more interested in converting your assets into income than in converting mass into energy. The focus of this book derives from a lesser-known statement that Albert Einstein was reputed to have made, that *compound interest was the greatest mathematical discovery of all time!* Who are we to argue with Einstein? And what does this mean to us?

Compounding means plenty to each and every one of us; it is the way to build wealth. Anything that grows by compounding grows logarithmically. For those of you who having been doing your best to forget high school algebra, this means that as something increases, the amount of increase itself increases as time goes on. If you have a stock dividend that pays $1 per share and the dividend increases at 10 percent per year, the dividend will double in size every seven years. Thus, at the end of seven years, you will receive $2 per share. At the end of the next seven years, you will have increased your dividend, not by another $1 per share but by $2 a share, now totaling $4. Go on for another seven years and you will be at $8 per share. Another seven years and you are at $16 per share, then $32 the next seven years, then $64, then $128. Now you get the picture.

This book is about increasing your wealth, for retirement and for your loved ones after your death, through the magic of compounding. I will show you the ways to get a steady and fairly high rate of return over the many years that it takes to give compounding a chance to work. Historically, going back two centuries, the stock market has outperformed bonds, gold, and any other common investment vehicle, and this is where your money should be. I will show you how it is important to position your money early in life and not to wait for the day of retirement to decide what investments are needed or for the day they call for the priest to start planning for the disposal of your estate.

Most important, I will guide you through the traps that destroy your ability to compound your money. The two main traps are taxes and fees. John D. Rockefeller said, "The surest way to accumulate wealth is to make sure that you never pay taxes on income you don't use." You will find the way taxes destroy your wealth. Every time you sell a stock and take a capital gain, or every time you buy a mutual fund that turns over stocks, you pay taxes, taking one step backward for every two steps that you might have moved forward. In many instances, you may not even realize that your investments are generating the high taxes that you pay. This book will allow you to spot these traps and circumvent them.

Similarly, fees destroy your ability to create wealth. Consider that if you pay a 1 percent fee per year to manage your money, after twenty years, when you are ready to retire, your nest egg will be decreased by 17 percent. Consider, also, that many mutual funds charge up to 3 percent in fees, and variable annuities charge fees that are even higher. Think of what this does to your ability to accumulate wealth. If the mutual-fund manager can guarantee you that they can get you over 3 percent more than you could realize by doing it on your own, it might be worthwhile to turn your hard-earned money over to them: Their dirty little secret, however, is that they can't. In this book, you will get a detailed analysis of the pros, and mainly cons, of investing in mutual funds, bonds, and annuities as opposed to investing your money yourself in blue-chip companies with a long history of raising their dividends.

How are you going to do this? The plan that I developed, which I call the Dividend Growth Investment Strategy, has two main advantages. The first is purely economic; this plan allows you to grow your wealth without losing your money to Washington and Wall Street in the form of taxes and fees. The second advantage is psychological. Many people, myself included, are afraid to invest in the stock market because of the roller-coaster effect: the dizzying drops that make your life flash before your eyes while you imagine your retirement nest egg evaporating. No matter how much you know that the stock market—rationally—is the right place for your money, fear prevents you from taking advantage of the gains available to you. The Dividend Growth Investment Strategy provides a way to bolster your courage in the form of an escalator of dividends that steadily increase over time. The escalator will stiffen your spine, allowing you to stick with the roller coaster over the years necessary to create your wealth.

In reading this book, you will encounter more numbers and statistics than you will know what to do with. While the numbers are accurate, during the time between my writing of the book and your reading it, some of the circumstances and numbers will have changed. (Indeed, the numbers in the stock market change minute to minute.) I will stress that you should look to the broad principles that I put forth and use the numbers that I provide as illustrations and examples only. They are not meant to be used as specific rationales for specific investments. For instance, when I say that a mutual fund may charge 3 percent fees, there will be some managers that object, saying that their fund charges a lesser amount. This may be true, but it still does not get around the general principle that fees destroy compounding. *An overriding principle in this book is that you should be responsible for creating your own wealth.* When it is time for you to implement the Dividend Growth Investment Strategy, you will be ready to take charge and evaluate the specific numbers for any investment that you make. This is the reason that I included a chapter on researching your investments. The investments will be yours, not mine, and therefore you need to be comfortable that you are making the right decision. I hope that this book will help demystify the world of investing. You are capable of guiding your own future. You don't need to put your fate in the hands of a mutual-fund manager, a variable annuity salesman, or me.

Once you have mastered the principles of the Dividend Growth Investment Strategy, there is more to the book that you may find useful. I have included a large sample portfolio that may act as a starting point for your investment career and a large section on the specialized world of investing in tax-deferred plans, such as 401(k) or IRA accounts.

Throughout the book, I have also tried to stress how wealth accumulation can only occur in a capitalistic system. The trends toward bigger and bigger government, increasing government regulation, redistribution of wealth, and higher and higher taxes all decrease your ability to take care of yourself. Stay away from these traps as much as humanly possible. If you value your right to provide yourself a comfortable retirement, you should consider supporting that part of the political apparatus that calls for less government and lower taxes. Adam Smith, in *The Wealth of Nations,* said:

> The statesman who should attempt to direct private people in what manner they ought to employ their capitals, would not only load himself with a most unnecessary attention, but assume an authority which could safely be trusted to no council and senate whatever, and which would nowhere be so dangerous as in the hands of a man who had folly and presumption enough to fancy himself fit to exercise it.

# THE DIVIDEND GROWTH INVESTMENT STRATEGY

# 1

## THE ESCALATOR AND THE ROLLER COASTER

We all want, at some time in life, to have the freedom to retire. This may be to play golf, to change careers to something more enjoyable but less remunerative than your former job, to take care of your grandchildren, or to just relax after a hard life. Retirement means freedom. It gives you the freedom to do what *you* want, not what others tell you to do. To achieve this, you absolutely need *financial* freedom. Without adequate financial resources, you have no freedom at all. The great tragedy in many people's lives is that this goal is within reach but, through lack of planning and foresight, slips through their fingers.

How do you ensure your financial freedom? Social Security is great if you believe that it will be there when you retire and if you project that you can live comfortably on an income of under $12,000 a year. Pension plans and 401(k) plans are great, but not everyone has one. Both of these alternatives, moreover, rely on someone else coming up with a plan for you. You don't let anyone else plan for your marriage, for raising your children, or for the hobbies you pursue. Why should you leave the planning for one-third of your life to a complete stranger? The fact is, the person responsible for providing for your prosperous retirement is *you*.

"But that's not so easy," you say. "I don't make enough money to invest. Even if I had some extra cash, what do I do with it? The stock market is risky and complicated. Bonds don't pay much. There are three million mutual funds; I don't know which one will not lose my money. Ah, well, I might as well buy that new car."

The U.S. Trust Company recently surveyed investors to find out what drove their investment decisions. Their foremost worries were:

1. Inflation will diminish my retirement income.
2. The stock market will decline, and I will lose a significant portion of my principal.
3. My investments will not be able to support me in my retirement.
4. I myself do not have enough knowledge to properly manage my finances.
5. Markets and investments have become too complex for individuals to deal with.

At the same time, people respond to ads in the *Wall Street Journal* for investment vehicles that promise (with, of course, numerous caveats, disclaimers, references to the unknowability of the future, etc.) returns of 20 percent, 30 percent, 40 percent or more per year. They want to *get rich quick.*

Fear and greed are the two emotions that drive most investors. *It doesn't have to be this way.* This book is about the alternative, a long-term plan to continually increase your income and wealth with little risk and reasonable rewards. This investment strategy is as predictable as any investment tool that is available, and what is most important, it is a strategy that you can undertake yourself by easily understanding the underlying principles and by having confidence in the future.

Without a statistical doubt, the stock market is the best place to keep your money to grow for your later years. Most of us, however, view the stock market as a giant roller coaster; one that has more steep dips than upward climbs. It is simply too scary to put our money at risk in this way. In this book, I hope to convince you that the stock market also contains an escalator, one that allows you to stay invested and ride the roller coaster with something approaching peace of mind.

Before I describe the Dividend Growth Investment Strategy, I will illustrate the spectrum of approaches to retirement investing by successful and not-so-successful investors.

## APPROACHES TO RETIREMENT INVESTING

### Anne

Anne Scheiber was a lifelong federal government employee who never had a salary of more than $3,150 a year. She invested $5,000 in blue-chip stocks in 1944. When she died in 1995, her stocks were worth $22 million, and she was receiving annual dividend income from them of over $1 million. This is the goal that we should all be shooting for.

## Barbra

Barbra Streisand, the multimedia megastar, invested in a professional hedge fund. A hedge fund is an investment vehicle, often run by college professors and other geniuses, that are set up to balance assets that are going up in value along with "shorting" those that are going down. (Short-selling is borrowing securities, these could be stocks, bonds, national currencies, etc., from a brokerage firm and selling them, figuring to buy back the securities, at a lower price, return them to the brokerage house, and gain a profit from the decline in price.) The theory behind this is that you can make money in an up or down market. While some of these funds are conservative, others are very risky. Some are open only to those with hundreds of thousands to millions of dollars to invest, require investors to surrender their money for at least three years, give *no* information to the investors as to what the fund is doing with their money (indeed, they may remove you for even asking), and highly leverage their money, borrowing $100 to $300 for each $1 invested. Computers run the fund and do wonderfully as long as markets are acting as they are supposed to; occasionally, however, life doesn't act as planned (as when the Russian currency markets collapsed), and these funds can accumulate huge losses on both sides of their "hedge." According to news reports, Ms. Streisand, along with movie producer Jon Peters, lost millions of dollars in the collapse of one such fund. I will later show you how the principles illustrated by these hedge funds are exactly the opposite of those that we should embrace in order to assure a secure and prosperous retirement.

## Ron and Sue

Ron and Sue did not do badly for themselves, but they could have done a lot better. Ron, a successful certified public accountant, invested in municipal bonds during his working life. At retirement, he cashed them in and bought a basketful of utility stocks. These pay a high rate of dividends initially, but the growth of the stock price and dividends is very slow. Generally, electric utility stocks grow and raise their dividends at the rate of inflation. Their current portfolio is $1 million with an annual income of $60,000. Ron is recently deceased, and Sue is looking for ways to increase her income; the amount of her social security check was cut when Ron died, and her household expenses are fixed. Sue would have no reason to worry if they had used the Dividend Growth Investment Strategy. They should have invested in good-quality blue-chip stocks that grow on average 14 percent in annual dividends. Sue would now have a portfolio worth $16 million and an income from stock dividends of around $500,000. This would continue to double for her every five years. In the year 2003 her income would be approximately $1 million.

### Jack

Jack's recent dilemma is one that none of us wants to experience, but it is a common predicament. He is sixty years old. He happily retired at the end of 1997 with $630,000 in his 401(k) plan. He thought that he was set for life, until the market downturn in the summer of 1998. This market correction wiped out nearly half of his 401(k) mutual-fund investments, leaving him with a 401(k) value of $340,000. Jack was planning to spend down the $630,000 over his life expectancy. Now it is half gone after seven months of retirement, and Jack is wondering what to do.

### Beth

In the same market downturn, a local radio talk show received a call from Beth. She was distressed by the losses in her mutual funds in her retirement account and asked the host if she should sell all of her mutual funds and buy gold. This type of reaction is a pure panic attack. She needs a strategy that will allow her to know what her investments are and what they can be expected to do in the future according to historical data. High-quality stocks and their dividends will, over time, continue to grow in spite of occasional corrections. Gold, over the last two hundred years, has shown *no* net growth. If Beth had been utilizing the Dividend Growth Investment Strategy, the disastrous move of converting her assets to gold would never have crossed her mind.

### Airman Thompson

In the September 14, 1998, issue of *Newsweek,* Jane Bryant Quinn wrote about Airman First Class Marshall Thompson, who lost 30 percent of his $25,000 portfolio in the stock market over the summer slump. He took his money out and bought bonds. At the time of that article, the future was unsure, but from our perspective, we know that the market climbed 2,000 points and was reaching new highs again by the third week in November. Not only did Airman Thompson permanently lock in his 30 percent loss, but as we will see in chapter 4, he ended up in a dead-end investment.

## Bill

Bill, a dentist, had $14,000 in cash to spend. His broker had a hot tip on an initial public offering (IPO) of a computer chip maker for $14 per share, a no-brainer. Bill bought 1,000 shares, and when the stock dropped 50 percent in two weeks, Bill felt as if he had no brain. Within two years, the company was out of business, and Bill was out his $14,000.

## RoxAnn

RoxAnn (the name is familiar because this is the story of how I came to my investment philosophy) is a forty-something individual investor. In my twenties and thirties I worked as a periodontist (a DDS with a surgical subspecialty) part-time while raising my children. My husband is a physician who earns an income healthy enough to put us in the highest tax bracket. During the seventies and eighties we spent all the money we earned. I bought expensive clothes, we moved up in housing a number of times, and we bought expensive home furnishings and antiques as well as automobiles. At various times we had a second home.

Our investment strategy consisted of paying off the mortgage on our home. By 1993, we owned outright an expensive, beautiful home stuffed with stuff. What we didn't have was any money in the bank. We owned no stocks or bonds. My husband had a good pension plan that we vaguely felt would provide for our retirement.

At about that time we came to two very important conclusions. The first was that I was working for nothing. My part-time income, for tax purposes, was placed on top of my husband's, putting every dollar that I earned in the highest tax bracket of about 40 percent for the federal government, 8.5 percent for the state of Minnesota, and 15 percent for self-employed Social Security and self-employed Medicare. Add this up and it comes to 63.5 percent! Out of the remaining 36.5 percent I had to pay for my car, my work clothes, child care, and housecleaning. Add on to this the legal risks in running a dental practice (malpractice as well as the likelihood of running afoul of the ever-increasing mandates and regulations of the federal government) and it became obvious that my work was benefiting many people but not my family or me.

The second realization was that we wanted more freedom and security than the medical professions could afford us. We decided that for this, as well as other reasons, my husband might want to retire at fifty-five rather than the usual sixty-five. The problem was that his pension plan would not have matured enough by this age to support us for (hopefully) thirty years.

We needed to change the direction of our lives. The first two steps were psychologically hard but physically rather easy. I quit work, and we stopped spending money. I did the child care and housework myself, and we cut our ties with the antique dealers and landscape designers.

The third step, however, was more difficult. We knew that we had to save and invest for retirement, but how? In our previous life, our investments were limited to collectibles and a paid-up mortgage. We had no financial assets and were extremely distrustful of the stock market, viewing it as a big crapshoot. We were afraid that even if we invested in stocks that usually went up, we might end up like Jack, with a bear market destroying our wealth just when we needed it for retirement. We were also distrustful of financial planners in general, feeling that most of them had conflicts of interest between giving us the optimum advice and making a buck for themselves. I also felt that I was as intelligent as anyone that I could hire, so why shouldn't I be the one to best plan our finances?

We started in 1994. For the first time in our over twenty years of marriage, we actually had extra cash coming in (because we had stopped spending), and we could invest it. Our first plan was to invest in bonds. Over the first year we bought a load of tax-free municipal bonds and another load of treasury strips (I'll explain what these are later). Our plan was to hold them until maturity and then spend down the principal and interest until my husband's pension had grown enough to provide for our retirement. In other words, we were just trying to stretch our cash out for a few years without thinking of any growth.

Fortunately, wisdom prevailed, and I learned enough to abandon this dead-end strategy. Because I was home, I had more time to study our situation. I already knew that, whatever we did, we needed to think of the taxes that our investments would generate. During my dental practice, I attended law school at night with the goal of doing medical malpractice. I found myself, however, more interested in estate planning and taxes. This background was one of the prime reasons that we rejected mutual funds with their tax inefficiency as our investment vehicle (more about this in chapter 4.).

I started reading and doing research (more on this in chapter 6) and was convinced that the stock market was not the scary place I thought it was; with some diligence and patience the small investor could do well.

What did all of my research produce? We now have a healthy portfolio outside of our pension fund that will allow us to retire in a reasonable time. We have taken control of my husband's pension money and invested that using the Dividend Growth Investment Strategy. When we retire, we will live off the dividends our stocks produce without having to sell any stocks or spend down our principal. Our dividend income and stock value will continually grow. We have minimized our fees and taxes, and we are secure in riding the dividend escalator; we no longer fear the breathtaking drops in the stock-price roller coaster.

## RISK

All investors are concerned about risk. Go back through the list of investors that we have just met and see which type of risk was most important to each. Ann Scheiber may have been aware of the different types of risks but managed to ignore them and proceed in the best direction for her investments. In each of the other stories that I have presented, the investor concentrated on one or more of the risk categories and, as a result, derailed the potential for growth.

Risk comes to the investor in five ways. All of these forms of risk are inherent in investing. Investors tend to concentrate on one or two while ignoring the others. For instance, women tend to have principal risk aversion, fearing that they will lose their nest egg while tending to be afraid of stocks. Men, on the other hand, have market risk aversion. Specifically, they are afraid that the market itself will increase when they are not invested. This leads men into more volatile stocks for investment.

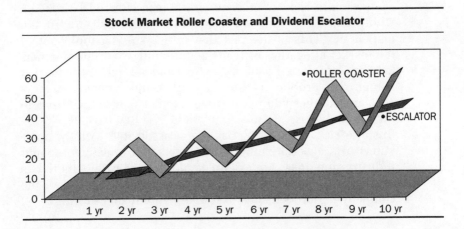

**Stock Market Roller Coaster and Dividend Escalator**

Psychological research by Brad Barber and Terrance Odean has established that men are more prone to overconfidence than women. Thus, models of investor overconfidence predict that men will trade more and perform worse than women. Using account data for over thirty-five thousand households from a large discount brokerage firm, Barber and Odean analyzed the common-stock investments of men and women from February 1991 through January 1997. Consistent with the predictions of the overconfidence models, they document that men trade 45 percent more than women and earn annual risk-adjusted net returns that are 1.4 percent less than those earned by women. These differences are more pronounced between single men and single women; single men trade 67 percent more than single women and earn annual risk-adjusted net returns that are 2.3 percent less than those earned by single women.

We all, however, have to be aware of *all* types of risk. I believe that the Dividend Growth Investment Strategy is the best way to deal with risk in all of its forms.

## The Five Forms of Risk

1.  Principal risk   Will I lose my money? This is the risk that many investors focus on primarily; they then end up buying CDs.
2.  Interest-rate risk   This is the risk that investors are exposed to when interest rates fluctuate. This risk is what makes the investor pay a premium for a bond with a higher yield when interest rates are falling.
3.  Market risk   This risk is the perception that investors have of the market as a whole. This overall market risk is referred to as "systemic risk." For example, a recession will drag the whole market down, and a booming economy will lift the market up. This is the risk that either keeps people out of the market altogether or leads people to try to "time the market," invest when the market is low, and sell when the market is high. The problem is that the market undergoes its own cycles, and neither you nor anyone else is smart enough to predict these cycles.
4.  Business risk   This is the risk that is associated with the operations of a specific company. Management effectiveness and industry timeliness are examples of business risk. This risk is related to the fundamentals of the company, to how well the company performs its business and maintains its earnings.

5. Inflation risk   This risk occurs when the annual rate of inflation is not adequately covered by the interest rate of the investment. This investor is typically a bond investor, who wants to avoid principal risk but actually is losing principal through taxation and inflation.

Which type of risk are you most concerned about?

## "BUT I'M NOT RICH!"

At this point you are saying to yourself, "Doctors, dentists, movie stars, little old ladies with no kids or expenses. If I was one of those, I could easily become rich, too, but I have no money to invest." This book is not about "them," but about *you*. You can do it, and in the next chapter I will show you how. Until then, let's see how little it really takes to provide for yourself.

Most of us can't throw around thousands of dollars to buy or sell controlling interests in major corporations, but most of us can come up with $2,000 a year. If that seems like a lot of money, consider that this breaks down to $5.50 a day. Surely you can do something to save that amount. The average Minnesotan spends $2,000 a year on gambling. Since the four people in my family spend, in total, $0, someone out there is spending a lot more to bring the average up. How about putting that money toward investing? What about taking your lunch to work instead of going out? Or making your own morning coffee instead of going to a coffee shop? How about buying a less-expensive car instead of a status car? If you hire people to do your laundry, clean your house, or do your yard work, you can eliminate these costs by doing these chores yourself. You can give up smoking, cut back on going out for dinner, or take a less expensive vacation. These are just a few suggestions that would allow you to accumulate your $2,000, or even a lot more.

Can this really make a difference? Consider spending $2 a day on making your own lunch instead of going to the restaurant and paying, with tax and tip, $7.50. There is your $5.50 per day. As you will learn later, it doesn't help to start this program six months before you retire; you need to start early. If you do, the rewards will be tremendous. Taking your lunch to work over a thirty-year period and investing the $5.50 difference, assuming a very modest 8 percent yearly return, will give you *$100,000* at the end of that period.

You can do even better. The next chart will become clearer to you as you go through the book, but the lesson is simple: Start early by saving modest amounts and the rewards can be great. This chart compares three types of investments, a stock whose share price and dividend grow at 14 percent per year, which is high but achievable; a stock whose share price and dividend grow at 10 percent per year, around the historical average; and one whose share price and dividend grow at 7 percent per year, a very poor performance over a thirty-year period. These stocks are compared to a bond yielding 7 percent, an interest rate difficult to achieve in the current low-inflation climate. The results are tabulated to show you how much the stock price has appreciated over thirty years, what the total amount of dividends that you have collected would be over thirty years, and what the annual dividend income would be in the thirtieth year.

After looking at these returns, instead of thinking, I can't afford to start investing for my retirement, you should be thinking, I can't afford to *not* start investing for my retirement! This program is not for those who are wealthy and want to become wealthier; it is for those who want to take some responsibility for their financial security, use discipline, and secure their future.

## THE DISCLAIMER

Every self-respecting financial adviser enters a disclaimer at some point in his presentation. Louis Rukeyser, a TV analyst on PBS's *Wall Street Week,* always tells viewers that the management does not guarantee the suggestions of his guest. A local talk-show host in my area always starts his program with "Past performance does not guarantee future results." Intuitively, everyone knows that the future is unpredictable and that anyone who guarantees results in the investment world is a fraud. Think about what it would mean if the future was "knowable"? If it was common knowledge that General Electric (GE)

| Invest $2,000 Each Year for 30 Years | | | |
|---|---|---|---|
| Annual Growth Rate | Stock Appreciation 30 Years | Total Dividend Payments | Dividend Payment in Year 30 |
| 14% Stock | $763,524 | $80,729 | $10,704 |
| 10% Stock | $345,437 | $45,283 | $ 4,935 |
| 7% Stock | $195,534 | $30,460 | $ 2,833 |
| 7% Bond | $        0 | $31,500 | $ 4,200 |

was going to outperform all other stocks by fivefold over the next ten years, all investors would try to buy GE. Its stock price would go into the stratosphere, and its price/earnings ratio would be in the hundreds, if not thousands. At this point, investors would think this to be too expensive, and Microsoft, Coca-Cola, etc., with price/earnings ratios beaten down below 200 would look like great buys. The money flows would reverse. This is the self-correcting free market, supply-and-demand capitalism. As soon as you think you know the future, this knowledge changes things, so the future changes right under your watchful gaze.

Not to be outdone, I will offer my caveat: *My investment strategy will work for you if you believe that the future will be like the past.* My strategy is based on analyzing historical data to estimate future performance. If the future is markedly different from the past, my strategy might not work.

We should look into this possibility a little further. If you believe that the future is going to be much different, what investment strategy should you use? First, if there is a huge change in our society, all current investment vehicles will be unstable and will not perform the way they are now projected to perform. Second, it is not enough to simply say that things will be different; you must say *how* they will be different. Inflation? Deflation? Depression? Armageddon? Earthly Paradise? Will the socialist wing of the Democratic party control the country? Will California fall into the sea? Dow at 25,000? Dow at 250? Each of these scenarios calls for a different strategy. A betting man would say that the best odds would ride on the future resembling the past. My bias is that this is a prudent assumption and that my strategy is a prudent way to proceed.

# 2

LEARNING TO RIDE THE ESCALATOR
AND IGNORE THE ROLLER COASTER

What is this Dividend Growth Investment Strategy that I have been talking about? It is a strategy that I came to after years of studying the market, trying to fit our investment strategy with our retirement needs. I searched the literature for an approach that I thought would work, but I found nothing approaching the strategy that I am going to present to you. In order for you to understand the Dividend Growth Investment Strategy, you must first understand what common stocks are.

A common stock is an investment in the ownership, or equity, of a corporation. Common shareholders expect a return on their investment from the dividend payments and share price appreciation as the company's earnings increase. The common shareholders are owners, however, their rights to corporate assets on liquidation are subordinate to corporate creditors, corporate bondholders, and the preferred shareholders.

I started my investment career in the traditional way. I researched a number of companies and came up with a list of those whose stocks I felt would be safe and provide a reasonable increase in the price of the stock. The first group that I bought in 1995 included:

Home Depot, Inc.
PepsiCo, Inc.
Walgreen Co.
Wal-Mart Stores, Inc.
Cifra S A De CV Adr
Rubbermaid, Inc.
Coca-Cola Co.

In retrospect, this is a pretty good list. Cifra is a Mexican discount chain that I put a little money into after the Mexican economy crashed. Rubbermaid has had its problems and has shown no appreciation over the last few years. The other companies have done well and likely will continue to do so. When I bought these stocks, I took no serious note of their dividend payouts. Most of them paid in the 1 percent range, which we thought was insignificant.

Over the next three years I bought and sold a large number of stocks. Many of our holdings were meant to be long term, but many were made for short-term gains. I immersed myself in the minutiae of the high-tech and telecom industries so that I could understand what I should invest in and what to stay away from. All of the specific information about individual companies also had to be factored in to the general trends of society and the world economy. I did very well with this approach, making "total returns" in the range of 30–40 percent annually. Total returns are the sum of the percentage of price appreciation of the stock and the dividend yield.

This was great on paper, but I found some grave defects with this approach. First, every time we sold a stock at a profit, a large portion went to the federal and state governments. The second problem was even more fundamental: What happens in the coming dreaded correction? I didn't believe that I could time the correction and sell all of our stocks at the top of the market. Using investment gimmicks like selling short was not a viable option. Making 40 percent gains in a falling market also was not a likely possibility. I know that corrections end, and the stock market always rebounds, but this may take a long time. If your retirement income depends on selling stocks, it is disastrous to have to sell when their value is down 25–50 percent. This led me to look to investments that produce income. Bonds will give a guaranteed return, but the return is decimated by taxes and inflation (more details about this later). Stocks with high-dividend yields also seem superficially attractive. Many utilities pay in the 5 percent range. The problem with these is similar to that found in bonds. The dividend remains static, and the growth of stock price for utilities historically underperforms the market as a whole; thus, you are giving up significant growth. These stocks performed very well in 2000, but don't let that fool you into thinking that there is a fundamental change in the potential of these stocks.

As this unfolded, I started focusing on the numerous small dividend checks that each of our companies sent us each quarter. These checks ranged from $2 to $200 and, in the aggregate, began to add up to significant sums. Could this be the answer? I started looking more closely into the dividends that companies pay out. There are many companies, mainly high-growth, high-tech companies such as Microsoft and Dell Computer, that pay no dividends. Most publicly traded companies, however, reward their shareholders with quarterly dividends. Each year, the board of directors declares a dividend of so many dollars and cents per share, usually paid out in four quarterly payments. The yield of the stock is defined as the dividend divided by the share price. This is expressed as a percentage, ranging from less than 1 percent to up to 6 percent or 7 percent. You can see from this that the yield (percentage) will change as the stock price changes. The dividend payout, however, remains static unless the board of directors votes to change it.

The conventional wisdom that we would likely have used as we neared retirement is illustrated by Ron and Sue, whom we met in the first chapter. This wisdom tells them to get rid of their growth stocks and buy high-yield bonds as retirement nears. They wanted income, so they bought utility companies, instead of bonds, that gave a high yield, in the 5 percent to 6 percent range. These stocks are similar to bonds in that they grow little or not at all and the dividends usually increase only to match inflation. Ron would never have considered investing in a company that had a yield of less than 1 percent, but this is precisely what he should have done, especially early in his career, when he was buying municipal bonds. The secret that he did not realize was that *companies raise their dividends.* There are many high quality companies that raise their dividends 14 percent a year and have a history of continuously raising dividends for decades. At a 14 percent increase each year, the dividend payout will double every five years, geometrically increasing to retirement and beyond. A stock that pays 1 percent when you buy it, with a dividend that doubles every five years, will pay 16 percent on your original investment in twenty years and 64 percent at thirty years. This does not include the increase in the price of the stock over that period. Contrast this to a 6 percent bond that, in thirty years, will still be worth its face value and still pay 6 percent. We will examine bonds in more detail later.

### The Stock Market Roller Coaster

- Most people investing in the stock market worry about their principal being destroyed by a market downturn.
- They also know the stock market is the best protection against inflation, but they cannot stomach the market's volatility.

### The Stock Market Also Has an Escalator

- The escalator has a gradual upward incline that takes you up without the volatility.

- The escalator is the dividend payment that many companies increase annually.
- You can live off the dividends, and they continue to grow.
- Invest to keep your dividends doubling every five years.

## DIVIDEND GROWTH AND THE STOCK MARKET

The Dividend Growth Investment Strategy is about psychology as much as actual numbers and percentage returns. It is meant to steer the middle course between two extremes. The first extreme is the pure stock-market roller coaster, giving you the psychological bolster of dividends to ride out the dizzying drops without letting yourself bail out at exactly the worst moment. The other extreme is taking your money out of the stock market and investing in bonds, which barely keep you abreast of inflation, let alone grow your wealth. You may want to invest in high-flying tech stocks, such as Cisco or AOL, but you should also have a large portion of your portfolio in the Dividend Growth Investment Strategy; you can look at this investment as the portion that conventional wisdom tells you should be diversified into bonds. Your dividends will outpace the bond yields, plus you will realize a substantial capital gain.

This continuous increase in dividends serves as the cornerstone for the Dividend Growth Investment Strategy. I will now present the entire strategy as the eight Ds.

## THE EIGHT DS OF THE DIVIDEND GROWTH INVESTMENT STRATEGY

### 1. Discipline

You can only invest your money if you have money to invest. Does this mean that only the rich can use my strategy? Absolutely not! The truth is that everyone can afford to put something away each month and that small amounts invested over time become large amounts. It just takes a disciplined approach to your finances. In order to save, it is important to allocate a portion of your income each month, to make the necessary small sacrifices to free up that money. (E.g., stop smoking, bring a bag lunch instead of going out every day, buy a less expensive car than the neighbors', etc.) You then need the discipline to follow through with the strategy over the long haul. Don't sell your high-quality stocks in down markets. Don't succumb to the temptation to buy the the latest high-tech hot tip from your neighbor or broker. You also need to realize that stocks don't go up in a straight line. Just about every stock that I have purchased has dipped lower after the purchase before starting to rise. Stick with it! If you bought a good company, have the discipline to stay the course through this first discouraging period.

> Laszlo Birinyi Jr., a well-respected investor, recently said: In my experience I have known good, bad and indifferent managers. Some of the successful ones were tall and some short; some talked a great deal and others listened. Some had offices that were immaculate; others had reports and papers stuffed in every nook and cranny. Some had photographic memories, while others probably had to look up their own phone numbers. But the one common denominator with all of the good ones was discipline.

## 2. Decades

If you are looking to get rich quick, the Dividend Growth Investment Strategy is not for you. The strategy is for those who can be patient over the long haul. The earlier you start, the better, for *it literally takes decades to work.* The long-term rewards, however, are great and as predictable as anything in the financial world. This is the "get rich slowly" that Warren Buffett, head of Berkshire Hathaway, talks about. Put time to work on your side. Compounding of your investments is the magic that will lead to your secure retirement. Give the magic as much time as possible to work.

## 3. Direction

Cynthia Danaher, a manager at Hewlett-Packard, was quoted in the *Wall Street Journal* as dividing the people she has worked with over the years into three types: "There are those who say, 'There is a rat in the room and I am going to kill it.' A second group says, 'There's a rat in this room; let's figure out a plan to kill it.' And a third group asks, 'Did anyone notice there's a rat in the room?' " You should train yourself to be one of those people that are ready to kill the rat yourself; don't wait for someone else to do it for you.

You will not have the discipline to invest money and leave it for decades unless you have confidence in the appropriateness of your investments. You cannot do this if you give someone else carte blanche to manage your portfolio because you think they know better than you. The typical mutual fund does just that. This is why Beth panicked and wanted to transfer all of her money from mutual funds to gold. It is important that you take direction of your investments either by doing it yourself or by finding a financial planner that has your same philosophy and works closely with you to optimize your portfolio. You will come to the realization that you are not buying lottery tickets but are buying a piece of a company. When you know what that company does, how it has performed in the past, and what to expect from it in the future, you will have become an investor and not a trader. You will be able to ride out the corrections and recessions much more placidly than your acquaintances who are still riding the mutual-fund roller coaster.

When you take charge of your own finances, the "experts" will do everything they can to dissuade you. Listen to what Jonathan Clements writes in "The Myth of the Dumb Investor" in the *Wall Street Journal* on November 30, 1998:

> We have all heard the denigrating comments from brokers, market strategists, and money managers: Small investors are stupid. Really stupid.
>
> According to Wall Street lore, the little guy always buys heavily at market peaks. In this favored caricature, small investors also panic when the stock market dives. In fact, small investors are apparently so dumb that you can make decent money by doing the exact opposite of whatever they do.
>
> All this is good for a hearty, patronizing chuckle, and certainly helps promote the idea that you need the hand holding of a money manager, broker, or financial planner.
>
> But there's just one problem with these comments about investor incompetence: *They aren't true.*

As an adjunct to the direction you must impose on your investments, you should limit your investments to companies that you understand. Everyone can relate to Coca-Cola and PepsiCo (which includes Frito-Lay). Anyone who consumes ketchup knows about H. J. Heinz; anyone using a lightbulb knows General Electric (although many don't know that a large percentage of GE is now a financial stock). In your occupation or avocation, you may understand computers or

telecom equipment, making Microsoft or Cisco more rational investments. My husband and I have spent many years in the health-care
industry. We know how valuable the drug companies have become.
Alternatively, we know what a mess the health-care delivery system
has become. We would never touch the stocks of HMOs or management companies. When we see analysts recommending these stocks,
we know that they have no experience to back up their foolhardiness.
If you don't know much about these industries, you must study them
intensively before investing; otherwise, you are just buying a lottery
ticket.

Bill, the dentist whom we met in the first chapter, violated both of
these rules. He put his money in the hands of a stockbroker who had
him invest in a risky computer-chip maker in an industry that neither
of them understood at all. He would have been infinitely better off in
taking the money himself and investing in a safe stock, such as H. J.
Heinz. Bill does understand ketchup.

Steve Forbes, publisher of *Forbes* magazine, tells us about his
grandfather's advice to him: "You make more money giving advice than
you do taking it."

## 4. Department of Revenue

All of the investment characteristics that we have talked about to this
point have been aimed at giving your investments time to grow by *compounding,* that is, having your new gains grow as well as the original
money that you put in. Compounding is the most powerful tool that
you have to grow your wealth. Albert Einstein, in his infinite wisdom,
described compounding of interest as the greatest mathematical discovery. Because of this, you want to do nothing that diminishes your
compounding.

The three biggest enemies of compounding are taxes, taxes, and
taxes (with fees paid to professionals a strong fourth). Every dollar
paid in taxes is one less dollar that is available for growth. We will
talk about taxes in depth later, but in the meantime you need to know
that they are something to be avoided. Taxes are owed in two ways on
your investments. Dividends paid to you by corporations and interest
on bonds are taxed each year at your marginal (highest) rate. This applies even if you reinvest the dividends and never see the cash. The
Dividend Growth Investment Strategy minimizes these taxes in the
following way: During your working years, when your income will be
relatively high, your dividends will be low and will thus generate little in the way of taxes. These dividends will grow into large sums

over time, but presumably this will occur after your retirement, when your total income will be less, and thus you may be in a lower tax bracket.

The second type of tax that you will pay is the capital-gains tax. This tax is owed on the gain, or profit, that you make when you sell a stock. The rate of the tax is dependent on how long you own the stock before the sale. For any stock held less than one year, the rate is the same as your highest marginal personal rate, which may be as high as 50 percent (federal and state). There is one sure way to avoid this tax. Since the tax is owed only when you sell your stock, *don't sell your stock!*

Here is an interesting exercise to show you what this means to your growth of wealth. Assume that you have a dollar to invest and that you are smart enough to invest it so that it doubles in value each year for the next twenty years without selling it. Elmer, your neighbor, has the same investment insight but sells his investment at the end of each year and reinvests in a new stock after paying the taxes. Each of his new investments also double in a year. How much will each of you have at the end of twenty years?

Obviously, Elmer will have somewhat less because he pays taxes of $13,000 over the twenty years, leaving him with $25,200. Not bad starting at $1. If you think that your investments may end up double, or even triple, this number, or even reach $100,000, think again. Your one dollar, doubling each year for twenty years without paying taxes will be worth $1 million!

If you don't believe me, do the math.

---

*How $1 Doubled Each Year for 20 Years Is Worth $1 Million*

| | | | |
|---|---|---|---|
| 1. $2 | | 11. $2048 | |
| 2. $4 | | 12. $4096 | |
| 3. $8 | | 13. $8192 | |
| 4. $16 | | 14. $16,384 | |
| 5. $32 | | 15. $32,768 | |
| 6. $64 | | 16. $65,536 | |
| 7. $128 | | 17. $131,072 | |
| 8. $256 | | 18. $262,144 | |
| 9. $512 | | 19. $524,288 | |
| 10. $1024 | | 20. $1,048,576 | |

---

To see the difference in graphic form is even more impressive:

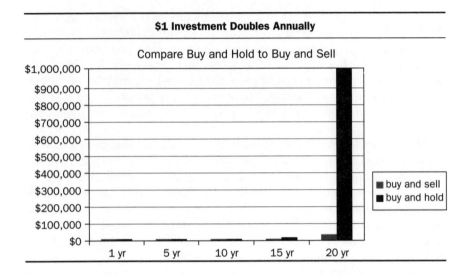

**$1 Investment Doubles Annually**

You can see the astronomical difference that taxes make in your investments and how important it is to avoid them if at all possible. You also have to understand that a large amount of the gain reported by your mutual funds comes from dividends and from selling stocks owned in the fund, generating capital gains and income taxes. This tax liability is passed on directly to you.

*Beware of the mutual-fund industry.* The mutual-fund company will not subtract these taxes from your gain. You will receive a statement that you probably will send to your tax preparer, and the taxes will be paid with the rest of your household taxes. You may not consciously associate them with the mutual fund. The pocket that these taxes come out of does not matter. As long as you are paying out the cash, you will have that much less cash to invest.

## 5. Don't Sell

The fifth principle is a direct outgrowth of the tax issue that we have been talking about. The best attitude toward your stock purchase is to regard it as a lifelong relationship. Occasionally, the fundamentals of a company that you own will go south and you will be forced to sell, but this should be a rare occurrence. *Buy and hold* should be your watchwords for investing.

The trap that many investors fall into with holding their stocks is succumbing to the false promise of market timing. You may own a good stock that you think is higher than it should be. Why not sell it and buy it back later at a cheaper price? This is called a "wash sale." When a stock is sold for a loss, however, you have to wait thirty-one days to repurchase the stock or the loss can not be used to reduce the gains in your portfolio.

Setting the tax consequences aside, this approach becomes a crapshoot, with as much chance of disaster as success. If the professionals could time the market accurately, the indexed mutual funds would not outperform 90 percent of the actively managed mutual funds, as is now the case. The fact is that while the stock market has shown steady gains over a period of two hundred years, these gains do not happen in a straight line. Most of the gains in the market happen in a few trading days each year. Most individual stocks rest at one price for an extended period, only to jump up dramatically in one or two days. It is impossible to predict these days. If you are not invested in the market when these days happen, you will lose out. If you try to buy the stock as it is going up, you are too late.

The rational strategy is to buy the stocks that likely will appreciate in value, and give them their chance to perform. Warren Buffett says that you should not look at your investments for five years after making the purchase. Peter Lynch, a former manager of Fidelity Management's flagship Magellan Fund, says:

> Timing the Market is an expensive hobby, expensive because of all the gains you miss when you sell at the wrong time. Stocks make most of their gains in short bursts that are impossible to predict.

## 6. Dominant Companies

To buy and hold for twenty or thirty years means that you must own companies that will continue to grow for that period. This means buying companies that have a long track record of growth and performance. Most of these companies will be the dominant player in their industry and will be household names, such as General Electric, Coca-Cola, H. J. Heinz, or Automatic Data Processing. You may have to pay more than you like for these stocks, but you get what you pay for. If you buy a competitor that is cheaper, you may make a short-term gain but sacrifice the long-term potential for growth. Some years ago, I had the choice of buying Cisco Systems or Cabletron, two internet switch manufacturers. They had roughly the same market capitalization at that time. Cisco was recognized as the superior company but had a much higher price/earnings ratio. I went for the cheap stock. Over the next few years, Cisco's strong growth persisted, while Cabletron's growth languished. Cabletron now has a market cap only a fraction of that of Cisco. The purchase of Cabletron was penny wise but pound foolish.

What you want to look for is a "blue chip" stock. This is stock in companies that have a long track record of growth and regular payment of substantial dividends. These companies have an excellent reputation for providing good products and services.

The companies that I have included in my sample portfolio not only are dominant but have a winning combination of fundamentals (low manufacturing costs, high profit margins, and the habitual purchase of their products) that make them superior performers. Many of these stocks have outperformed the market averages.

Please note that there is no room in this strategy for speculation in risky, high-flying stocks that zoom up and down the roller coaster. These stocks have as much potential for crashing and burning as they do for making a decent gain. If you cannot imagine the company that you are considering still being a dominant company twenty years from now, don't buy it.

## 7. Diversification

No one can predict the future; if we could, we would all be rich. Picking the stocks that go into your Dividend Growth Investment Strategy portfolio is based on projecting growth of a company using a long track record of historical data. While this will be highly useful in most cases, occasionally the company that you invest in, for many reasons, will go in the wrong direction. In order to protect yourself from this potential problem, you need to diversify. If you own twenty high-quality companies, the adverse effects of one of these companies crashing will be minimal; if all of your money is in two or three companies and one goes under, the consequences for your retirement will be disastrous. At the end of this book, I will present a sample portfolio with many suggestions for diversifications.

Keep in mind that you should be diversified across industries as well as companies. Due to a whole host of factors, different industries perform at different levels at different times. For instance, the pharmaceutical stocks were extremely depressed in 1992 by the hostility of Hillary Clinton and her health-care-reform task force. With the collapse of her effort, the drug stocks rebounded and were among the best performers in the market. The trend is now reversing again with the possible advent of drug coverage under medicare. Financial stocks, food processing stocks, toiletries, drug stocks, insurance stocks, and data processing, etc., all have their seasons of rest and growth. Rather than trying the futile game of guessing when these cycles will occur, own some of each to take advantage of the growth as it happens.

## 8. Dividends

For most average investors, money is earned in one of three ways, by means of: the Shooting Star, the Sure Thing, or the Forgotten Orphan.

The Shooting Star refers to capital gains. Capital gains are collected when you sell an asset, in this case a stock, for more than you paid for it. The profit is your gain on your capital. This is very seductive and carries the promise of enormous returns as in, "I bought Tech Squared Software at its initial public offering at $5 a share and sold it the next day at eighty-five dollars a share!"

The problem with this approach is that if you hold on to this stock until the third day, after the savvy investors have taken their profits, it will be worth $3 a share. Capital gains are not the sole outcome in this scenario; there is also such a thing as capital losses. Investing for capital gains is not like riding a shooting star; it is more like riding a roller coaster. There is nothing wrong with this approach, but you must be ready, both financially and psychologically, for the sharp, deep dips.

If this approach is too gut wrenching for you, you may opt for the Sure Thing, which is collecting interest. Interest is usually a fixed percentage (although sometimes these may vary with cost of living, fed rates, etc.) that a bank, corporation, or government pays you for lending them your money. The percentage is fixed by contract at a set amount and for a set period of time and is guaranteed as long as the entity that you lend it to doesn't go bankrupt. The problem with this approach is that, at the end of the set period, your principal will be the same as when you deposited it, except that the real value of that money will have been significantly eroded by inflation. Likewise, the interest will not grow throughout the life of the bond and will also be eroded by inflation and, in most cases, taxes.

That leaves us with the heart of the Dividend Growth Investment Strategy, the Forgotten Orphan: *dividends.* When I told a mutual "Fund of Funds" manager about my idea, he told me that no one would be interested because "Dividends aren't sexy!" Sexy or not, they work for you.

What are dividends? Unlike interest, you, as an investor, have no contractual right to expect dividends on any stock that you purchase. The dividend is paid to stockholders out of corporate earnings. This payout is totally a prerogative of the corporation's board of directors. They can increase, decrease, or cancel the dividend as circumstances dictate. Although this makes the process seem random, this is far from the case. The dividend record is public, and by studying the payments, profiles can be set up for any corporation. There are many companies that have histories of continuous dividend payouts and yearly dividend *increases* going back twenty, thirty, or even over forty years. This does not constitute an iron-clad guarantee of future performance, but can be used as a very powerful predictor of that performance.

---

**Dividend Growth**

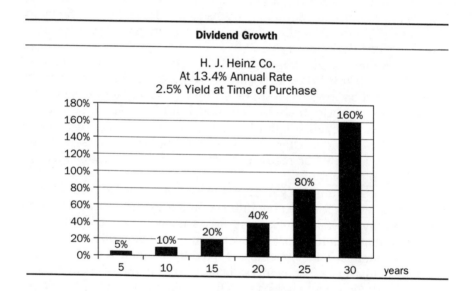

How are dividends paid out? The board of directors of a corporation votes a dividend of so many cents per share per year (paid out quarterly). If you look in the newspaper stock tables, you may see under International Poly Conglomerate (a mythical company) that the dividend yield is 1 percent. The yield is not fixed by the board of directors but is calculated by dividing the dividend payout by the stock price. You can see that this will vary with the price of the stock. As an example, if IPC has a dividend payout of $1 per share and a share is selling for $100, the yield is 1 percent. What if the stock price changes?

| Share Price | Dividend per Share | % Yield |
|---|---|---|
| $100 | $1.00 | 1% |
| $200 | $1.00 | 0.5% |
| $50 | $1.00 | 2% |

International Poly Conglomerate shows us an important principle. Its stock price may change, up or down by 400 percent from $50 to $200 (or vice versa). This changes the dividend yield over a range of .5 percent to 2 percent. Notice, however, that the dividend paid per share does *not* change, whatever the stock price. Whether the stock is at 50 or 200, you still get your dollar for the year. If you are buying and holding, not selling, it is of no concern in the short run if the stock price goes up or down: You get to pocket your dollar.

Furthermore, you picked IPC because it has a long history of raising its dividends each year, averaging 14 percent per year. In all probability, this will continue into the future. By growing at 14 percent, this means that the dividend will double each five years. The dividend and yield on the $100 that you paid for your share will grow as follows:

| Year | 0 | 5 | 10 | 15 | 20 | 25 | 30 |
|---|---|---|---|---|---|---|---|
| Yield (%) | 1 | 2 | 4 | 8 | 16 | 32 | 64 |
| Dividend ($) | 1 | 2 | 4 | 8 | 16 | 32 | 64 |

In thirty years, the $100 that you invested will be yielding 64 percent and paying you $64 per year. The roller coaster of the ups and downs of the stock price doesn't have to concern you. You will realize a large capital gain, but you need not count on it. Instead, you are on the dividend escalator that goes up steadily at ever-increasing rates. If you can buy the stock at a lower price, with a higher yield, you can do even better. If you catch IPC at $50 per share, you can buy two shares for your $100. The yield becomes:

| Year | 0 | 5 | 10 | 15 | 20 | 25 | 30 |
|---|---|---|---|---|---|---|---|
| Yield (%) | 2 | 4 | 8 | 16 | 32 | 64 | 128 |
| Dividend ($) per share | 1 | 2 | 4 | 8 | 16 | 32 | 64 |
| Dividend ($) total | 2 | 4 | 8 | 16 | 32 | 64 | 128 |

Thirty years later you receive $128 per year on your $100 investment.

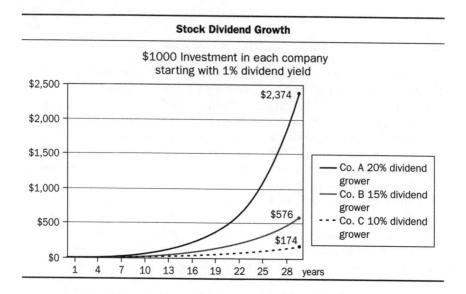

**Stock Dividend Growth**

Contrast this to a bond. If you take out a thirty-year bond at 7 percent (hard to find in the current climate) for your $100, you will get $7 each year for thirty years. For the first ten or fifteen years, you will collect more than you would from your stock dividend. This is not too helpful as these years are high income years when a large portion of your interest will go to taxes. If you retire at twenty years, your bond will still pay you $7, while, in the first example, the dividend will be $16 per year. Ten years into your retirement, the bond will still be paying $7, while the stock dividend has grown to $64 each year, with more growth to come. At thirty years the bond reaches maturity and must be redeemed. You will get your $100 back, which, due to inflation, is worth less than half of its worth when you purchased it. The stock, by contrast, is now worth in the range of $4,000–$5,000.

The other point to consider is that you must buy stocks that grow their dividends aggressively, in the 13 percent or greater range. Ron and Sue bought electric utilities with average yields of 5 percent. This sounds wonderful, compared with the yields of Coca-Cola or Hewlett-Packard, which are less than 1 percent. Utilities, however, have very slow dividend growth and act more like bonds than growth stocks. In later years, the dividends will be only slightly increased over what they were in year one. Coca-Cola, Hewlett-Packard, and many other great companies that will be profiled later in my sample portfolio, will act like IPC in our example. You will not realize much income in the high income years while you are working, but you will reap great benefits in retirement.

## SUMMARY OF THE DIVIDEND GROWTH INVESTMENT STRATEGY

To grow your wealth to a secure and comfortable retirement, you should invest in individual stocks in companies that dominate their industries and have a long history of high dividend growth. You should have an active role in setting up your portfolio. Once you buy your stocks, you should hold them for the long term, both to allow their dividends to grow as well as to minimize taxes. You should buy a number of different companies to decrease the risk that one may underperform your expectations. Lastly, you need to show the discipline to continuously save small amounts of money and to stick to your strategy in the face of the ups, downs, and fads that infect the market.

## A VOICE IN THE WILDERNESS?

Admittedly, this strategy is not sexy and won't make you rich overnight. You don't see these principals elucidated each night on the business news or each morning in the *Wall Street Journal*. Are they, therefore, out of line? The conventional wisdom takes some time to shift directions, but I am encouraged that it is moving in my direction. In evidence is a recent article in the *Wall Street Journal* from November 17, 1998, by Jonathan Clements. He had been writing a weekly column for four years and writes about how his ideas had matured over that period. Some excerpts:

> *Investing is 90 percent emotional.* I now believe that the biggest reason investors fail isn't a lack of knowledge but an excess of emotion.
> We often don't have enough self-discipline when it comes to spending and saving. We are far too confident in our ability to pick winning investments and forecast markets. We fret too much over short-term performance, even though we are supposedly investing for the next thirty years.
>
> *Without good savings habits, there is nothing.* The real key to investing is good savings habits. The fact is, if you don't

save a healthy amount each month, it doesn't matter whether you earn 8 percent a year or 18 percent.

*There are no gurus.* Four years ago, I was a fan of index funds, which simply buy stocks that constitute a market index in an effort to match the index's performance. Today I am a true believer.

With every passing year, there are yet more star fund managers who burn out, no-lose propositions that prove otherwise, and market gurus who drop the crystal ball.

*Churn and get burned.* From the earliest columns, I have emphasized the importance of holding down investment costs, like mutual-fund annual expenses, brokerage commissions, and other trading costs. But it is only in the last few years that I have realized just how damaging taxes can be.

Sound familiar? It's nice to see that this columnist is coming around to the commonsense approach that I advocate. Hopefully, in the future, he will bridge the remaining gap and recognize the superiority of the strategy of buying blue-chip stocks that raise their dividends over mutual funds.

# 3

==

# MUTUAL FUNDS: STOP SENDING YOUR MONEY TO WASHINGTON AND WALL STREET

There are, of course, many alternatives to the Dividend Growth Investment Strategy, perhaps the most popular are mutual funds.

## WHAT IS A MUTUAL FUND?

A mutual fund is a publicly registered, professionally traded managed trust that has been established by an investment company. All the money of investors is pooled and used to buy and sell stocks or bonds. The value of a share in a mutual fund is the net-asset value (NAV), which is calculated at the end of the business day by dividing the total portfolio value by the number of outstanding shares. The performance of the mutual fund can be tracked daily through the NAV and compared to the performance of other similar funds or the benchmark Standard & Poor's (S&P) 500.

There are now over six thousand four hundred mutual funds from which to chose. There are also many rating services that independently rate mutual funds. Some of these services include Morningstar, the *Wall Street Journal, Money* magazine, Kiplinger, and *Business Week*.

Why do people invest in mutual funds? The most common reasons are diversification and professional management. Small investors see these funds as a way to own a large number of companies with a small investment. Many investors also doubt their own abilities to manage their money in the sometimes mysterious and incomprehensible stock market and believe that a professional could do a better job. Neither of these reasons holds up to scrutiny. Over time, using my strategy, you can accumulate a portfolio of fifteen to thirty high-quality companies that will make you well diversified while putting you in charge of your own money.

## MUTUAL FUND MANAGEMENT

The management of mutual funds is often not what it appears to be, i.e., fiscally conservative, highly experienced managers looking out for your financial welfare. Many of the mutual fund managers are in their twenties and thirties. At that age, I had not had enough life experience, and probably lacked a certain amount of judgment and wisdom, to handle millions of dollars of other people's money. I'm sure that many of these professionals fall into this same category. Since these managers charge a lot to invest your money for you, you would hope that the high fees would be made up by high returns. This doesn't turn out to be the case. The Vanguard Indexed 500 fund, which owns stocks indexed (i.e., they own roughly equal amounts of shares of every stock listed on the exchange) to the Standard & Poor's 500 large company stocks, regularly outperforms 85–90 percent of the actively managed funds. The returns from mutual funds do not justify the high fees that make these managers millionaires.

The real problem with mutual funds, however, is that they don't deliver the returns that you think you are receiving. You may get a statement that says you have earned X percent for the year, but taxes and fees, which may be hidden in your household finances and not recognized as originating from the mutual fund, will seriously erode your chance at wealth creation. Now that you have sacrificed your Starbuck's coffee and Ralph Lauren sweater in order to invest for your retirement, don't send your hard-earned money to a mutual fund that acts as a conduit for distributing your profits to tax collectors and money managers. You need every dollar that you earn to compound in your account, not in an account in Washington or Wall Street. *Fees and taxes are the sledgehammer that destroys compounding that is so important for your wealth to grow and accumulate.*

## MUTUAL FUND FEES

Fees are collected seamlessly by the fund manager and subtracted from your total return, leaving you, the investor, clueless as to their impact on performance. Fees take a sizable bite out of annual returns. The facts show that the average mutual-fund investor does not understand the extent to which performance is affected by all the various fees. These fees hurt more when the market is going down and returns are lower than in the great bull market of the past few years (1995–99). This is because fees remain constant. They are fixed costs that are charged regardless of the mutual funds' performance.

There are a variety of annual fees mutual funds charge. Mutual-fund companies charge annual management fees, marketing and distribution fees, and fees when an investor redeems shares (sells) before a set period of time. Funds sold through brokers also charge a fee called a "load," or up-front commission. All funds charge an annual management fee, which is called the "expense ratio" to pay for the cost of managing the fund. This is how the fund manager is paid. The expense ratio can range from less than 1 percent up to 2 percent in typical mutual funds.

The "12-b" fees are collected to cover the cost of marketing and distributing the mutual funds. These 12-b fees are not paid to the fund manager but to the mutual-fund company. Some mutual funds also charge fees for reinvesting whatever dividends are collected on the stocks held in the fund.

The loads are brokerage sales commissions charged by mutual funds. They can be up-front commissions or deferred sales charges paid by the investor upon redemption (when you sell your shares in the fund). For example, Fidelity Investment's Magellan Fund, the nation's largest mutual fund, charges a 3 percent load.

Deferred loads, or brokerage commissions, are sometimes charged as higher fees embedded in the fund's overall expense ratio and are paid by you, the investor, over time. These are called "B" shares.

The mutual funds report their annual performance based on the market returns of the stocks it holds; they do not deduct the expense ratios, 12-b fees, and brokerage commissions that investors are paying. Thus, your actual return will be a few points less than what you see on your statement. These are fixed fees unrelated to the fund's performance. Even if the fund is losing money, the investor pays these fees.

The Securities and Exchange Commission now requires mutual-fund companies to list their expenses in their mutual-fund document, called the prospectus. The companies are also required to provide examples of a hypothetical investment of $10,000 and how much they pay in fees over one year, three years, five years, and ten years. They do not, however, have to put this information in the monthly statements and typically don't.

In addition to the expenses charged by the mutual fund, some investors have financial planners or advisers who charge a fee to help investors buy the right funds. There are also the "fund of fund" managers that charge investors management fees to select a basket of mutual funds. These management fees are typically 1 percent to 2 percent, which are added on top of the 1 percent to 3 percent that you are already paying to the mutual fund.

These fees may seem trivial, only 1 percent annual decrease in your wealth. You should think otherwise. Even a 1 percent per year fee, after twenty years, decreases your total wealth by, not 1 percent, but 17 percent. A $1 million nest egg is reduced by $177,000, leaving a retirement nest egg of only $823,000.

All of these fees and expenses add up: When the market is going up, they deplete the compounding of wealth. When the market is going down, these fees deplete the investor's capital. *Be aware that the percent gain that your mutual fund reports does not include these fees and expenses.*

## INDIVIDUAL TAXES GENERATED BY MUTUAL FUNDS

Taxes are the other, and most important, major expense incurred when an investor uses a mutual fund. Most people do not realize that the gains they make in mutual funds are taxed at their highest marginal rates. These taxes are usually mixed in with the taxes they pay on their income and may not be recognized as originating from the mutual fund. Thus they may turn over 36 percent of their profits to the IRS at the end of each year. Why is this?

1.  When a stock is sold by your fund manager taxes are owed on any gain that is realized from the sale.

    | Merck is bought for | → | $100 a share |
    |---|---|---|
    | Merck is sold for | → | $200 a share |
    | | | $100 a share gain |

    This is termed a "capital gain."

2.  Taxes on capital gains are always owed when an asset is sold. In the example above, Merck is sold and there is $100 gain on each share. The gain is the profit or the money made on the investment in the stock. The taxes on the capital gains that are owed depend on the length of time the stock was held:

    a.  The gain on a stock held less than a year is a short-term capital gain. The tax rate is the same as the individual's ordinary income tax rates:

| If taxable income is: | | Federal tax is: |
|---|---|---|
| Under $36,900 | → | 15% |
| Over $36,900 but not over $89,150 | → | 28% |
| Over $89,150 but not over $140,000 | → | 31% |
| Over $140,000 but not over $250,000 | → | 36% |
| Over $250,000 | → | 39.6% |
| *(These rates are for a joint return filed by a married couple.)* | | |

Example: Stock in Merck is sold after being held for a year or less. The $100 gain is taxed as ordinary income ($100 × 36 percent = $36.) The 36 percent tax bracket was assumed, and $36 of taxes are owed on the gain; state income taxes also are owed ($100 × 8.5 percent = $8.50 in Minnesota.) Total taxes owed by Minnesota residents are $44.50.

b.   The gain on a stock held more than one year is a long-term capital gain and receives favorable tax treatment, with a lower rate of 20 percent.

Example: Stock in Merck is sold after being held for more than 1 year. The $100 gain is taxed as a capital gain at the lower tax rate of 20 percent ($100 × 20 percent = $20.)

3.   A stock that is not sold owes no taxes on its gains. The gains are not taxable until the stock is sold. This third alternative is the best one for compounding the retirement nest egg. *Buy and hold = No taxes.*

Investments in mutual funds are taxed at the highest rates. This is because of "churn."

Churn is the turnover of stocks in the mutual fund that the manager has bought and sold. Mutual-fund managers are often highly criticized for churning stocks in their funds. Some money managers even do some day trading; they buy and sell on the same day. The fund manager looks good because the fund reports only its performance, year-to-date (YTD). This performance reflects any capital gains that the manager has gleaned from this churning but *does not reflect the taxes* that the investor will pay on these returns. These taxes destroy the compounding of wealth.

Churn is why mutual fund investors receive a large tax bill at the end of the year. All funds have different churn rates. Some mutual funds have reported churn rates of over 100 percent. The industry average is probably around a 90 percent churn rate in any given year. Index funds have a low churn rate of around 10 percent, due primarily to "redemptions" and not manager induced churning. Redemption is when investors want to get out of the fund and call on the fund manager to return their money. The fund manager has to sell stock to raise the money to pay out to the investors leaving the fund. This sale of stock causes every investor in the fund to pay taxes on the gain.

Taxes destroy the growth of the retirement nest egg. Here's how:

If a mutual fund has a 20 percent return for the year with a 90 percent churn rate and $10,000 was invested.

1. Profit is $2,000
2. Churn rate × profit (90% × $2,000 = $1,800)
3. Taxes are due on $1,800 (36% × $1,800 = $648) The 36 percent federal tax rate is used, state income taxes would also be due. In Minnesota that is another 8.5 percent (8.5% × $1,800 = $153).
4. Total taxes owed are $801, leaving the mutual-fund profit that you actually realize at $1,199.
5. The *real* mutual-fund return is 12 percent after taxes.

REMEMBER: These taxes are *not* paid out of the mutual fund. The tax liability is spread through all of the investors in the fund. The fund sends you a statement at the end of the year listing the capital gains. You hand this to your accountant who figures it in with the rest of the taxes you owe from your income. Thus, the taxes are not linked directly to your profits on your mutual fund. *Most investors never make this connection.*

We can add the deleterious effects of fees to the $10,000 investment example that we just completed:

Annual fees and expenses of 3 percent on $10,000 are $300.

1. Deduct $300 annual expenses from the mutual fund account: ($1,199 − $300 = $899)
2. Profit to you after taxes and fees is 9 percent.

The mutual fund reports an eye-popping 20 percent performance return, but after taxes and fees it may be a more realistic 9 percent.

These calculations are based on many assumptions, and they probably will not fit any one given situation. The point is to demonstrate the impact of taxes and fees. Mutual-fund investors should be aware of the gap between what the mutual fund reports as the annual performance returns and the real returns after taxes and fees are deducted.

You will probably hear individual fund managers say, "Our fees are only 1.5 percent, not 3 percent"; "Our funds beat the S&P 500 three years in a row." They may be right: there are a few funds that beat the S&P 500; there are many funds with total fees well under the 3 percent average that I used. (Three percent is high if there are no loads or commissions.) There are also funds that have a churn rate of less than 90 percent (but remember that even low churn rates have significant effects on compounding). The 44.5 percent tax rate used was chosen arbitrarily as a conservative average of federal and state taxes combined; many of you are paying more in taxes, depending on your state income-tax rates. All of these figures are meant to be reasonable approximations of the situation that you will find yourself in the real world. It is not my purpose to give precise financial numbers for every situation (an impossible task even if I desired to do this). The purpose of the book is to explain the basic concepts of how wealth grows and how it is passed on to your loved ones. If you are going to invest in a mutual fund, you can get the specific numbers for that fund and utilize your marginal tax rate. Do the math for yourself.

---

*Mutual Funds*

| | | |
|---|---|---|
| Performance return reported | → | 20% |
| Real return after fees and taxes | → | 9% |

---

If your investment grows at 20 percent per year, your money will double every three and one-half years. At 9 percent, your investment will take eight years to double. The difference is hardly trivial. What's worse, in years that the funds reported performance is small, or even negative, the fees and churning go on, driving your returns deeper into the red, cutting into your capital.

How does this performance compare with buying and holding individual stocks as you will do in the Dividend Growth Investment Strategy. If you have 20 percent reported returns for your mutual funds versus 20 percent growth in individual stocks (with no fees and taxes), and invest $1,000, after twenty years you will have $8,061 from a mutual fund but $38,200 from individual stocks.

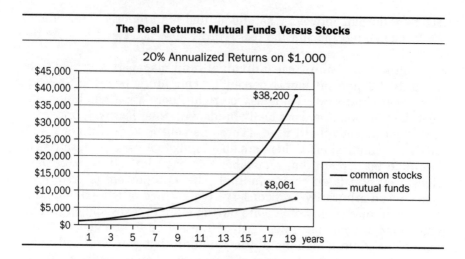

**The Real Returns: Mutual Funds Versus Stocks**

20% Annualized Returns on $1,000

If you think 20 percent is too optimistic (which it probably is), how about assuming a 13 percent growth rate on $1,000 for thirty years that will yield $13,800 from a mutual fund versus $63,200 from individual stocks.

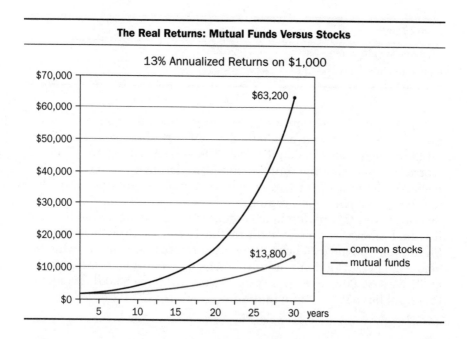

**The Real Returns: Mutual Funds Versus Stocks**

13% Annualized Returns on $1,000

These results just indicate capital gains, the dividends that you receive are an extra added attraction.

The obvious lesson is: Don't send your retirement money to Washington and Wall Street. Use the Dividend Growth Investment Strategy.

A further problem with mutual funds is the loss of control over your money. There is no good way to evaluate the fundamentals of a mutual fund. All you have to go on is the performance of the funds in previous years and a list of stocks that it has owned in the recent past. Knowing past performance does little to help, as all funds have their ups and downs. You can evaluate the fundamentals such as earnings, P/E (Price Earnings, i.e., price of a share divided by the annual earnings) ratios, etc. of the companies that the fund holds; however, you have no control or guarantees that the manager will continue to hold those stocks. There is nothing to prevent her from panicking and doing something that you regard as less than smart. With the Dividend Growth Investment Strategy, *you* have the control; in any event, mistakes are much less likely when you buy and hold the safe, dominant, large-cap companies recommended in my strategy.

BEWARE: There are mutual funds that advertise themselves as offering "Dividend Growth." These funds have little in common with the strategy that I have described and much in common with the rest of the universe of mutual funds. These funds, like any others, will generate capital-gains taxes for you every time someone redeems their shares. There is less opportunity for your nest egg to grow over time, for in one such fund there was a greater than 110 percent turnover per year. This fund reported holding the same stocks that I recommend in my portfolio: from the standpoint of taxes, fees, and control, you will do much better by holding the stocks yourself.

## MUTUAL FUND SUMMARY

Mutual funds represent perhaps the most widely used investment instrument for small investors. There are, however, many reasons why the Dividend Growth Investment Strategy is much superior to mutual fund investments in planning for and living through retirement. The dividend strategy allows you to know and control what is in your portfolio rather than let an anonymous manager make crucial decisions that can have a huge impact on your life. There is evidence some stocks picked for the Dividend Growth Investment Strategy generally perform slightly better than the S&P 500 (mainly because they are the top performers in that index), while most fund managers fall well below this benchmark. The overriding factor, however, is the destruction of the compounding of your investments by the fees and taxes generated in the mutual funds. The Dividend Growth Investment Strategy generates virtually *no* fees and minimal taxes, and thus lets your nest egg grow unencumbered.

# 4

BONDS: THE SNAIL IN THE
RACE AGAINST INFLATION

"And you are . . . ?"

"Bond. James Bond."

In the early 1960s, these words ushered in the ultimate adolescent male fantasy. James Bond was suave, daring, sexy, high risk, and ruthless. This was a dash of what all adolescent American males felt that they were deep inside, even if the outside didn't appear quite the same. Never mind that few could tell the difference between a shaken and a stirred vodka martini.

"And you are . . . ?"

"Bond. Municipal Bond."

It somehow doesn't have the same ring to it. Bonds, far from being sexy, high risk, daring, etc., are safe, stodgy, risk-averse, and as unexciting as you can imagine. They, should, it follows, be the perfect investment vehicle for the long-term, risk-averse investor getting ready for retirement. In fact, this is the conventional wisdom. Here is what *Kiplinger's Retirement Planning Guide '98* says about bonds, "The safety of bonds makes for a steadier ride toward retirement, and diversifies your portfolio as well." They offer safety and predictability. We will examine whether this is enough.

## WHAT ARE BONDS?

Basically, bonds are a loan that you give to someone with a guaranteed interest payment over a set period of time. The someone that you give

your money to may be a government (federal, local, or foreign), it may
be a corporation, a bank, or an insurance company. Your money is safe
and you are guaranteed to get your principal back at the end of the borrowing term (maturity) as well as your interest payments *as long as* the
entity that holds your money stays in business. Occasionally, corporations go bankrupt, which may mean that you lose some or all of your
investment. Government bonds are usually safe, but remember that Or-
ange County, one of the richest counties in California, defaulted on its
bonds a few years ago.

There are many variations on the way bonds are structured and
paid out. Some bonds carry insurance against the entity defaulting.
You pay for this with a slightly lower yield. Municipal bonds issued by
local government agencies may be free of federal and, in some cases,
local taxes. Again, this advantage is offset by a lower interest rate. The
federal government now issues bonds whose yields vary slightly with
the rate of inflation. Bonds can be issued for different times to maturity: in general, the longer the period, the higher the yield as the lender
is assuming more risk because the future is unknowable. Zero coupon
bonds are sold at a discount. The buyer receives no interest until maturity, at which time he receives it all in a lump sum. This may be advantageous if you have these bonds in a college or retirement fund where
you will need the money at a much later date. The disadvantage is that
each year that you hold the bond you must pay taxes on the income
generated, even though you receive no cash. This is the dreaded "phantom income." Certificates of deposit (CDs) issued by banks and guaranteed investment contracts (GICs), issued by insurance companies, are
similar in their effects to bonds.

Bonds also vary as to safety. There are bond rating agencies such as
*Moody's* and *Standard & Poor's* that evaluate and rate the entities issuing bonds, both corporate and governmental. The higher the rating, the
less risk and thus the lower interest rate that investors will accept. The
lowest rated are "junk" bonds and thus must pay very high yields to attract investors. Bonds can also undergo capital appreciation. If you
own a high yielding bond in an environment of falling interest rates,
investors will pay you a premium to get a greater yield than they could
purchase in newly issued bonds. Your gain will also depend on the maturity of your bond: No one will pay a lot for a high yielding bond that
will mature in three months, but if it is good for fifteen years, it may be
quite attractive. Obviously, the converse is also true. Your low-yield
bond in an environment of rising interest rates will be worth less than
you paid for it. These capital gains and losses are only analogous to
those seen in the stock market to a point. The rise and fall of interest
rates in bonds is finite. Only a limited change can be expected over the

life of the bond. With stocks, however, the possibilities are almost limitless. Your company could go bankrupt, or could double in size many times in a few years. Microsoft, Intel, and Cisco are names that come to mind. Even a staid corporate giant like General Electric falls into this category.

## THE RISKS OF BONDS

From the foregoing, it is clear that, while relatively safe, bonds do have their risks. As in all of finance, these fall under the headings of inflation and taxes. Inflation, while currently low, is nonetheless still with us. At 2 percent to 3 percent a year, this is much lower than the double digits that we experienced in the 1970s, but it is still more than the 1 percent in the post–World War II years. Remember, President Richard Nixon put in wage and price controls when inflation hit only 4 percent to 5 percent during his administration. If you are getting a 6 percent return on your bond, and inflation is 3 percent for the year, the math is easy: 6−3=3 percent, your real gain on your bond. Without blinking, you have lost half of the value of your interest that you collect. To illustrate why this is so, let's buy a $1,000 bond at a 6 percent interest rate and assume that inflation is 6 percent. At the end of the year, you now have $1,060 by adding your principal to your interest that you have earned. The 6 percent inflation rate, however, means that you need $1,060 at the end of the year to equal the buying power of the $1,000 that you started with. Hence, you have kept pace with inflation, but have made no extra money for the year. Similarly, if you use the same example with a 3 percent inflation rate, you still end up with $1,060 at the end of the year. You needed $1,030 to keep up with inflation, so your real gain in purchasing power was $30.

The other risk from inflation is the market value of your bond. Since interest rates generally track with inflation, if you have a low-yield bond, your bond loses value as the inflation rate increases. If you wish to sell, your bond will be worth less than you paid for it, and you will have suffered a loss of capital as well as a decrease in yield.

This section brings us to a consideration of the "time value of money." This means that money changes its value over time. If we have deflation, the money that we hide in our mattress will be worth more in ten years than it is today. More likely, inflation will erode that value. Whenever you consider an investment strategy, you must calculate not only what your investment will do over time, factoring in inflation, but what your financial needs will be. Consider this: It is 1998, you are forty years old, make $100,000 a year, can buy a refrigerator for $750 and a cup of coffee for $1.50. What will these figures be in 2038 when you are eighty years old if there is 4 percent inflation?

I would bet that many of you guessed that you would need less than the $480,000 yearly income that you will need to keep your same standard of living, and were surprised that the refrigerator will cost $3,600 and the coffee $7.20 (regular, not cappuccino). If you are fortunate to live to ninety, the numbers become even worse!

We are not going to consider death in this section, but will address the other unavoidable: taxes. Interest on bonds is taxable (with the exception of tax-free municipal bonds). The taxes are due the year the interest is credited to your account, even if you receive no cash. Zero coupon bonds are the prototype for this generator of "phantom" income. If you are in a mutual fund that includes bonds, you will get a yearly tax statement telling you in no uncertain terms to pay taxes on your portion of the interest. The taxes are paid from your household budget, along with the taxes paid from your ordinary income. Furthermore, the interest is added on top of the income from your labor and, therefore, is taxed at the highest marginal rate, which may be up to 39 percent, not counting the taxes that your state may also collect (in Minnesota, this is 8.5 percent with no chance to deduct federal taxes from your income). To simplify, if you pay 30 percent in taxes on the 6 percent interest from your bond, you pay, for each $6: 6 × .30 = 1.80 or $1.80, leaving $4.20. Remember, that we already lost $3 to inflation. This leaves you with $1.20. Here is a similar calculation: If you have a $1,000 bond at 6 percent yield, your income per year will be $60; now subtract for inflation and taxes: $1,000 × 3 percent inflation = $30; plus taxes $60 × 34 percent = $20; so your real return is only $10. And this calculation does not take into account the compounding effects of inflation.

**Time Value of Money**

*4% Rate of Inflation*

| Year | Your age | Your Salary | Refrigerator | Cup of Coffee |
|------|----------|-------------|--------------|---------------|
| 1998 | 40 | $100,000 | $750 | $1.50 |
| 2008 | 50 | $148,000 | $1,110 | $2.22 |
| 2018 | 60 | $219,000 | $1,640 | $3.29 |
| 2028 | 70 | $324,000 | $2,430 | $4.87 |
| 2038 | 80 | $480,000 | $3,600 | $7.20 |
| 2048 | 90 | $710,000 | $5,330 | $10.66 |

These calculations may seem somewhat theoretical, so let's go to some actual calculations. Robert T. Willis, in his article "Prudent Investor Rules Gives Trustees New Guidelines" (1992), has calculated the real yield of bonds from 1950 through 1991. The average bond yield for that period was 6.1 percent. Inflation over that period (which included long periods of both high and low inflation rates) took away 4.3 percent from that yield. Taxes, which he calculated at 25 percent (low by current standards) took away another 1.53 percent. This left a total of *0.27 percent* in your pocket for the real return each year. I doubt that a bond salesman would like to use that figure in his sales pitch.

## ZERO RISK

These results seem pretty dismal, so why do investors buy bonds? The same Kiplinger report that I quoted earlier on the attractiveness of bonds contains the following statement, "Stocks are winners by a big margin in the long-term performance derby." According to the author's statistics, from 1975 through 1992, large cap stocks (i.e., stocks from large companies with $5 billion or more in capitalization) outperformed bonds by a 2.5 to 1 ratio and small cap stocks (i.e., stocks from small companies with $1 billion or less in capitalization) outperformed bonds by a ratio of 5 to 1. Why then would anyone invest in bonds? The authors of the Kiplinger report answer it this way:

> Not all individuals feel comfortable enough with stocks—despite their winning performance—to put an entire nest egg in that basket.

They go on to offer the conventional advice:

> If stocks are just too unsettling for you or if you have less than ten years to go to retirement, the bonds' lower volatility is important. The net effect of holding a small portion of your entire nest egg in bonds is to cushion the entire basket.

Whenever you read about retirement planning, the conventional wisdom is similar. Asset allocation is paramount. You should have a certain percentage of your money in stocks, a certain percentage in bonds (30 percent?), some in real estate (your homestead), insurance, and cash. As you near retirement, you should decrease your reliance on those risky stocks and increase your percentage of safe, income-generating bonds. Heaven forbid that you should own a fast-growing stock such as Microsoft or Cisco Systems, for this would throw off your

asset allocation, forcing you to sell off stocks that are repeatedly doubling in value to buy safe bonds. You must keep your assets in the
proper balanced percentages.

Jonathan Clements writes in his December 1, 1998, *Wall Street
Journal* column:

> Investing is plagued by uncertainty. Get used to it. That, of
> course, is the last thing most investors want to do. They find
> the daily turmoil unnerving, and they do everything possi-
> ble to escape it.
>
> The cure, however, is often worse than the disease.

Clements makes the point that we have covered, that U.S. treasury
bonds, for instance, may have certainty and be safe, but they are not
risk-free. They, in fact, contain a grave risk, namely that they will not
provide an adequate amount of money for retirement. One way he suggests to get around the problem is to split your portfolio into low-risk
and higher-risk portions.

These sources that I have quoted give us a clue as to why bonds are
attractive to investors. There is no good investment rationale for buying
them; it is all psychological. People want bonds because they can't handle the day-to-day volatility of the stock market. They can't accept Warren Buffett's advice to buy a stock and not look at it again for five years.
(They must believe that he earned his billions through extreme luck.)
The question remains: If you have ten years left until retirement, why
put a significant portion of your assets in a sector that is guaranteed to
underperform the rest of your money by a factor of up to *five* times?

## STOCKS VERSUS BONDS

The idea that stocks outperform bonds over the long run is nothing
new. Jeremy J. Siegel, professor of finance at the Wharton School of
Business, University of Pennsylvania, in his excellent book *Stocks for
the Long Run* traces the performance of the stock market against other
investment vehicles over the last two hundred years. Obviously, this
included periods of expansion and depression, inflation and deflation,
bull and bear markets: in short, any type of financial environment that
we are likely to encounter in our lifetimes. He charts the performance
of stocks, bonds, gold, and the consumer price index (CPI), the measure
of inflation, from 1802 to 1997. He does not take out taxes and reinvests
all interest and dividends. He does make the point that this is somewhat artificial, because, in real life, investors usually take some of the
proceeds from their investments to live on.

Siegel comes up with the following results from investing $1 in each of these asset categories in 1802:

1. In 1997, the CPI has risen to: $13.37;
2. Gold did not do as well as inflation, worth only: $11.17;
3. Bonds seem to perform far better, your one dollar having risen to: $10,744;
4. Do you think that the stock investment would be worth 2.5 to 5 times this figure, as the Kiplinger article hinted at? Most people would consider $50,000 to be a pretty good return on $1. Consider again. If left in the stock market and not touched, with dividends reinvested in your stocks, your $1 would have grown to $7,470,000

Think back to the story of Beth, the poor woman who called the radio talk show, who was so spooked by the market that she wanted to sell her mutual funds and buy gold!

## DIVIDENDS VERSUS BONDS

Now we are face to face with the conundrum: Most people say to themselves, "I know that the stock market is the place to be, but I can't stand the risk, the uncertainty, the volatility." I can certainly empathize with this feeling (for it certainly is about feelings, not logic). For years our pension money was in GICs (guaranteed investment contracts) for this very reason. Our first foray into individual investing was to buy a basket load of bonds. This is the precise reason why I developed the Dividend Growth Investment Strategy. This strategy allows you to ride the roller coaster (capital gains) to let your stocks appreciate while at the same time ascending the escalator (dividends) to give you a measure of safety and certainty.

We already know that the stock-price appreciation will outperform bonds by many multiples, but how do dividends stack up against the interest that you earn on bonds? This depends on the stocks that you pick. If you buy Microsoft or Dell Computer, you may get a large capital gain, but they pay no dividend. Utilities pay high dividends, in the 4 percent to 5 percent range, but only raise them with the inflation rate. The heart of the Dividend Growth Investment Strategy is to pick stocks that have a long history of continuous dividend raises. Doing this, you could average a 14 percent increase in dividends every year, which means that the total dividend payout will double every five years.

For the comparison of stock dividends to bond interest, let's (only for the sake of this discussion!) forget that there is any capital gain in the stock. What are the advantages of dividends over bond interest? The first is that dividends are not fixed. In most cases, a strong company's earnings will increase with inflation, and thus the directors will also increase the dividends. With bonds, you are stuck, and inflation can destroy your gains.

What about taxes? Both dividends and interest are taxed as ordinary income to the investor. This means that you will pay your highest marginal tax rate on any income that you receive from these sources. There is, however, one crucial difference: The bond will pay out the same rate of interest throughout its life. A 6 percent bond will pay you 6 percent a year from year one through maturity. This means that during the years that you are still working and earning a relatively high income, much of the interest that you earn in those years goes to taxes.

Stock dividends are different. They start low and grow over time. During your high-earning working years they may be only 1 percent to 1.5 percent of your investment, generating very little in tax. In your retirement years these dividends may hit 100 percent or more of your original investment. At this point, however, your total income will likely be smaller, and thus the tax bite less painful. Further, at maturity the bond's interest payments cease and you get your original principal back. With the stock, both the principal and the dividend payment continue growing throughout your retirement. With a stock that grows at 14 percent per year, both the stock price and the dividend payout will double every five years.

As I have said, stock dividends grow over time. How does this affect your total return? Let's assume 2 percent to 3 percent inflation and let's spend $20,000. We will buy a 6 percent bond with $10,000 and buy a stock such as Johnson and Johnson with the other $10,000. Assume that this stock pays out a dividend of 1.5 percent but raises it 14 percent per year. What happens in thirty years when you are ready to retire? In year one, you get, and pay taxes on: $600 from the bond and only $150 from the stock. In year thirty, you still get $600 per year from the bond, but the stock is now paying $9,600 per year, almost at the level of the original investment. In another five years, that figure will double again. This increase has been relatively constant over the thirty-year period. Considering inflation, the real payout from the bond is only $300, while the stock is paying out $4,800.

I said earlier we would forget about the capital gains, but now is the time to re-remember them. What has happened to the $10,000 that you invested in each of your choices? The bond has reached its maturity, so you get your principal back. The $10,000, however, due to inflation, is now worth $5,000. All you can do with it is buy another 6 percent bond. The stock, on the other hand, has been appreciating at 14 percent per year. The increase has not been a straight line; some years you may get 30 percent, some years, no or even negative growth, but over all 14 percent. The stock is now worth $640,000. Even taking inflation into account, the stock is worth $320,000.

| Bond Versus Stock | |
|---|---|
| *Inflation of 2–3% a Year for 30 Years* | |
| *$10,000 Bond* | *$10,000 Stock* |
| •Bond (6%) does not appreciate | •Stock appreciates at 14% a year for 30 years |
| •$10,000 → $10,000 | •$10,000 → $640,000 |
| •Yield $600 → $600 | •Yield $150 → $9,600 |
| •After inflation value —$5,000 —$300 | •After-inflation value —$320,000 —$4,800 |

You may ask, "What if the stock and its dividend don't grow at 14 percent?" Intuitively, even if the stock performs only half as well as predicted, it still out performs the bond by a mile.

Let us consider in more detail the possibility that your stock doesn't perform as well as expected. For this example, we are going to spend $2,000 on a bond paying 7 percent over thirty years (a hard thing to find in the current environment), and we will invest $2,000 each in stocks that turn out to grow an average of 14 percent, 10 percent, and 7 percent respectively, starting with a 1.5 percent yield. What happens?

| Invest $2,000 Each Year for 30 Years | | | |
|---|---|---|---|
| *Annual Growth Rate* | *Stock Appreciation 30 Years* | *Total Dividend Payments* | *Dividend Payment in Year 30* |
| 14% Stock | $763,524 | $80,729 | $10,704 |
| 10% Stock | $345,437 | $45,283 | $4,935 |
| 7% Stock | $195,534 | $30,460 | $2,833 |
| 7% Bond | $    0 | $31,500 | $4,200 |

In the best-case scenario for stocks, 14 percent, you have collected 2.5 times the total dividend payments over the thirty years as you have with the bond ($80,729 versus $31,500). Your payout in year thirty is 2.5 times greater as well ($10,704 versus $4,200). Your capital gain, the money you have made on the increase in your stock price, is $763,524 versus $0 for the bond. At 10 percent, which is more conservative, but definitely within the expected year over year performance of the broad stock market, your total dividend payout over thirty years is still 50 percent larger ($45,283 versus $31,500) and the yearly payout is $735 higher and growing. The $345,437 capital gain is also nothing to sneeze at. Even in the worst-case scenario of an anemic 7 percent growth in your stock, you don't fare too badly. Your total dividend payout over thirty years is slightly less than that for the bond, and your payout in year thirty is two-thirds of that you receive from the bond; however, your dividend from the stock will continue to grow and eventually surpass the payout of the bond. More important, you have still made a capital gain of $195,534 against, need we say it again, $0.

Sometimes, it is easier to picture the differences in different growth patterns graphically. Following is a chart comparing the growth in dividends between a 6 percent treasury bond, an 8 percent corporate bond, and a common stock that grows its dividend at 14 percent per year.

Your eye is first drawn to the thirty-year column, where the stock massively outperforms the bonds. Consider that, even if the stock divi-

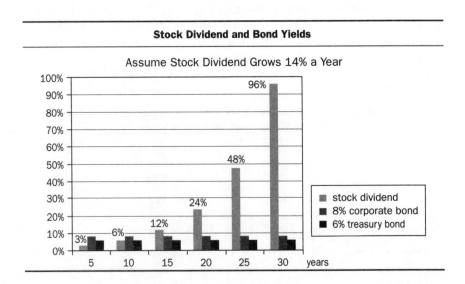

**Stock Dividend and Bond Yields**

Assume Stock Dividend Grows 14% a Year

dend grows only half as much as predicted, you're still way ahead of the game. To appreciate a little more detail, look at years five and ten, where the bonds are paying out more than the stock. It takes time for your dividends to grow, but once they start up the steep part of the curve, the growth is phenomenal. (As a review, remember that the dividend payout is based on the original amount of money invested, not on the current dividend compared to the *current* stock price—the yield. If a stock originally pays out a 1.5 percent dividend yield, the dividend payment amount grows at 14 percent per year, and the stock price also grows at 14 percent per year, the yield will stay at 1.5 percent throughout, even as the dividend payment amount grows in relation to the *original* investment.)

Comparing the capital gains of bonds to stocks is even easier. The following graph shows what happens to the capital appreciation of $1 invested in a 6 percent bond and a 14 percent growth stock such as Johnson & Johnson.

At year thirty, I think all of us would rather have the $64 than the $1 that we started with. As I said before, bonds can show some capital gains or losses in their value. This, however, depends on the expectations of interest rate changes. Over a thirty-year period, these ups and downs of interest rates should cancel each other out and the gains or losses should be nil.

**Capital Appreciation of $1 Stocks Versus Bonds**

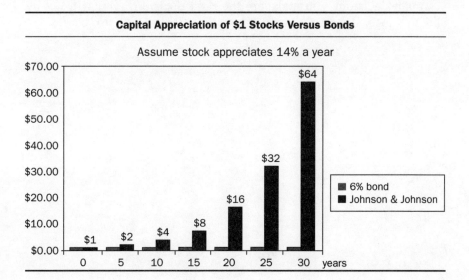

Assume stock appreciates 14% a year

Legend: 6% bond / Johnson & Johnson

## WHAT PERCENTAGE OF YOUR PORTFOLIO SHOULD BE ALLOCATED TO BONDS?

The conventional wisdom says that this should be a fixed percentage of your portfolio, depending on your tolerance for risk, that increases as you approach retirement. My answer is somewhat different. I see that the only reason that most people have for investing in bonds is to psychologically escape the stress and strain of the risky stock market. I will again ask the question: "Is it logical to invest in a vehicle guaranteed to underperform the stock market for the illusion of safety?" I believe that the Dividend Growth Investment Strategy gives you the tools to invest in the stock market roller coaster while maintaining your psychological needs by safely ascending the dividend escalator. Anne Scheiber, our first example of a most successful investor, must have conquerred the psychological demons of the stock market. In sticking with her investments over the long haul, she went through the 1970s, a decade that saw no stock-price appreciation, without wavering. We can only surmise that her dividends were sufficient during this period to satisfy both her financial and psychological needs and allow her to stay the course.

True to my philosophy that you should take *direction* of your investments for yourself, I believe that you should not take my word for this somewhat unconventional approach. Do the reading and the math for yourself, think about what I have written, and come to your own conclusion. Unless you are completely convinced that whatever investment decisions you make are the right decisions, you will not be able to muster the *discipline* to stay with your strategy for *decades.*

# 5

## THE ANNUITY BRIAR PATCH

In the process of evaluating my investment philosophy, I consulted with my brother-in-law, who has a doctorate in statistics and is also an insurance actuary. I was hoping to get some input as to the statistical methods that I used in my analysis (he did give much valuable assistance, for which I am extremely grateful). Along with the statistical help, I received an earful from the insurance side of his persona. "But how does this compare to annuities?" "People will still buy annuities." "I don't think that this will replace annuities." Every other sentence contained the A word; he seemed stuck in that box. I attributed this to his insurance background, giving increased importance to a small part of the investment world that he was overly familiar with; an option that I had never considered for my family. Because he was so emphatic, however, I thought that I would humor him and look into the subject. I couldn't have been more wrong. Annuities are the investment vehicle of choice for large segments of our population. According to the *Wall Street Journal,* $1,200,000,000,000 (yes, that's 1.2 trillion dollars) was invested in annuities by the end of 1997. In 1998 alone, $100 billion went into these vehicles. That ain't chicken feed.

Annuities are definitely popular, but are they a good idea and are they suitable for you? *Forbes* magazine said, on its February 9, 1998, cover: "Don't Be a Sucker! Variable Annuities Are a Lousy Investment!" *Forbes* concluded that these annuities "are sold, not bought," implying that they benefit the insurance companies and agents that sell them more than those buying them. And you thought that those large insurance skyscrapers sprang up from the pavement with just a little water and sunlight.

We need to look in some depth into annuities to understand them. If you are going to succumb to the temptation, it should be because you know enough about them to "buy" rather than have someone "sell" you a product that doesn't fit your needs. It should be instructive to observe how people view the annuities that they purchase. Deferred annuities are purchased some time before the payouts are to begin (usually at retirement). At the time that the payout is to begin, the annuitant has the option of receiving the payments per the original contract or take a lump-sum distribution of the accumulated money. I, and probably you as well, would be shocked to learn that only 5 percent of the participants elect to continue with the monthly payments, and 95 percent take a lump sum. Why would they pay all of the fees and forgo other investment opportunities that would have been available? Maybe they are telling us something.

What is an annuity? This is an investment vehicle in which, by contract, you turn over your money to someone, usually an insurance company, and at a time specified in the future, they are obligated to make payments to you, usually to support your retirement. This sounds very vague, and it is, because there are numerous permutations and combinations in the way you pay in the money and the way you receive your payments in return. The simplest form of contract consists of the participant giving the insurance company a lump sum of money either before or at the time of retirement. Based on their calculations of your life expectancy and the rate of growth of the money (usually calculated at 3 percent), they give you a monthly payment guaranteed for the rest of your life. At your death, the remainder of the money is kept by the insurer, leaving nothing to your heirs.

As I have said, these contracts can be written in almost any way that you and the insurer want. Some of the common terms used in defining annuities are:

*Straight Annuities* a series of fixed payments.

*Variable Annuities* a series of payments in amounts that depend on the investment results realized by the payer.

*Life Annuity* an annuity payable only until the death of the owner (annuitant), regardless of when death occurs.

*Annuity for Term Certain* (annuity certain) an annuity payable for a specified period regardless of when death occurs.

*Deferred Annuity* an annuity under which payments start at a specified time in the future.

*Immediate Annuity* payments start immediately upon deposit of the principal.

*Joint and Survivor Annuity* an annuity payable until the second of two individuals dies.

*Indexed Annuity* an annuity where the payments vary with a specified index (such as the Standard & Poor's 500).

These terms aren't mutually exclusive. For instance, a variable annuity can be either immediate or deferred. A straight annuity can be either a life annuity or an annuity certain.

All of these options, while different, have a basic core in common:

1. You hand over your nest egg to an insurance company.
2. They invest your money.
3. You receive payments that are less in total than the insurance company realizes from its investments.
4. You pay no taxes during the accumulation period but pay ordinary income on any gains that are withdrawn.

## STRAIGHT ANNUITIES

These are the simplest types of annuities and the easiest to understand. You give your money to the insurance company either in a lump sum or as a series of payments, and they guarantee a fixed income for you for the rest of your life, after which they keep the remainder. The main point to remember is that the insurer calculates the payments based on life tables estimating your life expectancy (annuities are the opposite of life insurance in this regard: With life insurance, the insurer wins if you live a long life; with the annuity, they are the winners if you die young) and using a 3–5 percent growth rate for the money that you turn over to them. You should recall that the growth rate of stocks since 1925 has averaged 10.2 percent. This annuity gives the difference, 7.2 percent, to the insurer. Why not keep the entire 10.2 percent for yourself?

## DEFERRED ANNUITIES

A deferred annuity provides income payments that start later, often many years after the original payment. Deferred annuities have an "accumulation" period, which is the time between the point when you start paying premiums and when income payments start. The time after income payments start is called the "payout" period. The deferred annuity allows the value of the contract to increase *tax-free* during the accumulation period. The owner of the deferred annuity can elect to do any one of the following at any point of the contract:

1. Surrender the contract for a lump sum.
2. Take staged withdrawals.
3. Elect a one-life or two-life annuity either with or without a guaranteed minimum (annuitization).
4. Leave amounts on deposit to pay interest to the annuity owner.

While the annuity owner has these four elections that can be taken at any time, there are penalties if taken too early. These penalties are:

1. The premature surrender or early withdrawal triggers penalties under the annuity contract. Typically, the annuity contract's surrender charges are about 7 percent and expire at the rate of 1 percent per year; over seven to nine years the penalty declines to zero. For example, if the annuity owner takes a premature withdrawal after two years into the contract a 5 percent penalty may be charged.
2. The Internal Revenue Code also imposes a 10 percent premature withdrawal penalty for withdrawal prior to death, disability, or age 59 and a half.
3. If the owner of the annuity elects to annuitize (take payments over his lifetime or a set number of years), this election must be made within sixty days of the date the contract provides for a lump-sum distribution. When the lump-sum distribution is paid out the annuity owner will owe ordinary income taxes on the entire amount.

## VARIABLE ANNUITIES

Variable annuities came into existence after World War II, when inflation was rising and people started living longer. The variable annuity was an attempt to ensure that the annuity's return would increase in value with inflation. The variable-annuity owner received the entire return from the investment assets (stocks and bonds), which were held in a segregated asset account by the insurance company. The insurance company charges commissions and annual fees on the variable annuity instead of receiving the spread between the investment return and the interest guaranteed to the fixed-annuity owner. The variable annuity owner was able to get the higher returns from the stock market, but also had to assume the risk that the investments would decline in value.

### History

In the 1970s the "investment annuity" evolved. This allowed an investor to own and control his investment portfolio and to defer taxation on both income and capital gains. The insurance company acted as a passive trustee-custodian for the investment annuity. The investment annuity owner could put unlimited amounts of money in the annuity for purposes of investing. The investment income from churning or turnover of stocks was not taxed until the money was eventually removed from the annuity. Taxes were deferred until annuitization or money was withdrawn from the annuity. This tax deferral allows the nest egg growth to compound even when there is churning and turnover in the annuity. *Turnover of stocks has no tax consequences in a variable annuity,* unlike a mutual fund, which passes gains through to its holders at year end, forcing them to pay taxes on all the gains from the turnover. This tax-deferral feature is the main selling point for variable annuities.

The other big advantage of the investment annuity, the ability to self-direct or invest in stocks and bonds directly, has been lost. Congress and the IRS saw this as a great loss of revenue and a tax-avoidance scheme by annuity owners. To curb this perceived abuse, Congress placed restrictions on annuity owners, requiring annuities to be invested by a third person (generally a professional money manager—this was the start of the mutual-fund boom). The owner of the variable annuity could direct the premiums among a group of subaccounts (these subaccounts are managed like a mutual fund) with no taxes owed on the turnover, but could no longer buy and sell individual stocks and bonds. It is interesting that the government perceived the investment annuity as a potential tax avoidance vehicle, which ultimately led to the establishment of the mutual fund. Mutual funds keep both the government and Wall Street content because so much of the holder's profits are siphoned off each year without much understanding or notice. This is the destruction of compounding by taxes and fees that we came to understand in earlier chapters. The poor investor trying to save for retirement outside his pension plan just about runs in place.

If you are inclined to invest in variable annuities, there is one situation that may be appropriate: using them as a vehicle to invest in a stock fund that has a high turnover rate with a high growth rate, an aggressive high growth stock fund (In 1999, for example, an Internet stock fund). A mutual fund with these highly volatile stocks will generate a large amount of taxes, taxes that the annuity fund holder will not be subject to. If you go this route, you will probably want a diversified and professionally managed stock fund. You must have a long-term-investment time horizon (twenty-five years) to break even for the cost of converting capital gain to ordinary income and offsetting the higher annual fees charged by an annuity. The longer you allow your assets to grow tax-deferred, the more advantageous the variable annuity becomes.

**Warning!**

Your ability to switch your annuity funds from one subaccount to another subaccount without a tax cost may be coming to an end. There is proposed legislation by the Clinton administration to tax the movement of funds from one subaccount to another.

## INDEXED ANNUITIES

These vehicles are relatively new. They differ from variable annuities in two important respects:

1. The performance of your fund is not tied to investments in specific stocks and bonds, but rather increases or decreases with a standard index. Any index of bonds or stocks, such as the Dow Jones Industrial Average, or the Russell 2000 index may be chosen, however the Standard & Poor's 500 index is the most common.

2. These accounts provide a floor for your investment, not allowing them to fall below a certain level regardless of how badly your index performs (they may have a ceiling as well). The variable annuity, like a mutual fund, is unforgiving in a bad market; you are at risk for both high losses as well as high gains.

If you are going to invest in one of these annuities, read the contract carefully. There are different ways to apply the chosen index to your fund (point-to-point, high water mark, and annual reset, also known as ratcheting). There will be a fixed term over which the indexing applies, generally from one to ten years, and floors and caps on the variation. There also is a "participation rate" which is a percent that applies to the change in the index. For instance, if the S&P 500 rises 10 percent in one year, and you have a participation rate of 60 percent, your investments will rise by 10 percent × 60 percent = 6 percent. You must be aware of all of these variations if you choose to follow this path. By this time, you should see that these investments do not meet the criteria for the Dividend Growth Investment Strategy.

## WHY OR WHY NOT?

What is the advantage to investing in annuities? The reasons that most annuitants are sold on these investments are simple: security and certainty. If you invest in a straight annuity, you give up your money for a fixed income for the rest of your life. You don't have to worry about the stock market roller coaster (although we will see later there is a lot that you should be worrying about). If you purchase a variable annuity, you are at risk for poor market performance, but you do have some tax advantages over mutual funds. You also may get a death benefit with this type of annuity, however, the amount that your heirs would receive would be small. You would get your principal returned, but little else.

There are many more reasons not to let yourself be sold an annuity. Some are the same reasons that I gave for staying out of mutual funds and bonds, but some are specific for annuities.

### Loss of Inheritance

If you have a desire to leave an inheritance for your descendants, annuities are not for you. With a straight annuity, when you are gone, so is the money. The benefit to the insurance company is that after supporting you in life, they keep your money at your death. Variable annuities often have a death benefit as part of the contract. This, usually, is more of a promise than a fact. Often, this benefit disappears as the annuitant reaches seventy-five or eighty years old. If any money is left for your heirs, wish them luck, for after paying 40 percent income tax on any gains that you have realized and up to 55 percent estate tax on everything distributed, they may be left with only pocket change. The only way to avoid taxes on money in this account is to leave it to charity.

### Taxes

Annuities have a tax advantage over mutual funds in that all gains in your annuity account are deferred until you withdraw the money as payments, while in a mutual fund you pay taxes each year on the dividends and capital gains. You have a distinct disadvantage, however, in comparing your annuity's tax bill to that of the Dividend Growth Investment Strategy. When you own individual stocks and sell them after holding them over one year, you pay capital gains tax rates of 20 percent. In the annuity account, you pay ordinary income tax on any gain as you receive your payment. This rate can be as high as 40 percent. You have lost the favorable treatment of capital gains. Let's see how this works:

Variable Annuity
$100,000 × 40 percent (income tax rate) = $40,000 taxes due
You will have after taxes: $60,000

A Portfolio You Hold Outright
$100,000 × 20 percent (capital-gains tax rate) = $20,000
taxes due
You will have after taxes: $80,000

After the year 2000, for stocks bought and held for more than five years the capital-gains rate will be 18 percent, leaving you with $82,000 after taxes.

The tax man also will take a big chunk of your annuity if you wish to make an early withdrawal: Any money withdrawn before you reach fifty-nine and a half years is subject to a 10 percent penalty.

## Fees

I showed you how fees hurt the compounding of mutual funds; annuities are much worse. The reason that annuities are so aggressively sold to clients is not that they are the best alternative for the investor but that they are a great deal for the agent. The commission for an agent or broker selling an annuity averages 5–7 percent, double the 3 percent average for a mutual-fund salesman selling a fund with a load. Annual fees that all annuities have are substantial. There is an annual contract maintenance fee of around $30. Fees for managing your assets in each fund can run as high as 2.5 percent of total assets every year. There is an annual assessment of approximatley 1.25 percent per year to cover administration; mortality and expense charges. These fees average about 2.25 percent per year, excluding the sales commission at the front end. The total fees could run as high as 4 percent a year on the average cash value of the annuity contract. Remember: Even a 1 percent yearly fee for twenty years decreases the value of your nest egg by 17 percent.

## Inflation

Variable and indexed annuities are protected against the effects of inflation to the extent that their investments rise with inflation. Straight annuities, on the other hand, have no inflation protection. For instance, at 3.5 percent inflation, your money's value is cut in half every twenty years. If you retire at age sixty with an income of $20,000 per year, and that income stays fixed, it will be worth $10,000 a year at age eighty. If we have periods of higher inflation, the results will be devastating.

## Regulations

By buying an annuity, you commit to a long-term relationship with both the insurance company and Uncle Sam. Annuities are currently highly regulated by the federal government, and the contracts that you sign with the insurance company are highly restrictive. At least these contracts with the insurer are binding and can't be changed arbitrarily and unilaterally. The federal government, however, recognizes no such restrictions. If you doubt this, think back to the Clinton tax increases if 1993. These increases were applied *retroactively* for a whole year before the law was passed. If you commit to an annuity today, who can predict what the laws governing these accounts will be twenty-five years from now? As we have seen, the government previously outlawed self-direction of your annuity account and is currently considering proposals to tax transfers between subaccounts. What do they have up their sleeve for the future?

Putting aside the government, you are still subject to your contract restrictions by the insurance company. If, after a few years of making payments, you become disenchanted, you can take your money out. If you are over fifty-nine and a half, you owe the government no penalty, but you may have to pay a penalty of up to 9 percent of your balance to the insurance company. Contrast this to a stock that you no longer have confidence in. You can sell this over the internet for a brokerage fee of as low as $7. Do you really want to get snarled in the annuity briar patch?

## Security

As I stated earlier, the main reason people allow themselves to be sold annuities is for the security of having a guaranteed fixed income. The contract that guarantees this income is, however, only as good as the insurance company backing it. Insurance companies can and do go bankrupt, leaving many of their creditors emptyhanded. I have first-hand knowledge of this. A few years ago, we had about 15 percent of my husband's pension fund invested in a GIC (guaranteed insurance contract) with a major U.S. insurance company with good ratings. We were poised to switch that money into an S&P indexed fund when a Canadian subsidiary of the U.S. company went under, throwing the whole company into receivership. Our funds were frozen as the company was taken over by federal regulators. After two years of uncertainty, we finally had our principal returned, along with some interest, less than called for in the original contract. At that point, we were overjoyed to get anything; looking back now, we see all that we lost with that money sitting dormant through two years of the great bull market.

The odds of an insurance company defaulting on your annuity are small, but if it happens, it can be devastating. If, this far into this chapter, you are still so inclined, protect yourself. Before you commit to an annuity contract, check out the insurance company carefully. There are good rating services that evaluate the credit worthiness of these insurance carriers. These services, with their "very high ratings" are:

Standard & Poor's AA+, AA, or AAA
Moody's Aa2, Aa1, Aaa
Duff & Phelps AAA
Weiss B+, A−, A, A+

If you are turning over your retirement nest egg to an insurance company you may want to choose an insurance company that has at the very least "high ratings" given by all of these ratings firms. It would also be wise to look at the data underlying these ratings:

1. company surplus
2. profitability
3. liquidity
4. asset quality
5. risk-based capital ratios

## Opportunity Costs

As with any investment, buying an annuity is a choice that precludes using that money in other ways. If your money is tied up in an annuity, what gains have you passed up? As we have seen with a straight annuity, the insurance company builds its office towers off the spread between the 3 percent that it pays you on your money and the 10.2 percent growth in the stock market. With variable and indexed annuities, you get the investment income, but the company charges you high fees to manage this money. What have you received for the money that you turned over to the insurance company? Basically, they do the same thing with your money that you could do for yourself. If this is the case, why not do it yourself and keep the fees? In order to justify fees of 4 percent per year, the money manager would have to beat your performance by more than 4 percent. Since 90 percent of mutual fund managers under perform the S&P 500, this is unlikely.

## Life Insurance

Annuities often are sold with life insurance policies and lumped together. This is a huge mistake. If you have done this, when you die, the payments from your insurance will be part of your estate and will be taxed as such. If insurance on your life is kept separate from your estate, as it should be, your heirs will save the 55 percent estate tax.

### IRAs and Qualified Plans

Over half of annuities are sold to investors as part of an IRA or other plan that allows tax deferral. This is also a huge mistake. The main advantage of a variable annuity is that it allows you to defer the taxes on the gains for your investments. If your money is already in a tax-deferred plan, you are simply paying high fees twice over by buying an annuity with this money.

### Buying at Retirement

A large proportion of variable annuities are sold to people at or close to retirement. These are the people that will benefit the least from these investments. As I stated previously, estimates show that it takes twenty-five years of allowing your investments to grow in an annuity before you make up for all of the fees as well as the shift of your taxes from capital gains to ordinary income. At retirement, most people don't have twenty-five years to wait. If you buy one of these investments at all, it only makes sense to do it when you are young.

### Non-Spouse Beneficiary

If you designate a beneficiary to your annuity that is not your spouse, or have a joint ownership with a non-spouse, the annuity must pay income and estate taxes at the time of the first partner's death, leaving about a quarter of the original amount for the survivor.

## ANNUITIES VERSUS DIVIDEND GROWTH INVESTMENT STRATEGY

It is clear that holding a portfolio of stocks outright is far superior to both a variable annuity and a mutual fund. Holding the stock portfolio outright is the only way you can avoid commissions, annual fees, and receive the favorable tax rates of 20 percent should you decide to sell your stocks. If you use the buy and hold Dividend Growth Investment Strategy and continue to hold your stocks, you will not pay any taxes on the capital appreciation of your assets. You will, however, pay ordinary income taxes on your dividends.

The Dividend Growth Investment Strategy has as one of its underlying principles that you should start early and stick with it through your retirement. Approaching retirement, you don't want to be in the position of having to cast around for an annuity to shift your money into. As with any task that you do in life, you should do it right the first time. If you start investing in high-quality, dividend-growing stocks when you are young, you will have no temptation to pay the high fees for the lesser performance offered by the annuity salesmen.

## SUMMARY

When I think of investing in an annuity, the image that comes to mind is of jumping into a briar patch—a tangle of fees, regulations, taxes, and poor investment options that claws at you as you try to extricate yourself. I would, however, never tell you, or anyone else, how you should invest your money. If you want to invest in an annuity, my hope is that you do it with an open mind and a fund of knowledge.

I personally believe that the Dividend Growth Investment Strategy is the best vehicle for most people to provide for their retirement. More important, however, than the specific vehicle of investment for your retirement is starting early and positioning your money to grow to and through the date of your retirement. Yesterday was the right time to start, today is still not too late—but don't wait until tomorrow! Don't expect to show up at the door of the AARP or an insurance agent on your sixty-fifth birthday with a small pile of money looking to buy an annuity. Give yourself a retirement present thirty years in advance.

# 6

## BACK TO THE LIBRARY

Throughout this book, I have tried to make it clear that your investments and your retirement depend on *you*. Your broker, Louis Rukeyser, Peter Lynch, or RoxAnn Klugman cannot do as good of a job for your retirement as you can. All of these people, and many more, may help, but the responsibilities are still yours. Once you accept this responsibility, I'm sure you will puff yourself up, look around, and say to yourself, "Now what?" The "what" is to educate yourself. Financial and economic education is a lifelong process: as you get into it, I am sure that you will develop your own sources that you will trust. In the meantime, to get you started I will give you the sources that I have used over the years. The list is long, but remember: this is a lifelong process. There will be *no* test on this eclectic collection next month.

The resources that I give you can be divided into a number of categories: general knowledge of the world and how it is working, general information on the world of investing, specific information on stocks and other investment vehicles, and finally, the place that you can get all of the above and more—the Internet.

### KEEP UP WITH THE WORLD

Investing does not occur in a vacuum. Any corporation, any real-estate investment, any bond issue, has its worth determined by the immutable laws of supply and demand. This, in turn, is dependent on many trends in society, government, economics, war and peace, and many more variables. The quality of how well a munitions manufacturer produces cruise missiles may be wonderful, but if the politicians are cutting back on defense spending, his quality won't save him. Conversely, if we are in a prolonged confrontation with Iraq, cruise missiles will sell like Beanie Babies. It pays for you to have some sense of these possibilities if you are going to invest in the defense industry. You know the sources that will get you this information: newspapers, TV, news magazines, and so forth. Many of these sources have to be read with a healthy dose of skepticism. Once you enter the world of investing, I hope that you develop pride of ownership in the companies you buy and learn not to fall for the networks' line that every dispute can be explained in terms of a malevolent corporation exploiting consumers or workers. The *Wall Street Journal* is a good source of general as well as financial news. Trends in fashion, communications, sports and other leisure activities, and many other areas may give you a head up on the areas in which to invest.

The political arena is particularly important to the world of investing. In general, you will want to watch for trends that increase freedom, decrease taxes, decrease government regulation, and decrease the power of lawyers and the likelihood of litigation. All of these things are good for the business world and good for your investments. The converse, increasing taxes, regulation, and litigation, is, predictably, bad for your investments. There are, on top of this, specific political actions that have an impact on specific industries. When the federal government passes a law subsidizing ethanol production from corn to add to gasoline, this directly benefits Archer Daniels Midland (ADM), the country's largest corn processor. Whether this is good or bad, it is the law, and if you are an ADM investor, you should be aware of it.

A striking example of the need to keep your eye on the ball involves the nation's pharmaceutical industry and the Clinton administration. As you may recall, the Clintons rode into town in 1993 with what they thought was a mandate for the federal government to take control of the nation's health-care system; they had one hundred days to accomplish this. Hillary Rodham Clinton was put in charge of the task force to accomplish this coup. As part of the process, Clinton continually bashed the drug companies for their obscene profits and led everyone to believe that taking control of drug prices would be a prime focus for her efforts. Since investors buy stocks on the expectations of future earnings and since Clinton was telling them there would be no future earnings, the expected happened, and the drug stocks dropped. Merck, for example, hit a high of $56.60 dollars a share in 1992 and dropped to $28.60 in 1993, staying at that level through 1994. At that point, it became obvious that the Clintons' plan had failed and there was going to be no sudden cataclysm in the health-care industry. As a matter of fact, most managed-care organizations became aware that the new high-cost drugs were more cost efficient than higher-cost surgery. In 1995, with good earnings continuing and the fear that they would be curtailed receding, the drug stocks rebounded strongly. By 1998, Merck had reached $158 per share, over five times what it was selling for in 1993. The story isn't over yet. A series of articles in the *Wall Street Journal* focuses on how expensive drugs have become, especially with all of the new drugs available. It seems inevitable that politicians will take it upon themselves to "protect" the consumers and curtail drug prices. In the long run this won't work, because we need the new drugs. A new generation of antibiotics will win out over price controls. In the meantime, investors may have a great buying opportunity.

## GENERAL SOURCES ON INVESTMENT

There are a number of general investing sources that I have used over the years, some more and some less useful. Television has its moments. I watch *The Nightly Business News* with Paul Kangas when I can and try as well to catch *Wall Street Week With Louis Rukeyser* each Friday. Both of these programs are on PBS.

There are a number of periodicals that I read on a regular basis. I read the *Wall Street Journal* daily. This is an excellent source for facts and comments. There is also a wealth of data that you can glean from these pages: the daily prices of stocks, their highs and lows for the day and the year, their price-earnings ratio (P/E), mutual-fund values, commodities values, and much more. Indeed, when Hillary Clinton was asked how she parlayed $1,000 into $100,000 in two years by trading cattle futures, she said she did it by reading the *Wall Street Journal* (although the *Journal* does not routinely cover cattle futures). *Barron's*, also published by the Dow Jones Company, comes out each Saturday. Besides general news and comments on the markets, I read the lists of insiders buying and selling shares in their companies. I always figure that they know more about their company than most of us, and we should watch how they vote with their cash on the health of their company. They also have a useful feature of consensus estimates of the earnings for the next year for the thirty Dow Jones Industrial Average stocks. These are compared to the same estimates four weeks previously. In a nutshell, you can see what the trend is in the analysis in these thirty dominant companies: Are the analysts bullish or bearish about earnings of each of these corporations?

*Forbes* magazine is an excellent source of information. I occasionally look at many other monthly publications, such as *Money, Worth, Fortune, Kiplinger's Personal Finance Magazine, Better Investing,* and others. You need to pick and choose the articles that are relevant from this mass of information.

There are also a number of books that I have read, and already alluded to, that may help shape your general investing philosophy. The first book I read was *The Beardstown Ladies,* by Leslie Witaker, about an investment club of ordinary women who made some impressive gains. It tells mainly how they use *Value Line* to evaluate individual stocks, and is interspersed with their favorite recipes. Recent reports have come out showing that their accounting was faulty and their returns not as good as put forth. This, however, does not take away from the main value of the book, which is to let the individual investor say to himself, "This looks easy. If these women can do it, so can I!" It is a great tool for demystifying the stock market.

Two books about Warren Buffett, *The Warren Buffett Way: Investment Strategies of the World's Greatest Investor* by R. G. Hagstrom, and *Buffett Speaks: Wit and Wisdom From the World's Greatest Investor,* by J. Lowe, are also very helpful. Mr. Buffett may, indeed, be the world's greatest investor, and his words and strategies are well worth listening to, even more so because his advice is mostly common sense, with very little statistical and economic obfuscation. (In the interest of full disclosure, we own a few shares of Berkshire Hathaway.)

*Peter Lynch: Beating the Street,* by J. Rothschild, and *Bogle on Mutual Funds,* by J. C. Bogle, give the perspectives of two of the giants of the mutual fund industry: Peter Lynch who ran the biggest mutual fund, Fidelity's Magellan Fund, and John Bogle of the Vanguard Group, the most successful practitioner of indexed funds. *Stocks for the Long Run,* second edition, by J. J. Siegel, from which I have quoted previously, is an excellent background source to show you the long-term history of the stock market. If the future is going to be more of what we had in the past, it gives us some comfort to know that the history extends back two hundred years, not the three months that most investment advisers use as the limits of their memory.

Lastly, I would highly recommend *The Millionaire Next Door,* by Thomas Stanley and William Danko. *Millionaire* gives you no specific advice about investing, but gives you a large amount of insight into what it takes to create wealth. It should be of no surprise to you at this point that these are the old-fashioned virtues of hard work, self-reliance, and frugality. They found that the typical millionaire, rather than being a prep-school graduate spending his days playing squash at the Downtown Athletic Club, is more likely a plumber who drives a ten-year-old car and wears a Timex watch.

The two authors tell a priceless story of the beginning of their research. They contacted a number of deca-millionaires to meet them in a hotel room to be interviewed. They had plenty of French wine and fancy hors d'oeuvres for the group. The first man to show up had the look of a workman rather than that of an investment banker. When they offered him a rare French wine, he said, "I drink two kinds of beer, Bud and free." The assemblage of millionaires felt uncomfortable in the fancy hotel and didn't touch the appetizers. When they left, the well-dressed bank-trust officers in the room next door, not a millionaire among them, ate the food with appreciation and relish.

## Stock Indexes

In your reading you will come across a number of stock-market indexes that you may or may not be familiar with. The Dividend Growth Investment Strategy does not depend on tracking the daily or quarterly ups and downs of the market to succeed; it actually works better if you ignore these trends. Still, because these indexes are so embedded in the investing literature, I will briefly describe the major averages to give you the vocabulary to decipher these numbers.

The Dow Jones Industrial Average, the grandfather of all indexes, is taken by most of the public as a shorthand for the performance of the market as a whole. No one can go through life without hearing a statement such as "The Dow is down seventeen points today" or "Will the Dow hit ten thousand this year?" This index has been in existence for a century. It consists of thirty large industrial companies: AT&T, Alcoa, Home Depot, American Express, Boeing, Caterpillar, Intel, Coca-Cola, Disney, Eastman Kodak, Exxon Mobil, General Electric, General Motors, Honeywell, Philip Morris, IBM, 3M, International Paper, Citigroup, J. P. Morgan, SBC Communications, Johnson & Johnson, McDonald's, Merck, Wal-Mart Stores, Hewlett-Packard, United Technologies, Microsoft, Procter & Gamble, and DuPont. The companies are changed periodically to reflect changes in the market. General Electric is the only company remaining from the original thirty. The "Dow" is simply an average of the increases or decreases of the share price of these thirty companies.

The Standard & Poor's 500 is a somewhat broader measure than the Dow. This index contains the five hundred largest companies in America, and it thus contains most of the high-cap stock universe. The Vanguard 500, the largest indexed mutual fund, picks stocks designed to match the S&P 500.

The Russell 2000 index is similar, but contains mainly small and mid-cap stocks, thus acting as an indicator for this segment of the market.

NASDAQ, the over-the-counter stock exchange alternative to the New York Stock Exchange, is heavily weighted with high-tech stocks, such as Microsoft, Intel, Cisco, and Dell Computers. The level of this stock exchange can be used as a rough approximation of the performance of the high-tech sector of the market.

## RESOURCES FOR EVALUATING SPECIFIC STOCKS

The primary source on the performance of any company is the annual report put out by the company. The information that you need is all there, but is often not organized in the way that you would like it, and is often hidden below flowery rhetoric about the "mission" and "goals" of the company. Admittedly, I don't have the time to go through all of these documents each year, and I doubt that many of you will be thus inclined. If you are a registered shareholder of a company, you will automatically receive the company's annual report. If your shares are held by a brokerage in the "street name," you can request that the broker forward the reports to you. All of these reports can also be accessed on line.

For most of us, it is easier and more efficient to let others gather and organize the information from these companies. If you are going to make dividend growth the cornerstone of your investment strategy, it would help to have a good source to track dividends. That source is available and is published yearly as *Moody's Handbook of Dividend Achievers* (Moody's Investors Service, Inc., the Dun & Bradstreet Corporation). This book is usually not available in bookstores, but may be ordered at 1-800-342-5647 ext. 7601 or online at fis@moodys.com. The description that the authors give the book is: "Complete, concise profiles of more than three hundred companies with the strongest dividend records in America." Each of these companies is listed on a page with a wealth of financial data. The most important figure for our purposes is the listing of the dividend payout and the annual percent increase of the dividend over the last ten years. It also tells us the number of years that this company has continuously raised its dividend, an important bit of information if you are using past performance to estimate the future. There are also some very useful charts in the front of the book that list the top twenty companies in a number of areas such as return on assets, return on earnings, high or low price-earnings ratios, revenues, and any number of other ways to evaluate corporations. They also have a very useful composite list of the three hundred stocks both by growth rate of the dividend and by total returns over the last three and five years.

This brings me to my single most important primary source, *The Value Line Investment Survey* (Value Line Publishing, Inc., New York, New York, 1-800-634-3583). *Value Line* covers the seventeen hundred largest publicly traded companies on our stock exchanges. These are divided into approximately ninety-six industries. Each week, you get a magazine covering the companies in seven to eight of these industries, giving a full page to each individual company. This means that each of the seventeen hundred companies will be covered and updated on a rotating basis four times a year. A subscription is very pricey, costing over $500 per year. You can, however, get a short-term trial subscription for $55, to give you a chance to study and familiarize yourself with the information presented. If you don't go on to a full subscription, you may find it in most libraries (although they may limit the time you can have it to yourself).

## VALUE LINE

What can you learn from *Value Line*? Quite a lot. Let's start when you open up your weekly edition. *Value Line* is published in three parts every week: Part 1 is the Summary and Index; Part 2, Selection and Opinion; Part 3, Ratings and Reports.

### Part I: Summary and Index

The first thing that you see is a short summary of the market. In bold figures on the front of this packet are the average price-earnings ratio, the average dividend yield and the average appreciation potential for the seventeen hundred stocks that they cover. These indexes can give you a rough idea as to the valuation of the market as a whole: is it cheap or too expensive? For instance, on a recent week, the P/E ratio on average was 16.4. This is the ratio of the stock's price to the expected earnings. They also tell us that twenty six weeks ago the P/E ratio was 19.5; that the most recent recorded low P/E was 10.6 on 11/6/87, and the highest was 19.5 on 5/1/98. We can see that the market at this time is lower than one half year previously, that is, we can get more for our money. The low, in 1987, followed the precipitous market crash. You can see the immense buying opportunity that existed at that time. The current dividend yield averages 2.0 percent as opposed to 1.6 percent twenty six weeks ago. The average appreciation potential for three to five years is 60 percent, as opposed to 40 percent twenty six weeks ago. Again, you can see that the market has improved for buyers over the last one half year.

This section also includes an index of the industries, and the individual stocks, with summaries of some of the pertinent statistics of each stock. *Value Line* then gives you lists of stocks arranged by different screens, such as those with the highest and lowest P/E, the highest dividend yield, highest and lowest appreciation potential, stocks that they feel are "bargain basement" prices, etc. These lists can be very valuable to confirm the desirability of a stock that you have researched and are planning to buy. This section also provides the most current earnings and dividend payments on all seventeen hundred companies, in the "latest results" section inside. You can compare this quarter's earnings and dividend payments with same quarter earnings and dividends a year ago.

## Part 2: Selection and Opinion

This section features, on its front page, an article on the general economic and stock-market conditions prevalent for that week. Inside, two companies are highlighted, each with a one-page article about the company, discussing its business prospects. This section also features three stock portfolios, each with different investment goals: Portfolio I contains twenty stocks with above-average year-ahead price potential; Portfolio II contains twenty stocks for income and potential price appreciation; Portfolio III contains twenty stocks with long-term price growth potential. *Value Line* periodically reports on each portfolio's performance. This section reports on the various economic indicators, market indexes, major insider buying and selling, valuations and yields of bonds, market sentiment, market volumes, industry price performance, and changes in financial strength ratings.

## Part 3: Ratings and Reports

The major part of the *Value Line Investment Survey* is in a separate section called Ratings and Reports. The typical weekly edition will contain seven to eight industries, each one with its individual companies arranged in alphabetical order. This organization is important because it allows you to easily compare whatever stock that you are researching against the others in the same industry. Often, indexes such as P/E ratio, dividend yields, book values, amount of debt, etc. are different for different industries. You want to know how your company compares to the others in its peer group: hopefully, it is the dominant company.

Let's now get to the meat of the *Survey:* the analysis of the individual company. I have picked a recent page on Merck & Co. for our consideration. At first glance, all of the numbers, graphs, and words may seem a little daunting, but the information jumps out once you get used to looking for it. The first principle of organization is that there are two kinds of information on the page: there is objective information that *Value Line* gleans from the public record of these corporations, and there is information that reflects *Value Line*'s analysis and opinion. All of this can be useful.

# MERCK & CO. NYSE-MRK

| RECENT PRICE | P/E RATIO | (Trailing: 29.3 Median: 21.0) | RELATIVE P/E RATIO | DIV'D YLD | VALUE LINE |
|---|---|---|---|---|---|
| 78 | 26.1 | | 1.95 | 1.7% | 1263 |

| | | |
|---|---|---|
| TIMELINESS | 3 | Lowered 6/4/99 |
| SAFETY | 1 | Raised 1/30/98 |
| TECHNICAL | 3 | Raised 1/7/00 |
| BETA | 1.10 | (1.00 = Market) |

**High:** 13.5 15.2 27.8 28.3 22.1 19.8 33.6 42.1 54.1 80.9 87.4 79.0
**Low:** 9.4 11.2 13.7 20.3 14.3 14.1 18.2 28.3 39.0 50.7 60.9 52.0

**Target Price Range** 2003 | 2004 | 2005

**LEGENDS**
- 15.5 x "Cash Flow" p sh
- .... Relative Price Strength
- 3-for-1 split 5/88
- 3-for-1 split 5/92
- 2-for-1 split 2/99
- Options: Yes
- Shaded area indicates recession

**2003-05 PROJECTIONS**

| | Price | Gain | Ann'l Total Return |
|---|---|---|---|
| High | 90 | (+15%) | 6% |
| Low | 75 | (-5%) | 1% |

**Insider Decisions**

| | D | J | F | M | A | M | J | J | A |
|---|---|---|---|---|---|---|---|---|---|
| to Buy | 0 | 0 | 0 | 0 | 0 | 0 | 0 | 0 | 0 |
| Options | 0 | 2 | 1 | 0 | 0 | 3 | 1 | 5 | 4 |
| to Sell | 0 | 2 | 1 | 0 | 0 | 3 | 0 | 1 | 4 |

**Institutional Decisions**

| | 4Q1999 | 1Q2000 | 2Q2000 |
|---|---|---|---|
| to Buy | 590 | 584 | 566 |
| to Sell | 519 | 572 | 568 |
| Hld's(000) | 1244934 | 1209218 | 1222361 |

| Percent shares traded | 9.0 6.0 3.0 |
|---|---|

**% TOT. RETURN 9/00**

| | THIS STOCK | VL ARITH. INDEX |
|---|---|---|
| 1 yr. | 17.1 | 15.4 |
| 3 yr. | 56.8 | 25.2 |
| 5 yr. | 191.4 | 97.6 |

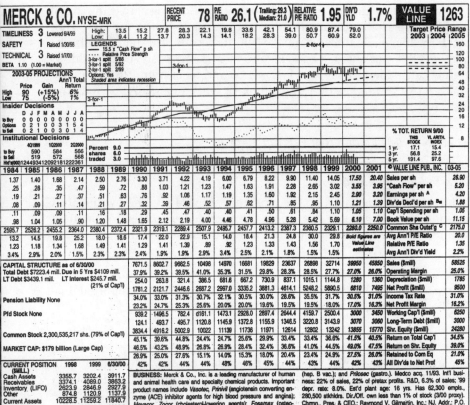

| 1984 | 1985 | 1986 | 1987 | 1988 | 1989 | 1990 | 1991 | 1992 | 1993 | 1994 | 1995 | 1996 | 1997 | 1998 | 1999 | 2000 | 2001 | © VALUE LINE PUB., INC. | 03-05 |
|---|---|---|---|---|---|---|---|---|---|---|---|---|---|---|---|---|---|---|---|
| 1.37 | 1.40 | 1.68 | 2.14 | 2.50 | 2.76 | 3.30 | 3.71 | 4.22 | 4.19 | 6.00 | 6.79 | 8.22 | 9.90 | 11.40 | 14.05 | 17.50 | 20.40 | Sales per sh | 26.90 |
| .25 | .28 | .35 | .47 | .59 | .72 | .88 | 1.03 | 1.21 | 1.23 | 1.47 | 1.63 | 1.91 | 2.28 | 2.65 | 3.02 | 3.55 | 3.95 | "Cash Flow" per sh | 5.20 |
| .19 | .21 | .27 | .37 | .51 | .63 | .76 | .92 | 1.06 | 1.17 | 1.19 | 1.35 | 1.60 | 1.92 | 2.15 | 2.45 | 2.90 | 3.20 | Earnings per sh ^A | 4.20 |
| .08 | .09 | .11 | .14 | .21 | .27 | .32 | .39 | .46 | .52 | .57 | .62 | .71 | .85 | .95 | 1.10 | 1.21 | 1.39 | Div'd Decl'd per sh ^B= | 1.88 |
| .11 | .09 | .09 | .11 | .16 | .18 | .29 | .45 | .47 | .40 | .40 | .41 | .50 | .61 | .84 | 1.10 | 1.05 | 1.10 | Cap'l Spending per sh | 1.05 |
| .98 | 1.04 | 1.05 | .90 | 1.20 | 1.48 | 1.65 | 2.12 | 2.19 | 4.00 | 4.46 | 4.78 | 4.96 | 5.28 | 5.42 | 5.69 | 6.10 | 7.00 | Book Value per sh | 11.15 |
| 2595.7 | 2526.2 | 2455.2 | 2364.0 | 2380.4 | 2372.4 | 2321.9 | 2319.1 | 2289.4 | 2507.9 | 2495.7 | 2457.7 | 2413.2 | 2387.3 | 2360.5 | 2329.1 | 2280.0 | 2250.0 | Common Shs Outst'g ^C | 2175.0 |
| 13.2 | 14.5 | 19.8 | 25.2 | 18.0 | 18.6 | 17.4 | 22.0 | 22.9 | 15.1 | 14.0 | 18.4 | 21.3 | 24.8 | 30.0 | 29.8 | Bold figures are Value Line estimates | | Avg Ann'l P/E Ratio | 20.0 |
| 1.23 | 1.18 | 1.34 | 1.68 | 1.49 | 1.41 | 1.29 | 1.41 | 1.39 | .89 | .92 | 1.23 | 1.33 | 1.43 | 1.56 | 1.70 | | | Relative P/E Ratio | 1.35 |
| 3.4% | 2.9% | 2.0% | 1.5% | 2.3% | 2.3% | 2.4% | 1.9% | 1.9% | 2.9% | 3.4% | 2.5% | 2.1% | 1.8% | 1.5% | 1.5% | | | Avg Ann'l Div'd Yield | 2.2% |

**CAPITAL STRUCTURE as of 6/30/00**
Total Debt $7223.4 mill. Due in 5 Yrs $4109 mill.
LT Debt $3439.1 mill. LT Interest $245.7 mill.
(21% of Cap'l)

**Pension Liability** None

**Pfd Stock** None

**Common Stock** 2,300,535,217 shs. (79% of Cap'l)

**MARKET CAP: $179 billion (Large Cap)**

| CURRENT POSITION | 1998 | 1999 | 6/30/00 |
|---|---|---|---|
| ($MILL.) | | | |
| Cash Assets | 3355.7 | 3202.4 | 3911.7 |
| Receivables | 3374.1 | 4089.0 | 3863.2 |
| Inventory. (LIFO) | 2623.9 | 2846.9 | 2927.9 |
| Other | 874.8 | 1120.9 | 1137.9 |
| Current Assets | 10228.5 | 11259.2 | 11840.7 |
| Accts Payable | 3682.1 | 4158.7 | 3923.7 |
| Debt Due | 624.2 | 2859.0 | 3784.3 |
| Other | 1762.5 | 1741.1 | 1340.2 |
| Current Liab. | 6068.8 | 8758.8 | 9048.2 |

| ANNUAL RATES | Past | Past | Est'd '97-'99 |
|---|---|---|---|
| of change (per sh) | 10 Yrs | 5 Yrs | to '03-'05 |
| Sales | 17.0% | 19.5% | 13.5% |
| "Cash Flow" | 16.0% | 15.5% | 12.0% |
| Earnings | 15.5% | 14.0% | 11.0% |
| Dividends | 16.5% | 13.5% | 12.0% |
| Book Value | 16.5% | 9.0% | 12.5% |

| Cal- endar | QUARTERLY SALES ($ mill.) | | | | Full Year |
|---|---|---|---|---|---|
| | Mar.31 | Jun.30 | Sep.30 | Dec.31 | |
| 1997 | 5567 | 5909 | 5927 | 6234 | 23637 |
| 1998 | 6058 | 6470 | 6838 | 7532 | 26898 |
| 1999 | 7537 | 8018 | 8196 | 8963 | 32714 |
| 2000 | 8851 | 9477 | 10508 | 11054 | 39950 |
| 2001 | 11000 | 11400 | 11650 | 11800 | 45850 |

| Cal- endar | EARNINGS PER SHARE ^A | | | | Full Year |
|---|---|---|---|---|---|
| | Mar.31 | Jun.30 | Sep.30 | Dec.31 | |
| 1997 | .42 | .48 | .50 | .52 | D1.92 |
| 1998 | .47 | .54 | .56 | .58 | 2.15 |
| 1999 | .54 | .61 | .64 | .66 | 2.45 |
| 2000 | .63 | .73 | .78 | .76 | 2.90 |
| 2001 | .72 | .81 | .83 | .84 | 3.20 |

| Cal- endar | QUARTERLY DIVIDENDS PAID ^B= | | | | Full Year |
|---|---|---|---|---|---|
| | Mar.31 | Jun.30 | Sep.30 | Dec.31 | |
| 1996 | .17 | .17 | .17 | .20 | .71 |
| 1997 | .20 | .21 | .21 | .225 | .85 |
| 1998 | .225 | .225 | .225 | .27 | .95 |
| 1999 | .27 | .27 | .27 | .29 | 1.10 |
| 2000 | .29 | .29 | .29 | .34 | |

| 7671.5 | 8602.7 | 9662.5 | 10498 | 14970 | 16681 | 19829 | 23637 | 26898 | 32714 | 39950 | 45850 | Sales ($mill) | 58525 |
|---|---|---|---|---|---|---|---|---|---|---|---|---|---|
| 37.9% | 39.2% | 39.5% | 41.0% | 35.3% | 31.5% | 29.8% | 28.3% | 28.5% | 27.7% | 27.0% | 26.0% | Operating Margin | 25.0% |
| 254.0 | 263.8 | 321.4 | 386.5 | 681.6 | 667.2 | 730.9 | 837.1 | 1015.1 | 1144.8 | 1280 | 1360 | Depreciation ($mill) | 1785 |
| 1781.2 | 2121.7 | 2446.6 | 2687.2 | 2997.0 | 3333.2 | 3881.3 | 4614.1 | 5248.2 | 5890.5 | 6810 | 7495 | Net Profit ($mill) | 9500 |
| 34.0% | 33.0% | 31.3% | 30.7% | 32.1% | 30.5% | 30.0% | 28.6% | 35.5% | 31.7% | 30.5% | 31.0% | Income Tax Rate | 31.0% |
| 23.2% | 24.7% | 25.3% | 25.6% | 20.0% | 20.0% | 19.6% | 19.5% | 19.5% | 18.0% | 17.0% | 16.3% | Net Profit Margin | 16.2% |
| 939.2 | 1496.5 | 782.4 | d161.1 | 1473.1 | 2928.0 | 2897.4 | 2644.4 | 4159.7 | 2500.4 | 3000 | 3450 | Working Cap'l ($mill) | 6250 |
| 124.1 | 493.7 | 495.7 | 1120.8 | 1145.9 | 1372.8 | 1155.9 | 1348.5 | 3220.8 | 3143.9 | 3070 | 3060 | Long-Term Debt ($mill) | 3000 |
| 3834.4 | 4916.2 | 5002.9 | 6002.2 | 11139 | 11736 | 11971 | 12614 | 12802 | 13242 | 13855 | 15770 | Shr. Equity ($mill) | 24280 |
| 45.1% | 39.6% | 44.8% | 24.4% | 24.7% | 25.6% | 29.9% | 33.4% | 33.4% | 36.6% | 41.5% | 40.5% | Return on Total Cap'l | 34.5% |
| 46.5% | 43.2% | 48.9% | 26.8% | 26.9% | 28.4% | 32.4% | 36.6% | 41.0% | 44.5% | 49.0% | 47.5% | Return on Shr. Equity | 39.0% |
| 26.9% | 25.0% | 27.6% | 15.1% | 14.0% | 15.3% | 18.0% | 20.4% | 23.4% | 24.9% | 27.5% | 26.0% | Retained to Com Eq | 24.0% |
| 42% | 42% | 44% | 44% | 44% | 48% | 46% | 45% | 44% | 43% | 42% | 43% | All Div'ds to Net Prof | 45% |

**BUSINESS:** Merck & Co., Inc. is a leading manufacturer of human and animal health care and specialty chemical products. Important product names include *Vasotec*, *Prinivil* (angiotensin converting enzyme (ACE) inhibitor agents for high blood pressure and angina); *Mevacor*, *Zocor* (cholesterol-lowering agents); *Fosamax* (osteoporosis); *Pepcid* (anti-ulcer); *Crixivan* (HIV/AIDS); *Recombivax HB* (hep. B vac.); and *Prilosec* (gastro.). Medco acq. 11/93. Int'l business: 22% of sales, 22% of pretax profits. R&D, 6.3% of sales; '99 depr. rate: 8.0%. Est'd plant age: 16 yrs. Has 62,300 empls., 280,500 stkhldrs. Dir./Off. own less than 1% of stock (3/00 proxy). Chrmn., Pres. & CEO: Raymond V. Gilmartin. Inc.: NJ. Addr.: P.O. Box 100, Whitehouse Station, NJ 08889. Tel. 908-423-1000.

**Merck posted strong, better-than-expected September-quarter results.** The revenue increase was a muscular 29%, with worldwide pharmaceutical sales advancing 18% (to $5.2 billion) and the Medco business expanding by 42% (to $5.4 billion), the latter was bolstered by the June addition of United Healthcare's 10-million lives contract. Drug sales were driven by five key products, which now account for 58% of the total. The company's newest medicine, *Vioxx*, launched in May, 1999, continues to perform remarkably well, generating sales of $615 million and rising by 29.5% on a sequential basis. Merck's largest-seller, *Zocor*, also remains on a sharp uptrend, surging 27% to $1.4 billion. As well, *Cozaar/Hyzaar*, *Fosamax*, and *Singulair* increased top-line contributions by 16% (to $405 million), 29% ($360 million), and 81% ($235 million), respectively. Meantime, per-share earnings rose by 22% (to $0.78), $0.04 and $0.05 above our and consensus estimates, respectively. **We have raised our estimate for 2001, but still expect the growth rate to slow considerably.** Year-to-date sales of four major drugs are down—*Vasotec* (-15%,

to $1.5 billion), *Pepcid* (-10%, $610 million), *Mevacor* (-15%, $395 million), and *Crixivan* (-17%, $410 million)—and the decline will undoubtedly accelerate in the coming months because the first three lose their patent protection in the 2000-2002 interval. Two other sizable profit contributors, *Prinivil* and *Prilosec*, will also start to encounter generic competition in this time frame. The drugs mentioned in paragraph one have ample growth possibilities, but we're skeptical that this will be sufficient to not only offset the patent-related decline but also to generate the robust double-digit growth Merck has historically generated. We've added a nickel to our bottom-line targets for both 2000 and 2001, to $2.90 and $3.20, respectively, but the latter represents growth of only 10%. **Most investors should probably wait for a more attractive entry point.** The company has consistently topped Wall Street's expectations this year, and it has a superb long-term track record. Nevertheless, we would note that the impending patent expirations significantly obscure earnings visibility for the next several years.

*George Rho*      *October 27, 2000*

We'll start with the objective information. Starting across the top of the page, we see the company's name, that it is listed on the New York Stock Exchange, its ticker symbol MRK. Its recent price before publication was $78 per share. The P/E ratio is 26.1. You can see that this is high because Merck's median P/E is 21.0 and its current P/E has a ratio relative to the market of 1.95. Merck is currently giving a dividend yield of 1.7%.

*What do these four different P/E ratios mean?*

### Price to Earnings Ratio (P/E)

*Value Line*'s P/E is based on the most recent price divided by the latest six months earnings per share plus the earnings estimated for the next six months. Merck's P/E is 26.1 at the share price of 78.

### Trailing P/E

The recent price divided by the sum of earnings per share reported during the last twelve months. Merck's trailing P/E is 29.3.

### Median P/E

The average annual P/E ratio over the past ten years. Merck's median P/E is 21, at a P/E of 26 Merck's stock is mildly overpriced. This is what people mean when they say the stock market is overpriced at some point in time. At a P/E of 21 and earnings of $2.90 a share the price should be $61 a share:

$$\$2.90 \times 21 = \$61 \text{ a share}$$

### Relative P/E Ratio

This ratio is the stock's current P/E divided by the median P/E for all stocks under *Value Line* review.

There are two other noteworthy areas of *Value Line* analysis. The first is seen in the box just under the company name. These are the *Value Line* ratings for timeliness and safety. The *Value Line* Timeliness Rank gives you a measure of the momentum of the stock over the next two to four quarters.

### Timeliness Rating

All seventeen hundred stocks are ranked by timeliness into five categories. This is a measure of a stock's earnings and price momentum. A rank of 1 is the highest rating. This stock is expected to be one of the best relative price performers during the next six to twelve months. Merck is ranked 3 for timeliness.

The *Value Line* Safety Rank gives a guide to the total risk that the stock presents over the next year. The rankings are done in the following way: The total list of seventeen hundred stocks are ranked from one to five for both timeliness and safety. The top 100 stocks are given the rating of 1, the bottom 100 given a 5. The second 300 from the top and the second 300 from the bottom are given a 2 and a 4 respectively. The middle 900 are all threes. From the viewpoint of the Dividend Growth Investment Strategy, it is important to choose safe stocks. Most of the stocks in my sample portfolio are ranked 1 and 2 for safety.

### Safety Rating

This is a measurement of risk based on the stock's price stability and financial strength. A stock with a Safety Rating of 1 is probably one of the safest, most stable, and least risky stock market investments. Merck is ranked 1 for safety.

The timeliness rankings are more useful if you are going to be a trader than if you use a buy-and-hold strategy. *Value Line* has some impressive data about how high your returns can reach if you invest in stocks with a rank of 1, shifting your portfolio as the rankings shift. While tempting, this is not the thrust of the strategy that I have been espousing in this book, especially in a taxable account. Finally, this box includes the company's "beta." This refers to the company's volatility in relation to the market as a whole. The market as a whole, by definition, has a beta of 1. Merck's beta is 1.10, very close to 1, indicating that it likely will fluctuate up or down relatively closely to the market as a whole. This is what we look for in the Dividend Growth Investment Strategy. High tech companies typically will be more volatile and will carry betas close to 2. Utilities, on the other hand, may have more stability than the market and will carry betas of below 1.

### Beta

The stock's sensitivity to fluctuations of the market as a whole. Merck's beta is 1.10; it will go up or down 10 percent more than the market fluctuations. Each tenth of a percent increment in beta increases the stock's price fluctuation by 10 percent relative to the market as a whole.

In the middle of the page is a rectangular box labeled BUSINESS: This tells what the company does, and what some of their most important products are. It also lists the number of employees, the number of shareholders, the percent of business done internationally, the percent of stock owned by the directors and officers (in Merck's case less than 1 percent), any large institutional investors, and the name, address, and telephone number of the CEO. Merck is a large company, so you wouldn't expect the officers to control a large part of the company. It often is a good sign, however, when directors do own a large percentage of the stock, for this gives them even more incentive to increase shareholder value. Wrigley and Tootsie Roll are examples of companies that perform well for shareholders where the founding families or insiders control large portions of the stock. For a related issue, look to the small box to the left of the graph titled Insider Decisions. Officers and directors are required to make public any trading of stock that they do in the company. While some of these transactions may be due to issues in their personal finances, trends in buying and selling may also be related to the prospects of the company that they work in day in and day out. Keep an eye on this box!

Next, your eye is drawn to the chart in the upper part of the page. This charts the price of the stock over the last twelve years, correcting for splits. (Remember, a stock split does nothing to the intrinsic value of the stock. A three-for-one split simply gives you three shares for your one, each at one-third of the original price: your total investment stays the same.) By paging through your issue, you can see the different shapes of these share price graphs, some going up explosively, some heading south precipitously, others very flat or slightly rising, while many will resemble the roller coaster, giving you a wild up-and-down ride. The ideal curve is one that steadily rises, easier to draw than to achieve. Merck's graph is impressive, showing strong, progressive growth, stumbling only in the midst of the Hillary care debacle of 1993–94. You will notice a shaded strip on the graph: this indicates times of recession. You will note that Merck performed relatively well during the 1990–91 period, a good sign. Even if times seem good now, the business cycle has not been abolished, and there will be recessions, so be prepared for them.

The other important part of the graph is the solid line that runs through the jagged price graph. This is the cash flow line, or what *Value Line* appropriately calls the "Value Line."

*Cash Flow*

Net profit plus noncash charges (depreciation, depletion, and amortization), divided by common shares outstanding.

Cash flow is defined as the annual earnings per share plus its depreciation per share times a multiple relating to its projected target price. Simply put, this line tells us how much cash the company has earned and is projected to earn. I have found this line to be valuable in valuing a stock. The graph of the stock's price always tends to return to the cash flow line. We can see how overvalued or undervalued the stock is by how far above or below the cash flow line the share price graph extends.

There are numerous other areas of objective data clustered in the center of the page. You can find the total debt of the company and the pension liability in a box on the left.

### Debt

The capital structure of the company as of recent date showing the percentage of capital in long-term debt (21 percent) and in common stock (79 percent). Ideally, the long-term debt should not exceed one-third of the net worth of the company.

The less the company's debt, the more agile it can be, especially in recessionary times. The company's net worth to long-term debt ratio is more important in evaluating companies with shorter track records, which tend to be riskier companies. The amount of debt that a company tends to carry also can depend on the industry. Capital-intensive companies generally will have more debt.

Just below the boxes listing the capital structure along with current assets and liabilities is a box for "Annual rates of change."

### Annual rates of change

Actual, past, and estimated future changes in sales, cash flow, earnings, dividends, book value. This deals with *Value Line*'s projections of the company's future growth potential. These are the analyst's estimates based on understanding the company, the business, and the industry as a whole. Merck's earnings and dividends are projected to grow at 11 percent and 12 percent annually from 2003 to 2005. Keep in mind that the analyst's estimates can and do change. It is important to use the most recent analyst consensus reports.

Below that, you can see the quarterly sales, earnings, and dividends paid for the last five years. In the center of the page there is a large chart that lists various indices going back approximately fifteen years as well as projected two years in the future. The most important lines in this chart are the yearly dividends and earnings per share.

Follow the earnings and dividend payment histories to make sure the trend is up and doubling every five to seven years.

### Earnings/Share

Net profit after taxes, expressed on per-share basis as reported by the company. Historical data goes back to 1984 and anticipated earnings are projected out to 2005.

The return on shareholder equity and the company's operating margins are important parameters that can be found in the same table. *Return on equity* is a measure of how much the management can do with the investment supplied by the shareholders. A value above 20 percent usually signals an excellently managed company. *Operating margin* refers to the ability of management to make profits from their products, that is, to get a profit from each sale. Taken together, these two measures are a good indication of management's performance.

### Return on Equity

The ROE is a measure of management's ability to enhance return on company's investments and demonstrates how well management grows the company using the shareholders' money. A high, consistent ROE and OM both demonstrate the company's management ability. Merck's ROE is 49 percent.

### Operating Margin

The operating margin (OM) is a measure of management's ability to extract profits from the sales of the company's products. Operating income is income from the sales of goods minus the cost of making and selling the goods (pretax). The operating margin is the pretax profit expressed as percent of sales. Merck's operating margin is 27 percent for 2000.

The ROE and OM numbers are reported for the past ten years. Look at the trend. It is best if these numbers are increasing or at least stable. When you first look at all of these numbers, they may seem overwhelming, and you may wonder what they mean. This is where comparison with the peer group in the industry is important. On this sheet, the operating margin for Merck is 27 percent for 2000 and the return on shareholder equity is 49 percent. These are very good numbers, well above the benchmark 20 percent. If pharmaceutical company XYZ has comparable numbers of 19.6 percent and 21.2 percent, it is obvious that Merck is a better performer than XYZ. Unless there is some reason to think that the fundamentals of these two companies are changing over the near term, Merck would be the better buy and may support a higher price earnings ratio than XYZ.

For many industries, especially banks, *book value* per share can be useful in evaluating the price of the share. The book value represents the value of the hard assets such as cash or real estate stripped from the rest of the corporation.

### Book Value

The book value per share is the company's net worth (including intangible assets), less preferred stock, divided by common shares outstanding. Merck's book value is $6.10 a share in 2000.

The subjective analysis of *Value Line* is a useful adjunct to all of the raw data. First, much of the hard data talked about earlier also contains projections into the next few years, helping you to get a feeling for the company's prospects. While not guaranteed, these are fairly accurate, and therefore useful as a rough guide.

### Potential share price appreciation

Projected average annual return, based on estimated three-to-five-year price appreciation plus dividend income.

### Upside-Down Ratio

The stock should have more upside potential than downside potential. The rule of thumb is three times more upside potential than downside potential. The projected share price out to 2003 to 2005 should have some upside. Merck does not have much upside potential in its share price at 78. Its projected share price is 75 (low) to 90 (high) out to 2005. These share price targets are frequently raised by the analysts, depending on the company's earning prospects. When the share price target is raised, you will first find this in Part I of *Value Line*.

About one quarter of the page, in the right lower quadrant, contains the narrative analysis, signed and dated by one of *Value Line*'s staff analysts. This is the part where you can learn in plain, non-jargon English what the analyst gleans from all of the data. In our example, George Rho tells us that Merck's core business showed stronger than expected growth in the preceding quarter and that some of its top drugs such as Vioxx and Zocor are doing very well. He warns, however, that Merck is about to lose exclusive rights to some of its older drugs, which may have a negative impact on earnings. He concludes, "Most investors should probably wait for a more attractive entry point." While these pronouncements may be helpful, I have found that, in many cases, *Value Line* underestimates the performance of the large blue-chip companies. *Value Line*'s evaluations are built on momentum and eval-uate mainly for the near term. You must correct for this when you are buying for the long term.

Finally, the small box in the bottom right corner gives an overview of the company's prospects. The company's financial strength is rated from the weakest grade of C to the highest of A++. We can see that Merck is extremely strong. The stability of the stock's price, the persis-tence of the growth in the stock price, and the degree of certainty of the ability to predict earnings are all ranked from a low of 5 to a high of 100. Again, Merck performs relatively well.

### Company's Financial Strength

This is a *Value Line* relative rating system with A++ being the strongest down to C the weakest. Merck's financial strength is A++.

### Stock's Price Stability

This is *Value Line*'s measure of the stability of a stock's price. It in-cludes sensitivity to the market (beta) as well as the stock's inherent volatility. *Value Line*'s stability ratings range from 100 (highest) to 5 (lowest.) Merck's stock price stability is 80.

### Price Growth Persistence

This measures the historic tendency of a stock to show persistent price growth compared to the average stock. Ratings range from 100 (highest) to 5 (lowest). Merck's price growth persistence is 75.

### Earnings Predictability

Measures the reliability of an earnings forecast, with 100 (highest) and 5 (lowest). Merck's earnings predictability is 100.

## THE INTERNET

When I first started my investing career, *Value Line* was the core of my information library. While still valuable, it has been supplanted by the marvel of the late twentieth century, the Internet. I find it difficult to talk in too much detail about this wonderful resource because, between the time that I write this and you read it, the Internet will have evolved through two or three generations. You have all kinds of information at your fingertips. Companies have their home pages, with their informa-tion about their business, their products, and their annual reports. Raw data and news releases are available at a myriad of sites. Analysis is abundant (Motley Fool), and Securities and Exchange Commission (SEC) filings are available (Edgar). There are many sites that you can post your portfolio, or multiple portfolios, for that matter, that will continuously update the stock price and total the value of your portfolio (Yahoo!). Chat rooms are of variable utility, but some high-tech chat rooms, such as the one for Loral Space and Communications, have some very high-level participants with interesting and entertaining information (The Silicon Investor). Video performances are available to see speeches of CEOs. Conference calls that financial analysts hold with industry representatives are also now available to you, the common investor.

Given the caveat that this list is from the stone age of the World Wide Web, and likely will be completely supplanted by the time you read this, I will still list some of the sites that I find the most useful:

| | |
|---|---|
| Yahoo! | quote.yahoo.com |
| Quicken | www.quicken.com |
| MoneyCentral | moneycentral.com |
| Edgar | www.edgar.online.com |
| The Silicon Investor | www.siliconinvestor.com |
| Morningstar | www.morningstar.net |
| Motley Fool | www.fool.com |
| Wall Street City | www.wallstreetcity.com |
| The Street | www.thestreet.com |
| Stockpoint | www.stockpoint.com |
| ZDNET Interactive Investor | www.zdnet.com |

You are now set. The publication of the Gutenberg Bible was thought to be one of the most important events of all time, allowing for the dissemination of knowledge via the printing press. It still took hundreds of years to make the printed word available to average citizens. Years ago, I had no clue to what futurists meant when they said that the Information Age was replacing the Industrial Age. Now I know. Information is increasing exponentially. It took centuries to spread the Bible, but only a second for the world's events to reach your computer screen. The Information Age means that you and I no longer have to rely on "experts" and "leaders" to distill our knowledge. We have the means to decipher the world for ourselves.

# 7

# THE NUTS AND BOLTS OF INVESTING

Okay, now you're all fired up about following the Dividend Growth Investment Strategy. Through research and contemplation and by doing your own calculations, you are now convinced that this is the wave for your future. Now what? How do you actually go about implementing the strategy. You have to decide what to buy, when to buy it, and exactly how to buy it.

## WHAT TO BUY

Three of the principles of the Dividend Growth Investment Strategy come to play in this decision: diversification, dominant companies, and dividends.

Diversification is an essential principle for risk management. If you are buying individual stocks you will want to diversify your portfolio in two ways:

1. Over time, buy a number of companies (at least 20–30).
2. Buy companies from different industries (drug, beverage, grocery, bank, financial services, drugstore, food processing, food wholesaler, household products, industrial services, insurance, medical supplies, retail stores, high tech, toiletries/cosmetics). This is a partial list of the various industrial sectors available to you.

Owning a number of stocks from different industrial sectors protects you from an industry-wide downturn. As an example of an industry downturn, I will return to the attempt by President Clinton, Hillary

Rodham Clinton, and the Democratic Congress to try to nationalize health care back in 1992 and 1993. Mrs. Clinton was bashing the drug companies for profiting on the sales of drugs, with the implicit threat that drug-company profits would be highly regulated and curtailed. This caused many investors to sell their drug stocks and flee the entire industry. The stock prices of all the drug companies went in the tank and stayed there until the threat of a government takeover subsided in 1995. The P/Es of drug stocks dropped to the 13 to 15 range during this period. Normally, drug stock P/Es are above the market average. This episode created a great buying opportunity for shareholders. At about this time, there was also a shift in the conventional wisdom that, while expensive, drugs were cheaper and more effective in the long run than other therapies, such as surgery. Share prices started to catch up, and the drug stock P/Es again exceeded the market's P/E average. But had the politicians succeeded in taking over the health-care industry and controlling drug companies' profits, the outcome of this story might have been radically different. The main point is that you cannot predict in advance what is going to increase or decrease the valuation of an industry, unless you have inside information. To protect yourself, you need to spread your investments around to catch the industry going up as another is going down.

There are many ways an industrywide downturn can come about; the threat of government takeover, regulation, and lawsuits are all real threats to companies and their shareholders. The tobacco industry comes to mind. A company such as Philip Morris currently sells for less than its Kraft Foods division would sell for if it stood alone, and it has been an excellent dividend raiser. The only thing that is certain about the future of Philip Morris is that it will be sharing its profits with the government, leaving less for its shareholders. The breast-implant litigation put a number of companies out of business, as did the asbestos class-action lawsuits. American Home Products has some diet drugs that were recently taken off the market because of some association with heart problems. Whether this is a serious medical problem or not, the trial lawyers are bound to seize on it, and it will end up being a problem for shareholders.

Fundamentals also play a critical role. In 1998, there was a worldwide oil glut, causing a depression in the prices of all of the major oil companies and of the support industries for oil exploration and drilling. In 2000, oil prices sky rocketed, further underlining the boom and bust cycle of this sector. These are all compelling reasons for diversification.

These are some of the obvious reasons why we need to diversify across industrial sectors. These factors make food and beverages and toiletries and cosmetics very attractive. The government seems to leave these industries alone, and their customers buy their products habitually. They are also not cyclical, so a recession, while it depresses share prices of all companies, does not hit these companies' earnings as hard. Consumers may put off buying a new washing machine in a recession, but they probably will continue to buy toothpaste or Coke. While these companies' share prices may decrease, their earnings will remain intact, as will their dividends. The escalator will continue to rise even as the roller coaster plunges.

There is also the chance that an individual company may be underperforming and its share price may be plummeting. The more stocks you hold in your portfolio the less effect this particular company will have on your overall financial well being.

Now you are ready to diversify, but you still have to start with individual stocks. Which ones? As stated before, these companies should be dominant in their industries. Here, again, I will list my criteria for including companies in my sample portfolio.

## 1. Dominant (Mostly Large-Cap) Companies

These companies should be market leaders in their industries, industries that are not subject to a high degree of government regulation or a high cost of manufacturing. Large-cap companies are also inherently more stable for the long term than are small-cap companies. There is a great temptation to see a promising small-cap that will multiply your capital ten times in a couple of years. There are two reasons that this is unlikely to happen. The first is that there is a large amount of risk inherent in this approach: for every ten-bagger, there will be a number of companies that crash and burn. The second problem is that, as the small company begins to reach its potential, it will be bought up by a dominant, large-cap company, giving you only a modest gain after you have assumed the risk and had your money at rest for a prolonged period of time.

## 2. Noncyclical—Consumer Nondurable Companies

Companies that engender repeat consumer business produce and sell relatively inexpensive items that consumers need, or are willing to purchase even in recessionary times, such as food, beverages, gum, toiletries, groceries, and drugs. Discount stores and drugstores also fit into this category.

## 3. Companies Consistently Demonstrating Good Fundamentals.*

- Safety ratings of 3 (average or above) as given by *Value Line*
- Sound financial strength ratings of B+ or better as rated by *Value Line*
- Sales have been increasing steadily and have doubled in the past five–seven years
- Earnings per share that have increased steadily and have doubled in the past five–seven years
- Increasing dividend payments, doubling in the past five–seven years
- A stable or increasing operating margin of ≥ 15
- A stable or increasing return on equity of ≥ 15
- Long-term debt that is less than one third of the company's net worth
- Current assets that are twice the current liabilities
- Cash and receivables ≥ current liabilities
- Projected annual growth of earnings and dividends is ≥ 14 percent
- Current PE does not exceed the median PE from the past five–ten years.

## 4. Demographic Considerations

Consideration of the aging population (drugs, hospital supplies, funeral equipment, and trust management services) or increased leisure time of the baby boomers.

## 5. Global Growth Opportunities

I would add one further criterion: I mainly invest in U.S. companies. I believe that the best way to take advantage of the opportunities in emerging foreign markets is to invest in American companies that are expanding into these markets.

I choose companies that have global-expansion opportunities and have demonstrated that they can be successful operating in different marketplaces. Future growth prospects for the company are brighter if they are able to grow internationally. Lacking these growth prospects

---

*These data for company fundamental analysis can be found in *Value Line*. These are general principles and will vary depending on the industry. This is another reason to study the entire industry before investing. *Value Line Investment Survey* is a good source for reviewing all the stocks in the entire industry.

the company may be facing a mature U.S. market, and growth would be limited. It is also a safer way of participating in the growth of global capitalism, instead of investing in emerging markets through mutual funds. The conventional advice that is being pitched at the public is to invest a certain percentage of your money into funds buying stocks in global and emerging markets. I would concur that, if you are going to invest in foreign stocks at all, it should be done through a professional; there is no way that you, as an individual, can research foreign companies. I would, however, question the wisdom of investing in foreign markets in the first place. Unless you are the first investor in and the first one out before the region's bubble bursts, you are likely to lose money. Just think of the travails in Japan, Korea, Thailand, Indonesia, Mexico, Brazil, and Russia, just to name a few. Even such stable, well-managed economies as Hong Kong, Singapore, and Taiwan were not immune to the recent bout of the "Asian flu."

One reason for the success and safety of U.S. companies that you may not be aware of is the standardized accounting principles they use as ordinary business practice. This allows us, as shareholders, to read and analyze the data in the annual and quarterly reports, which are audited and required by law to be sent to all shareholders. We can rely on the trustworthiness of the data, and if the company misleads its shareholders in any way, an army of trial lawyers is waiting to sue on their behalf. The development of trustworthy information promotes capitalism and entrepeneurship. We, as investors, can rely on the information when we make our investment decisions. The problem with investing in foreign companies through global or international mutual funds is that most countries have not developed these standardized accounting principles to the extent that we have in the United States, and the information that they are putting out (if they put out any information) may not be reliable. Furthermore, if the information is misleading, there are no consequences for the company. The company is not sued by shareholders for putting out misleading information to attract your investment money; you just lose your money, and the mutual-fund manager moves on to the next emerging growth market and starts hyping it. The cycle starts all over again with the initial wave of capital flowing in. These markets are small; it does not take much to create a tidal wave on these local exchanges.

Many of these so-called emerging growth markets are in countries that have corrupt governments. There is no way to make a long-term investment that makes money where there is government corruption. Government corruption, bureaucrats requiring bribes and protection money for every step a business wants to take, permeates many of these countries that are trying to attract your investment dollars. Your investment money is soon in the pockets of the country's bureaucrats. American investors do not appreciate the virtues of having a noncorrupt system. I personally experienced this government corruption when I spent three weeks in Romania in 1990 adopting my now ten-year-old daughter. We took $20,000 in cash with us and returned penniless and literally very hungry. Not only did every government official have his or her hand out; anyone and everyone who could stand in the way of our getting our daughter out of the orphanage, into a Romanian courtroom to adopt her, and then out of the country needed a payoff. There was never any certainty or a stable legal framework to operate under. The success of the whole operation depended on having money to pay people who would then allow us to go forward. This experience made it clear to us that it would be impossible to operate a business in an environment like this. This is typical of many political systems in emerging markets that are soliciting your investment dollars. I do not have any illusions about how difficult it is for American companies to set up operations in foreign countries.

While I want to invest in companies that are growing globally, I am also aware of the perils in which they operate. Investing in U.S. companies that are growing globally is probably the lowest-risk way to invest in international growth. I recently heard a mutual-fund manager who specializes in Russia soliciting capital for his fund say, "Russia is poised for a comeback." Until Russia builds a political system that encourages capitalism, investors with a longer-term time horizon will only lose. Some countries that we are invited to invest in will take a lifetime, if ever, to change their political system so that capitalism can thrive. I know this from another experience in Romania. We were all hungry most of the time in Romania. There was very little food; even if you had money, food could not always be bought; it just did not exist. When there was food, it was not very palatable (no such thing as ketchup or sauces). An American would see this as an opportunity, a country filled with people in a perpetual state of hunger, especially if you lived on a farm and knew how to grow food. The Romanian farmers, who at the time were being told by their government that they could sell their produce directly to the people instead of to the government, were revolting and refusing to farm if the government wouldn't continue to pay them to grow food. Dependency on government programs is going to be a difficult cycle to break in Romania. As an investor, I am under no illusion about how long it is going to take the people in these countries to change, for they do not know or see how entrepeneurship works. In conclusion, I avoid the conventional wisdom of investing in global or emerging market mutual funds but, instead, invest in global growth through the large U.S. blue-chip companies.

Many large U.S. companies are now doing more than 50 percent of their business outside the United States, and are attracting foreign investors. These companies are listed on many foreign stock exchanges and, with the explosion in popularity of the Internet, are beginning to sell stock directly to individual investors outside the United States. What impact will this have for the individual investor in India or Brazil? Will more capital flow into these giant U.S. blue-chip companies from foreign investors? Will this investor choose the big blue-chip company that uses standardized, trustworthy accounting practices or local companies that haven't introduced these accounting methods yet? What does this form of global capital do to this huge bubble the baby boomers are creating as they save for retirement? Conventional wisdom states that as the boomers reach retirement, they will sell their stocks and buy bonds (not those boomers who have read this book), and the bubble will burst. Will foreign investors step in to keep the bubble inflated? With capitalism going global, will national demographics have less impact on our stock market? All of these trends will be fascinating to watch over the next decades.

## 6. Dividends

P. J. O'Rourke, in a book about his journey into the world of economics, *Eat the Rich,* states that you just buy stocks in order to wait until someone else believes that that stock is worth more than you did when you bought the stock; that nobody cares about dividends. This may be true for most people, but if you have persevered to this point, you probably do care. I have a few points to reemphasize on this important topic.

The first point is not to get in the position of Ron and Sue, who did not position their money early enough to take advantage of the growth of dividends. It is better to buy stocks with a low dividend payout but with high dividend growth than to do as Ron and Sue did and buy stocks with a high current yield that does not show significant growth.

---

**The Rule of 72**

This rule is useful for estimating how long it will take for your investment to double if you know the growth rate. Divide the annual growth rate into 72. The answer is the number of years to double.

- Growth rate of 7% → 10 year double
- Growth rate of 10% → 7 year double
- Growth rate of 14% → 5 year double

---

*Cash Flow*

What dividend should a company pay, or, asked another way, what can it afford to pay? You probably hate formulas as much as I do, but if you are so inclined, you can figure out this basic fact about any company. One way to assess the safety of the company's dividend payment is to look at cash flow in the company's annual report or in the *Value Line Investment Survey*. Cash flow is the company's net income plus depreciation and amortization. An adequate cash flow for a safe dividend should be at least three times the dividend payout. This is a general principle; the ratio will vary depending on the industry. This is another reason to study the entire industry before investing. *Value Line Investment Survey* is a good source for reviewing all stocks in the entire industry.

*Historical Performance*

For most of us, the proof of a stocks propensity to raise its dividend is through its historic performance. People wonder how safe the reliance on the dividend is. Theoretically, any company can drop its payout at any time. Although there is no guarantee that this won't happen, the historical record makes this appear unlikely. Here is a list of companies most of which are included in the sample portfolio for the Dividend Growth Investment Strategy. These companies are listed with the year that they started paying dividends. They have all paid dividends *continuously* since that date. Note that all of these companies continued to pay dividends through the Great Depression and World War II. Do you think that we will have a cataclysm of this dimension over the next few years? If Coca-Cola has paid dividends continuously since 1883, what would happen in the next millennium to get them to discontinue rewarding shareholders?

| **Dividends Paid Since:** | | | |
|---|---|---|---|
| Coca-Cola Co. | 1883 | State Street Corp. | 1910 |
| Procter & Gamble | 1891 | Heinz (H. J.) | 1911 |
| Colgate-Palmolive | 1895 | Jefferson-Pilot | 1913 |
| Northern Trust | 1896 | Wrigley (Wm.) Jr. | 1913 |
| General Electric | 1899 | First Union Corp. | 1914 |
| Bristol-Myers | 1900 | Wilmington Trust Corp. | 1914 |
| Pfizer | 1901 | Abbott Laboratories | 1926 |
| Campbell Soup | 1902 | Becton Dickenson | 1926 |
| Johnson & Johnson | 1905 | Merck | 1935 |
| Gillette Co. | 1906 | | |

In chapter 8 I have my sample portfolio, with a complete discussion of each stock. In Appendix 1, I have listed the dividend performance of these stocks over the last eighteen years, listing the total percentage gain of the dividend over that period, the average yearly percentage increase, and the number of years that the dividend has been continuously increased. There also is a tabulation of stock-price appreciation over that same period. These lists are current but may be slightly different at the time that you read this book. This is a good starting place to evaluate the stocks that you are considering. Get out your calculator and your current information from the *Value Line Investment Survey* or the Internet, and make the best choice for your portfolio.

## WHEN TO BUY

This question basically has two parts: At what time do you start investing with the Dividend Growth Investment Strategy, and how do you time the purchase of an individual stock? The short answer is: As early as possible, and you don't.

### When Do I Start Investing?

To expand on the first question, when to start, we have to look at the conventional wisdom. I recently found this piece in a column in the *Wall Street Journal:*

> Update Your Asset-Allocation Strategy: If you are between twenty and forty years old, you can prudently put as much as 100 percent of your money into stocks because retirement is years away. As retirement comes closer the author suggests that the retirement portfolio of stocks undergo an asset reallocation to 40 percent–20 percent bonds depending on age and volatility tolerance.

The reader was encouraged to keep some money in stocks for inflation fighting.

Fidelity Investments, the company that has the huge Magellan Fund, has a similar outlook. You grow your money until retirement, at which time you convert to investments, including bonds, that will pay out 4 percent a year after adjustment for inflation, even if you need to dip into your principal to reach the 4 percent. This is a good principle, but requires that you have $500,000 for every $20,000 of income that you want to live on at retirement. The conventional wisdom would have everyone converting 40 percent of their growth stocks to bonds as they near their retirement years. The purpose is to create a portfolio that has an income cushion from bonds; the problem is that when people convert from growth stocks to bonds the government takes 20 percent of the appreciation that has occurred in capital-gains taxes. Everyone is afraid of a "bear market," in which you lose 20 percent of your principal through a decline in stock prices. This type of advice creates a *personal bear market* in your portfolio, a 20 percent loss of your assets to taxes.

Doesn't it make more sense to start growing your dividends now? If the stock market continues to grow at its current pace and we can average dividend growth of 14 percent per year, our income from dividends alone will double every five years. If the stock market resumes growth at its historic norm of 10.1 percent annual growth and dividends only grow at 10 percent a year, then income from dividends will double every seven years. Even if the market slows down and grows at 7 percent annually, dividend income will still double every ten years.

Assuming that, at the time you invest, your average dividend yield is 1.5 percent (this was about the market average yield in January 1999) you will need two doubles to be receiving a yield of 6 percent. These two doubles will give you a dividend yield that exceeds the 5 percent yield of bonds. Remember, you also have the capital-gain or stock appreciation to boot. The dividend income will continue to grow; after three doubles the yield will be 12 percent; after four doubles the yield will be 24 percent; after five doubles 48 percent; after six doubles the yield will be 96 percent; and on and on. These six doubles could happen within thirty to sixty years, meaning that many of us will live to receive a 96 percent yield on that dollar we invested back during our working days. This seems to be a better option than holding a portfolio of half bonds and half stocks and living off 4 percent (adjusted for inflation) of your portfolio.

This latter is, however, the conventional advice that you will receive from almost all financial planners, but this is not how Anne Schieber did it. Fortunately for her, Anne Schieber did not follow this conventional wisdom, followed her own counsel, and ended up with an income of over $1 million a year when she died in 1995.

Why settle for living off 4 percent of your nest egg? The Fidelity plan is in place for the investor who comes to them with a pile of money at age sixty-five along with the desire to retire immediately. At that point it is too late, and he may need to settle for their 4 percent plan. If you have been paying attention, however, you may now see that you can do much better. If you start early and position your money properly, you will far outpace the 4 percent return on your money.

Even if you start just ten years early, look what you can do: you can buy a blue-chip stock that has a dividend yield of 1.5 percent and grows its dividend at 14 percent per year. At retirement ten years later, your dividend will have doubled twice and will be yielding 6 percent on your original investment. Five years into your retirement, the dividend will have doubled again to a yield of 12 percent. While you live off of this dividend, you can let the stock price grow without dipping into your principal. The stock price should also appreciate greatly, but you don't need to count on this appreciation for your retirement well-being.

Another benefit of owning these blue-chip stocks outright is that it allows you to leave more money to your loved ones. This occurs because your loved ones can inherit the stocks with a stepped-up basis and continue receiving the dividends you were getting. The stepped-up basis means that they can use the value of the stock at the time that they inherit them as the basis, and don't need to pay capital gains taxes on all of the increase that the stock price has undergone since you bought the stock; the slate is wiped clean and they owe *no* capital gains tax. If your children sell the stocks, they will only pay capital gains tax (20 percent) on the appreciation that has occurred in their hands. Estate taxes are collected, however, and your stocks are valued at their fair market value on the day you die. Thus, you do not escape taxation on your portfolio's value when you die.

We are living longer these days, so positioning a retirement nest egg in good-quality blue-chip companies that have a history of commitment to growing their dividends is the best way to assure yourself of a growing income in retirement. If you keep 50 percent of your retirement money in bonds, your principal is destroyed by inflation over time.

To say it yet one more time, for this is the essence of a secure retirement: Invest your money as early as possible and position it properly the first time so that it will be in the right place when you need it. Those people stuck with converting their portfolios from stocks to bonds are also turning over 20 percent of their retirement nest egg to the federal government (20 percent capital gains taxes). Can you afford this tax bite?

## How Do I Time the Purchase of a Stock?

When do I buy a stock? How do I know when the stock is at the bottom and is ready to make impressive gains? Before we answer this question, we should discuss market volatility and the relative valuation of the market.

*Most stocks fluctuate 50 percent from top to bottom every year.*

This is the source of the anxiety over the stock market roller coaster. Everyone wants to buy at the lowest price and sell at the highest. The problem is that this is completely unpredictable. Early in my investing career, I attempted this. The two most common scenarios of this approach were that:

1. I would buy 100 shares of Amalgamated Consolidated at a price that had to be the lowest that it could go, only to have it drop another $5 the next day, or:
2. I would watch Tech High Industries fall for three days, but, knowing the current situation, I knew that the stock was bound to fall farther. Instead of buying, I then would watch it climb until I had to pay a price higher than it was at at the start.

Warren Buffett tells us that you shouldn't be in the stock market if you are not prepared to see your stocks fall 50 percent in value. If this scares you, you are in the wrong game. The Dividend Growth Investment Strategy is a way to psychologically bolster your courage; it allows you to stay in the market in spite of the roller coaster.

The other consideration is the valuation of the market as a whole. The debate in the financial press is endless on this subject, with some saying that the market is fairly valued, and others saying that all stocks are way too expensive. It is no secret that we experienced a great bull market that started in the early 1980s. Stock prices are high by all historical indicators, P/Es have expanded to historic highs, book values are low relative to stock prices, dividend yields are low. The Ibbotson figures, based on the S&P 500, show that from 1926 through 1990 the 10.1 percent average annual rate of total return consisted of 6.9 percent from price appreciation and 3.2 percent from cash dividends. Corporate earnings growth accelerated to 15 percent annually (more than double the long-term average of 7 percent) in the 1990s. Dividend increases have risen from 3.2 percent to 4.5 percent in this decade, but stock price increases have outraced the dividend increases, causing the yield to lag. Remember, the dividend yield is calculated by:

$$\frac{\text{Yearly Dividend per Share}}{\text{Price per Share}} = \% \text{ Yield}$$

Therefore, even if the dividend increases, if the share price increases more than the dividend, the yield will go down. The average yield of S&P 500 stocks is fluctuating between 1.5 percent and 2.0 percent. The rate of dividend increase generally varies with the industrial sector of the company and the company's growth. Stock prices have recently soared at an unprecedented 17.5 percent yearly pace, dividend increases have been averaging 4.5 percent.

What does this mean? Michael Edesess wrote:

> Isn't it possible that historic market levels were too low? In the past, the information investors needed to assess the value of an investment was far less readily available than it is today. Investments may, as a result, have seemed more risky than they really were. Investors may have been too cautious to anticipate the high corporate earnings growth rates that subsequently came to pass. The cumulative annual return is 12.3 percent for the past forty years, 16.6 percent for the past twenty years, 18.0 percent for the past five years. What accounts for this increase? Return can be viewed as the sum of dividend yield, corporate earnings growth, and growth in the P/E ratio. Over the past fifteen to twenty-five years, dividend yield has been declining while corporate earnings growth rates have shown a definite increase. Even more marked over that period has been the increased growth of P/E ratios, which are now around 30 as against their historic average of 14.5. High P/E ratios are a sign that the market believes future earnings growth will be high—the long-term historical growth rate of corporate dividends is about 8 percent, but over the past twenty years the rate has been about 10 percent.

Are we going to return to historic norms? This has been a much-discussed question. Is there a new investing paradigm as Mr. Edesess suggests, or is there just a stock-market bubble that is going to burst? If and when we do return to historic market norms (regression to the mean), we will have to pay back with lower stock prices, probably not lower dividend payouts. This payback could come in the form of a recession, a market correction, or just sideways movement of stock prices while earnings catch up. This is the stock-market roller coaster. When payback time comes, the dividend payments will increase faster than the stock price, meaning that the yield will increase, so new money invested will fetch a higher yield as well as buy more shares.

The statement by Peter Lynch, market guru of Fidelity Investments, bears repeating, "Timing the market is an expensive hobby, expensive because of all the gains you miss when you sell at the wrong time. Stocks make most of their gains in short bursts that are impossible to predict."

If you compare two investors, one who buys his stocks on the worst day of the year for thirty years from 1965 to 1995, and the second who buys when stocks are at their lowest point of the year for the same period, how much difference would there be between the two at the end of thirty years? The lucky investor, who was able to buy low, ended up with 11.7 percent gain per year. His unlucky counterpart, who bought at the high point each year, ended up with 10.6 percent gain each year. Thus, even if you could be a perfect market timer (which, as you now know, you can't) the maximum that you could hope to gain from your talent would be 1.1 percent per year.

Since we can't predict the day-to-day fluctuation of stock price, and since we don't know if the market as a whole is going up or down, how do we decide when to buy? The answer is: *continuously.* We should use a technique called "dollar-cost averaging." The principle is simple: Instead of putting your money into the market all at once, trying to catch the low, you invest over a long period of time, putting in money at regular intervals, such as a month or every two weeks. You don't worry too much about the price. You may want to keep a list of stocks that you wish to purchase and pick off the one that has dipped the lowest each month. By doing this, you smooth out the ups and downs of the market, some months paying a high premium, but other months catching a bargain, overall paying a fair, or "average," price. In the long run, whether you pay a couple of dollars more or less for any one stock is unimportant. You do, however, need a strategy to keep investing without torturing yourself about the price. Dollar-cost averaging is the way to pay a fair price for your stocks. This is an extremely useful adjunct to your Dividend Growth Investment Strategy.

## HOW TO BUY

You have decided to buy Amalgamated Consolidated Industries as the first stock in your portfolio. You want to spend about $5,000; the stock is at $50 per share; ergo, you want to buy 100 shares. To whom do you give the money? The answer is that there are many, many people anxious to accommodate you. This section will help you decide exactly how to complete the transaction.

### How Do I Choose a Broker?

The first decision you need to make is to decide on a broker (you will see later that this may not be necessary if the stock you wish to purchase is available through a direct stock purchase plan from the issuing company). There are three levels of brokerages that you need to consider, stratified by fees and services. The full-service brokers are the familiar ones with the household names, such as Merrill Lynch. Their job is not just to sell stocks, but to advise you and help you pick your investments, often selling you investments and funds out of their portfolio. For this service, you will pay a relatively high fee for each exchange. If you are committed to the Dividend Growth Investment Strategy, you will understand by this time that this is not the path that you should go down.

The second level has the discount brokers, such as Charles Schwab & Co. These brokers have discounted fees but still offer some investment advice and services. We dealt with a brokerage in this category for a while and found it very aggravating. The rules and fee structures were constantly changing, so that we never knew what any transaction was actually costing us until we got the bill.

The third level has the deep-discount brokers, such as the one we have been using, Scottrade. The advice that these brokers give is limited to the current stock quotes. No broker calls you at home with a "hot tip." Their fees are reasonable and are published and do not change. Currently, for a "Safe Keeping" account, the charge is $30 for buying or selling 100 shares with an added $5 for each 100 shares in the same stock. For an account in which you want to hold your own stock certificate, the fee is $35 for the first 100, again with $5 for each extra 100 shares.

If you are comfortable on the Internet, most brokerages now have accounts for Internet trading at considerably cheaper prices. I have seen fees as low as $7 per trade. These accounts do *not* allow you to hold your own certificates.

## How Do I Order Stock?

After deciding on a broker and setting up your account, you can place your order. This can be done in a number of ways. You can place a "market order," which simply means that you will pay whatever Amalgamated Consolidated is selling for at that instant. The order usually can be executed a few minutes after you get your quote, so (except in an extremely volatile market) you will have a rough idea of what you will be spending. A few minutes after you place the order, the brokerage will call you back with a confirmation of the sale, giving you the exact cost. They will also send out a confirmation on paper. Under current rules, you have three business days to complete the trade; they need your money and, in the case of a sale, any stock certificates involved. There are rumors that this period may go down to twenty-four hours in the near future. If you are holding your own certificates, the transfer agent for Amalgamated Consolidated will send them to you through the mail in approximately one month. Adhering to the principles of the Dividend Growth Investment Strategy and dollar-cost averaging, most of your transactions will be placed in this manner.

If you decide that you want Amalgamated Consolidated at $50 a share but find that it is selling for $53, you can place a "limit order" specifying that you will buy the stock when it hits your target price. You can also specify the period for which the order is good, twenty-four hours, a month, or open-ended. Nothing happens unless your company dips to $50, at which time the brokerage executes the trade and you owe the money. You can cancel any time before execution. Similar "limit orders" can also be placed for selling a stock. There are other ways to buy and sell stocks, but these do not fit into the Dividend Growth Investment Strategy.

## Who Keeps the Certificates?

There are other decisions that you must make in purchasing stocks. As alluded to earlier, you need to decide whether you will hold your certificates yourself or the brokerage will hold them for you in the "street name." There are advantages and disadvantages both ways. Holding your certificates is slightly more expensive than a safe keeping account and involves a lot more hassle. You must keep track of the certificates, to make sure that you receive all that are due you; you need a place to keep them safely; and each time you sell a stock, you need to retrieve the certificate and promptly return it to the broker. The certificates are not negotiable by other parties, so theft is of little concern, but they may be lost or accidentally destroyed. It costs about $50 to replace one, again causing a lot of hassle.

The advantage to holding your own certificate is that it allows you more control over your finances. When we switched from the discount broker to the deep discount broker, we either had to leave our stocks in the original account and sell them at a higher commission or pay a lot to have the account transferred to the new brokerage. If we had held our certificates, we could have taken them anywhere we chose to sell them with no extra fees. There have been occasional instances where companies and brokerages have made errors in the amount of a stock that we held; holding the certificates made resolving the dispute much easier. Lastly, although rare in recent times, brokerages can go bankrupt. Your account with them would be insured through SIPCO, but you can only imagine the delays and confusion involved in extricating yourself from that mess.

The disadvantages of allowing the brokerage to hold your stocks are the opposite of those listed above. The big advantage is convenience. You make a trade, and you are done. No trips to the brokerage with certificates, no safe deposit box, no lost certificates. This advantage may increase if the period to execute the trade decreases to one day.

## What About My Dividend?

The next decision you need to make concerns your dividends. You have two choices: you can get a quarterly check from each company, or you can have the company reinvest your dividend. Reinvestment is a process that most corporations offer to their shareholders (DRIPs, or dividend-reinvestment plans). Instead of sending you the dividend check, they use it to purchase a fractional share of stock. They may or may not charge a small fee for doing this. The company keeps these accumulating shares in an account in your name. Even though you never see the cash, you do owe taxes at the end of the year on all dividends invested in this way. There are two main advantages of reinvesting dividends. It is convenient, done automatically by the company, and it forces you to keep reinvesting your money, according to the principle of dollar-cost averaging, to increase your compounding.

There are two disadvantages as well. The first is that, perhaps, you don't want to keep investing more money in the companies that you already own. Maybe you want to take the aggregate of your dividends from all of your stocks and buy a new company that you do not own. The second reason is bookkeeping: If you hold a stock for ten years and then sell it, your basis, that is, what you paid for the stock, would be horrendous to compute. You would have your original purchase, plus forty quarterly purchases of fractional shares, each at a different price. We found this task too daunting. There probably is, somewhere, a computer program that can handle this calculation, but why bother?

You may want to belong to a company's DRIP program, reinvesting your dividends, as a way to acquire additional shares in the company. The DRIP program allows you to send extra money directly into the company for the purchase of additonal company shares, usually on a quarterly basis. A dividend-reinvestment program requires that you own the stock before you can enroll in the company's DRIP plan. The fastest way to purchase that first share of stock is through a broker. In order to enroll in the company's DRIP plan, the stock certificate must be in your name (not the street name or name of the broker). You must tell the broker when you buy the stock that you want the stock certificate mailed to you; that way it will be in your name and you can deal directly with the company. After receipt of the stock certificate, the company will send you an enrollment form for the company's DRIP plan. Now you can send optional cash payments to the company's transfer agent, and shares will be purchased for your account on a certain prearranged date. You will have a stock certificate that will require safekeeping. Many companies are now offering to hold your certificates in your account.

To make life even easier, many companies are now offering Direct Stock Purchase Plans (DSPPs), in which you can buy stock directly from the company or the bank acting as its transfer agent. These plans are also referred to as: direct stock plans (DSPs); direct investment programs; no-load stocks. They all allow you to purchase stocks directly from the company. There are now about 180 companies offering this direct-purchase option, and the list grows daily. The company holds your stock in your personal account. *No broker is involved.*

Although these plans may have slightly different features, they all allow dividend reinvestment or the option to receive cash dividends. Many also allow the shareholders to make automatic periodic purchases from their bank accounts, an excellent dollar-cost-averaging tool. Small fees may be charged. In appendix 2 is a list of the companies in my sample portfolio that offer this service and the features of their plan. I suspect that, by the time you read this book, the list will be greatly expanded. If you are interested in a specific company, information can be obtained through their shareholder services (investor relations), either through their home page on the Internet or through their telephone number listed in *Value Line.*

## SUMMARY

Once you are committed to investing in the stock market, you have many decisions to make. You have to decide what to buy, using the principles of diversification, dominant companies, and dividends. You need to decide when to buy it, remembering that market timing doesn't work and that dollar-cost averaging is a proven strategy. Next, you need to either pick a broker or decide to invest directly in the company that you chose. You need to decide whether you wish to reinvest your dividends or collect your cash and decide if you or the company or broker should hold your shares. Once you have made these decisions (and isn't it wonderful to have a system where these decisions are available to you), all you need is the money.

# 8

---

# A TEMPORARY ESCAPE
# FROM THE IRS

One of the main tactics of the Dividend Growth Investment Strategy, as you know by now, is to minimize the effect of taxes on your investments. Up until this point, we have mainly talked about money invested in your personal accounts: money subject to all of the taxation that the federal and state governments can bring to bear. For most of us, however, there is an entirely separate world of investing; indeed, for many of you, this world may contain your entire portfolio. This is the world of tax-deferred plans. Some of these plans are available to you as an individual (IRAs), but most are associated with your job and your employer. Because these plans are authorized and regulated by the government, and because the laws have evolved over the years with layer upon layer of regulations, this discussion is guaranteed to make your eyes glaze over. The purpose of this section is not to give you an ironclad understanding of the tax laws. Rather, it is meant as an overview of your tax-deferred retirement options so that you will recognize some of the options available and recognize points at which you need professional guidance. This is one area where you should have some anxiety. Withdrawing your money the wrong way from these accounts could cost you thousands of dollars in taxes. There are two main sections to this chapter: first, a description of the pension laws and how they affect you; and second, a discussion on investing your money in a tax-deferred plan. I have also included a discussion of what could become of your retirement income *if* you were free to manage your own social security account instead of leaving it to the government.

## TAX-DEFERRED PLANS FROM YOUR EMPLOYER

Start planning early so when retirement day comes you are prepared and you can enjoy your retirement. The day you actually retire is not the day you want to panic about what to do with your retirement money. Employers will not have the resources to help you understand all your retirement options, and many of them will require that you take your retirement money with you in a lump-sum payment. It is at this time that most employees need help so that they do not end up squandering their nest egg. Consider Gary, who worked for a large corporation in California. When Gary retired, he was given the choice of either taking a lump sum (taking all of his retirement money out of the plan in one payout) or annuitizing it and receiving a monthly check. A retirement counselor explained the company and the government rules controlling distributions of retirement money. The problem was that Gary did not seek out investment advice, and he chose the lump-sum payout. Gary's entire retirement nest egg was gone in five years. Gary could have benefited from both investing advice and advice on how to roll over his retirement money and make it last.

This is a situation that we all want to avoid. The rules that govern retirement benefits are complex; there are numerous options that any one retiree is going to have. You want to be able to select the option that will cause you to pay the least taxes now, keep your money growing tax deferred, so it will last as long as you and your spouse live with some left over for your loved ones. This may be a good time to consult with a professional on your rollover options. There are many tax traps for the unwary; good planning can help minimize the taxes you owe on your retirement benefits (income and estate taxes). A good example is Rene, who received company stock in her 401(k) plan. When she retired, she rolled it into a traditional IRA and later found out that she owed ordinary income taxes on the entire distribution. Had she taken one of two different options, she could have paid capital gains taxes (20 percent) instead of the ordinary income taxes (up to 39.6 percent). On $100,000 of retirement money, she paid an extra $20,000 in taxes. With good advice, that $20,000 could have been in her pocket instead of Uncle Sam's.

You probably cannot get all of the advice that you need about your defered retirement account from one source. Do not take investment advice from someone selling the products. Pay for it in a fee-for-service session. A broker is there to sell you products that earn him the highest commissions, not products that will help you the most. Many brokers, bankers, and financial planners may have the best of intentions, but they may not have the expertise to answer your pension questions and select the best investments for your needs. Remember, a little knowledge can be a dangerous thing. The more informed you become, the better armed you will be when it comes to seeking advice. After reading this book, you should have general knowledge about retirement money and how to invest it. This should represent a road map for both investing and pension planning to keep you on the correct path. Be informed enough so you don't fall prey to bad advice.

There are many rules that govern how your retirement money is paid out, how long it will last, and how it is taxed. The biggest risk you can take is not getting informed and turning over your retirement money to someone else to manage. If you take the correct approach, you will probably outlive your money. When you and your spouse reach sixty-five years old, there is a fifty-fifty chance that one of you will reach the age of eighty-eight (at the current state of medical science). The table below represents data from the National Center For Health Statistics. Their data is based on a probability of at least 20 percent. For example, a fifty-five year-old man has a 20 percent chance of living another thirty-two years and an eighty-year-old woman has a 20 percent chance of living another fourteen years or until she is ninety-four years of age. These life expectancies have continued to move up, giving us more years of retirement as well as longer lives. Planning is important if you don't want to outlive your money.

| | Years you should plan to live | |
|---|---|---|
| At Age | Male | Female |
| 55 | 32 | 36 |
| 60 | 27 | 31 |
| 65 | 22 | 27 |
| 70 | 18 | 22 |
| 75 | 14 | 18 |
| 80 | 11 | 14 |

## QUALIFIED RETIREMENT PLANS

You may or may not have a choice from your employer of the type of retirement plan in which you can participate. Possibly, the type of plan offered may influence which of two jobs you choose in the future. Regardless of choice, it is important to understand the features of any plan that is offered to you.

Qualified plans set up by employers for their employees' retirement have three tax advantages:

1. Income earned by the qualified plan is not taxable until the plan money is taken out of the plan.
2. Employer contributions to the plan are deductible.
3. The contributions to the plan by the employer are not taxable to the employee until the money is taken out of the plan.

There are two types of qualified retirement plans, a *defined contribution plan* and a *defined benefit plan.* The type of plan depends upon the method used to determine the employer's contribution and the employee's benefit. A defined contribution plan provides for an individual account for each participant, and the benefit is determined solely by the amount in the participant's account. The defined benefit plan provides for a set level of benefits to be paid in the future, usually at retirement age. In the past, defined benefit plans were the most popular, but in December 1997, the total assets in defined contribution plans finally surpassed the total assets in defined benefit plans. Currently, defined contribution plans, mainly 401(k) plans, cover 43 percent of U.S. workers, while only 25 percent are covered by defined benefit plans.

## Defined Benefit Plan

This type of plan provides the employee with a specified benefit, derived by applying a formula to the employee's compensation: this formula can be found in the plan document. Every year the employer contributes the amount that is actuarially estimated (insurance actuaries compute the life expectancy of the participant using current population and mortality data) to be necessary to fund the promised benefit at retirement. The amount of the employee's benefit is not dependent on the income, expenses, or gains or losses of the trust assets; the employer bears the investment risk. These benefits are insured by the Pension Benefit Guaranty Corporation (PBGC) up to $3,000 a month. The plan sponsor must pay insurance premiums to the PBGC to insure the plan. The maximum annual benefit that may accrue to a participant under a qualified defined benefit plan is the lesser of $90,000 (adjusted for inflation), or 100 percent of the participant's average compensation for his three consecutive most highly compensated years of employment. If you have a defined benefit plan, it is important to find out if there are any survivor benefits for your spouse upon your death or if the pension benefit terminates upon your death.

A defined benefit plan promises to pay the participant a pension, a stated amount, upon retirement. There are several types of defined benefit plans that differ from one another in the method of determining the participant's benefit. Types of defined benefit plans include:

1. A Fixed Benefit Plan promises to pay a stated dollar amount for the participant's lifetime (e.g., $500 per month for the participant's life).
2. A Flat Benefit Plan promises to pay a stated percentage of compensation (compensation may be the average of the entire career or the last three years of one's career).
3. A Cash Balance Plan represents a new wrinkle in defined benefit pensions.

Many employers are now using the "cash-balance" plan, instead of the 401(k) plan. There are some major differences, with advantages and disadvantages for employees. Employees have a hypothetical account into which contributions are made each year. The accounts earn interest, and the employer invests the money and promises to provide an interest rate of return on the account of 5 percent or so. The employer keeps whatever it earns above the promised rate of return. The employee does not have the opportunity to make investment decisions and receive the higher returns. This is the disadvantage to the employee, who misses out on the opportunity to make the higher returns.

A cash balance plan is a portable defined-benefit plan. The main advantage of this type of qualified plan is that the young employees usually can take their money in a lump sum with them when they leave the employer, if they are vested. Typically, the employee vests after five years. "Vesting" is the process by which you gain the rights to keep your employers contributions for yourself. This can be in one, two, five, or any number of years after starting employment, as defined in the plan of the fund. Typically, you may gain 20 percent per year, so that after three years you are entitled to 60 percent of your pension account, and after five years you own 100 percent of the fund. Like the defined benefit plan, the cash-balance account is a bookkeeping device for a pool of pension assets. Each year a percentage of the employee's pay is contributed to the account along with the interest credit on the account's funds. The employee receives a quarterly statement showing the account balance.

## Defined Contribution Plan

These plans provide individual accounts for each participant. Benefits are based solely on the amount contributed to the account (contributions from employer and employee), plus any income, expenses, gains, and losses, and any forfeitures of accounts of other participants that are allocated to the participant's account. The participant bears the investment risk. Plans are not subject to PBGC insurance.

Not all employers match your savings, but some do to various degrees, which sharply boosts the return on each dollar you save. You may have to remain on the job several years to become vested in your employer's matching contributions.

There are a number of rules governing these defined contribution plans:

1. The maximum annual contribution limit is $35,000 and will be raised to $40,000 in 2002.

2. Withdrawals of tax-deferred contributions and any investment earnings are taxed at ordinary income rates.

3. There is no tax on withdrawals of after-tax contributions, loans from your account, or rollovers to an IRA or new employer's 401(k).

4. There is an additional *penalty tax of 10 percent* for withdrawals made before age fifty-nine and a half.

5. There is no 10 percent penalty if early withdrawals are made:

   a. By your beneficiaries at your death

   b. On diagnosis of severe disability

   c. To pay medical expenses in excess of 7.5 percent of gross income

   d. Upon retirement after age 55

6. You must begin withdrawing money from your plan by April 1 of the year after you turn seventy and a half. The minimum payout depends on your life expectancy or the joint life expectancy of you and your spouse, or beneficiary. There is a *50 percent penalty* for failure to make the required minimum distribution.

Defined contribution plans come in many styles and forms, each with its own set of rules. These include profit-sharing plans, age-weighted profit-sharing plans, money-purchase pension plans, target-benefit pension plans, stock bonus plans, and employee stock ownership plans (ESOPs). You can find out from your plan administrator which kind you have and its rules and restrictions.

### 401(k) Plan

Currently, the most common tax-deferred vehicle is the 401(k) Plan. A 401(k) can be set up as part of a profit-sharing or stock bonus plan. This is an employee salary reduction plan where the employee opts to have his employer put some of his salary into the plan's trust account. The employee must have the option of taking the money as salary or putting it into the 401(k). These elective salary contributions and any employer contributions that are used in computing the ADP (actual deferral percentage) must be 100 percent invested. The employer can match the employee's contribution, subject to limitations. This salary contribution to the 401(k) is not taxed until it is withdrawn, and benefits may not be distributed earlier than upon separation from service, death, disability, termination of the the plan without the establishment of a successor plan, or the attainment of age fifty nine and a half.

## SELF-EMPLOYED PLANS

### Keogh Plan

There are also other types of plans, many of which the employee funds himself. The Keogh Plan is a qualified retirement plan for self-employed individuals. It can take the form of a profit-sharing or money-purchase plan or both. The existing $35,000 annual contribution limit will be raised to $40,000 starting in 2002. Rollovers are permitted into IRAs and other qualified plans. All withdrawals are taxed at ordinary income-tax rates, with an additional 10 percent tax on withdrawals made before age fifty nine and a half. The same rules of distribution apply to Keoghs as apply to 401(k) plans.

### Traditional IRA

A Traditional IRA, or individual retirement account, is set up by an individual to provide for his own retirement. An individual under age seventy and a half with earned income qualifies if:

a.  He has no company plan for either himself or his spouse

b.  Is single and has an income under $40,000

c.  Is married and has an income under $60,000; or

d.  Is married and only one spouse has a retirement plan, and their joint income is under $160,000.

Contributions can be made up to $2,000 per individual per year and up to $4,000 per couple per year ($2,000 in each spouse's name). Contribution limits will be increased up to $5,000 by 2008. After 2008, the limit will be adjusted for inflation.

All withdrawals are taxed as ordinary income and have a 10 percent penalty tax on distributions made before fifty-nine and a half years of age. Early withdrawals can be made from a traditional IRA (as well as SEP, and SIMPLE IRAs which are slightly different variants) without penalty:

a. By your beneficiaries at your death

b. On diagnosis of severe disability

c. To pay medical expenses in excess of 7.5 percent of gross income

d. To pay health insurance premiums while unemployed

e. To pay higher education expenses for yourself, spouse, children, grandchildren

f. To buy a first house for yourself or family members ($10,000 lifetime limit)

Traditional IRAs, SEPs, and SIMPLE IRAs have the same minimum distribution rules; you must begin withdrawing money from the IRA by April 1 of the year after you turn seventy and a half. The minimum payout depends on your life expectancy or the joint life expectancy of yourself and a beneficiary.

## Nondeductible IRA

Nondeductible IRAs are available to those who don't qualify for a traditional IRA or a Roth IRA and want to save outside a company plan, deferring taxes on earnings. As the name implies, the contribution is not tax deductible and the investment earnings are taxed at ordinary income-tax rates. These nondeductible IRAs have the same penalties and distribution rules as traditional IRAs. Rather than set up one of these plans, you would be financially ahead by using the buy-and-hold Dividend Growth Investment Strategy in your private account. The nondeductible IRA charges taxes at both ends, at the highest ordinary income tax rates. You lose the benefit of paying the lower capital gains tax rate on investment earnings.

## Roth IRA

The newest wrinkle in the world of tax-deferred accounts is the Roth IRA. This account is a nondeductible IRA (the money that you contribute to a Roth IRA is not tax deductible, whereas in the traditional IRA your contribution is tax deductible). For example, assume that you pay 40 percent in federal and state taxes:

Roth IRA: In order to place $2,000 in the Roth IRA account, you must earn $3,333. $1,333 goes to taxes.
Traditional IRA: $2,000 can go in the account and no taxes are paid.

The advantage of the Roth IRA is that when the money is withdrawn, *it is not taxed.* At this time, the government has promised that money and stocks can grow in a Roth IRA, and you will not pay any taxes on the capital gains or the dividends when it is withdrawn. This contrasts to the traditional IRA, where ordinary income taxes are paid on all withdrawals.

The Roth IRA is subject to the same rules and penalties that the traditional IRA is subject to. The money must be held in the Roth IRA for at least five years and the participant must be at least fifty-nine and a half years old at the time of withdrawal. As with all other retirement plans, qualified plans, and IRAs, distributions may occur without penalty if the participant becomes disabled or dies. Since distributions are tax free from a Roth IRA, an individual is not required to take distributions from a Roth IRA at any time in his life.

With the advent of the Roth IRA, there has been an avalanche of advice about converting your traditional IRA to a Roth. *Converting to a Roth IRA is not the no-brainer you have been led to believe!* When a traditional IRA is converted to a Roth IRA, ordinary income taxes are collected on the entire amount held in your traditional IRA. You cannot pay them out of your IRA funds because that would constitute a premature withdrawal and a 10 percent penalty would be charged. Taxes are paid from your household budget. This is money you could invest using the Dividend Growth Investment Strategy.

Which is the best vehicle for growing a retirement nest egg, a Roth IRA or a Traditional IRA? Studies have shown that it can be six of one and a half dozen of the other deciding which type of IRA is most advantageous. The Traditional IRA costs less to fund because of the income tax deduction; conversely, the Roth IRA takes more out of the participant's pocket to fund. You, however, may make up this loss of income at withdrawal with the Roth, because you pay no taxes at that end. After taking these differences into account there is very little difference in outcome between the IRAs, especially if your income-tax bracket is lower when you retire.

In summary, disadvantages of the Roth IRA:

1. You pay income taxes on your Roth IRA contribution;
2. The Roth IRA is subject to the same restrictions as the traditional IRA;

3. The Roth IRA does not have the same asset protection as the traditional IRA in many states (creditors have access to the Roth IRA funds);

4. There is always the chance that the government will change the rules on you some time in the future after you have committed to the Roth. Remember the retroactive tax increases of 1993.

Is the Roth IRA a good deal for you, or just another scheme to accelerate collection of income taxes while you are working and paying taxes at a higher rate? When you make your calculations remember to consider the time value of money. Take the income-tax deduction money (Roth IRA contribution–Traditional IRA = value of the income tax deduction) and invest it growing at the same rate and time of the IRAs. It may be more prudent, if after doing the calculations for your own situation and finding that you are in the six of one, half a dozen of another situation, not to convert to the Roth IRA. Tax attorneys, as a general principle, always defer income and accelerate deductions to put off paying taxes as long as possible.

### Rules of the Roth IRA

1. Contributions: Up to $2,000 per individual per year and up to $4,000 per couple per year ($2,000 in each spouse's name). These contribution limits will be increased to $3,000 in 2002, up to $5,000 in 2008. The Roth IRA cannot be used if an individual's adjusted gross income is greater than $110,000, or a couples' income is greater than $160,000.

2. Withdrawals are tax-free, including growth of income if you've held the Roth IRA for five years and the withdrawal is made:

   a. After you reach fifty-nine and a half years of age;

   b. By your beneficiaries after your death;

   c. Because of severe disability; or

   d. To buy a first house for yourself or family members (lifetime limit of $10,000).

3. There are no minimum distribution rules.

4. Premature withdrawals of principal are tax-free, and all withdrawals are deemed to consist of principal until the principal is depleted. Investment earnings drawn before age fifty-nine and a half are taxed at ordinary income-tax rates with a 10 percent penalty added to any tax due.

*Converting Company Stock in a 401(k) to a Roth IRA*

If you have company stock in your 401(k) plan, the Roth IRA may be for you. This is a specialized tax situation; company stock in your 401(k) gets preferential tax treatment that you don't want to lose. This tax benefit could save you a bundle, and many people blow it without realizing it. Many tax professionals and advisors are unware of the tax nuances. You will get capital gains treatment on the appreciation that has occurred while the stock has been in your account. To preserve this capital gains treatment, don't roll this stock into a traditional IRA (this is where people blow it). A traditional IRA will increase the taxation of the company stock to ordinary income rates when you take it out: the long term capital gains rate is 20 percent while the ordinary income tax rate is 39.6 percent (highest rate). You have several good options. There are special brokerage accounts that can be set up for this stock, which continues to defer taxes and preserves the capital gains treatment when you do sell the stock. It can be rolled into a Roth IRA, in this case you pay the taxes (capital gains on the appreciated amount and ordinary income on the cost of the stock when you originally acquired it in your account). The third option is taking it out in a lump sum, and paying the taxes as you would if you rolled it into a Roth IRA.

## RULES FOR TAX-DEFERRED ACCOUNTS

For those of you that have made it to this point in the chapter, have faith; the end is in sight. We just have to get through some general rules for tax deferred accounts regarding tax free rollovers, distributions, recalculations, and beneficiaries. These are all issues that you will face if you have one of these plans.

A "tax-free rollover" can occur if, after you withdraw your money from one plan, you place it in a second qualified recipient plan within sixty days. If you do this, no taxes are owed; if you don't reinvest the money, income taxes and any appropriate penalties are owed on the full amount.

Distributions from qualified plans to participants and beneficiaries may take many forms. Among the most common are the lump-sum distribution, the straight-life annuity, the annuity for a fixed term of years, and the qualified joint and survivor annuity.

Lump-sum distributions can be rolled over into an IRA and distributions can be made from the IRA, or, taxes can be paid and the money invested in a taxable account. The types of annuities available have been covered in a previous chapter.

You may also take installment payments. These may start at any time after age fifty-nine and a half, but you must begin withdrawing money from your plan by April 1 of the year after you turn seventy and a half. The required minimum payment amount depends on your life expectancy or the joint life expectancy of you and a beneficiary. There are severe penalties if these distributions are not made (50 percent penalty).

The only form of distribution that is imposed on plans by law is the requirement that certain qualified plans provide the spouse of the participant with benefits in the form of a qualified "joint and survivor annuity"; the spouse of certain vested participants who dies before retirement will receive benefits in the form of a qualified preretirement survivor annuity. This requirement can be waived if both the participant and the participant's spouse sign a written waiver request (spousal consent). This requirement applies to all pension plans and also to profit sharing plans that provide for payment of benefits in the form of lifetime annuities.

## Who Should Be Named as Your Designated Beneficiary?

In most cases you will want to name your spouse as the designated beneficiary of your qualified plan. Your spouse has the greatest flexibility when receiving qualified retirement plan and IRA benefits upon the participant's death.

1. A spouse is the only beneficiary who may roll over a distribution received by reason of the participant's death. A spouse can roll over or transfer such benefits to an IRA in the spouse's own name, and then defer distributions from that IRA subject to the required minimum distribution rules as applied to the spouse.
2. The spouse can also elect to begin taking distributions from the plan without paying any penalties; penalties are waived because of the death of the participant spouse. Distributions will qualify for the marital deduction, thus there is no estate tax on the transfer of these benefits to a spouse. The spouse may take distributions in the form of annuity payments, fixed installments, or a lump-sum payment.

A trust can be named as the beneficiary of your qualified plan. Before doing this get professional advice to make sure that this is your best option; generally, it will not be. There are special rules that must be followed when naming the trust as the beneficiary.

## Election to Recalculate

It may not be your greatest cause of anxiety at this moment, but, at some point in your life, you will have to consider an "election to recalculate." This is a decision that all people with qualified plans and IRAs will need to make when they begin taking distributions: Should life expectancies be recalculated every year? In order to calculate the minimum distribution payments that you are required to take out of your qualified plan, you can make these calculations in two ways:

1. You can use your actuarially determined life expectancy, or
2. You can chose to recalculate your life expectancy every year.

Recalculation slows down distributions by adding one more year each year, to preserve the nest egg in your plan. One disadvantage of recalculating is that, when you and your spouse both die, the money left in the plan is all paid out to the named beneficiary immediately, which means more taxes (income and estate).

You can also choose to have minimum distribution calculations based on your single life expectancy or on the joint life expectancy of you and your spouse or another beneficiary (a nonspouse beneficiary will not be calculated as more than ten years younger than you).

As this book is going to press, the rules on calculating required minimum distributions and inheritance of IRAs and other retirement plans have been completely overhauled. They have been simplified and clarified and, in general, give plan owners and their beneficiaries more favorable tax treatment.

There are new regulations that have gone into effect in 2001 that everyone with an IRA, 401(k), or other tax-deferred retirement plan should know about. The old rules on distribution have been simplified and clarified. Many of the traps for the unwary have been eliminated. The new uniform distribution table eliminates provisions that have cost some individuals and their families thousands in income taxes. People who have made paperwork mistakes, poor beneficiary choices, or other mistakes now have a fresh start. Under the old rules the government frequently required that IRAs and other tax-deferred plans to be paid out in a lump sum in the year following the death of the plan owner, or, less onerous, payout was required in five years. This hurts, because income and estate taxes can claim 75 to 95 percent of the IRA or plan amount; it is best to stretch the payout over the longest time possible. These new rules will in most cases allow a longer payout period.

The new proposed regulations simplify the rules by:

1. Providing a simple, uniform table that all plan owners use to determine the minimum distribution required during their lifetime. This makes it far easier to calculate the required minimum distribution because plan owners would no longer need to determine their beneficiary by their required beginning date

(seventy and a half) and no longer need to decide whether to recalculate their life expectancy each year in determining required minimum distributions.

2. Permitting the required minimum distribution during the plan owner's lifetime to be calculated without regard to the beneficiary's age, except when required distributions can be reduced by taking into account the age of a beneficiary who is a spouse more than ten years younger than the plan owner. When the spouse is the sole beneficiary and is more than ten years younger than the plan owner, the distribution period is measured by the joint life and last survivor life expectancy of the plan owner and spouse.

3. Permitting the beneficiary to be determined as late as the end of the year following the year of the plan owner's death. This allows the plan owner to change designated beneficiaries after the required beginning date without increasing the required minimum distribution and the beneficiary to be changed after the plan owner's death, by one or more beneficiaries disclaiming or being cashed out.

Under these new rules, distributions from an individual account are determined by dividing the account balance by the distribution period. Using the minimum distribution incidental death (MDIB) table, most plan owners will be able to determine their required minimum distribution for each year based on nothing more than their current age and their account balance as of the end of the prior year.

Upon the death of the plan owner, the distribution period is generally the remaining life expectancy of the designated beneficiary. The beneficiary's remaining life expectancy is calculated using the age of the beneficiary in the year following the year of the plan owner's death, reduced by one for each subsequent year. If there is no designated beneficiary as of the end of the year after the plan owner's death, the distribution period is the plan owner's life expectancy calculated in the year of death, reduced by one for each subsequent year.

In summary, these new rules eliminate the need to fix the amount of the distribution during the plan owner's lifetime based on the beneficiary designated on the required beginning date and eliminates the need to elect recalculation or no recalculation of life expectancies at the required beginning date. Under the new rules a uniform table determines the required minimum distributions. The table gives everyone the smallest required minimum distribution under the old system. Inheritance issues are also simplified. Under the new regulations, minimum distributions of inherited IRAs are based on the life expectancy of the designated beneficiary. The beneficiary now isn't determined until December 31 of the year following the death of the plan owner. The new rules will allow the IRA's or plan's assets to be distributed over a longer period of time, reducing the immediate income tax bite and allowing continued tax-deferred growth.

Even when you die, you can't escape the tax man. There are extensive taxes, although the new tax laws are phasing in relief. Estate tax rates are decreasing and exemption amounts are increasing between 2002 and 2009. The estate and generation-skipping taxes may be repealed in 2010.

### Taxes on Payments of Qualified Plan Money to Beneficiaries

1. Estate Tax   All qualified plan and IRA benefits are included in the estate of the deceased participant (surviving spouse) and taxed;
2. Income Tax   All qualified plans and IRA benefits are also subject to income tax upon receipt by a beneficiary of a deceased participant. These assets are considered "income in respect of decedent." The recipient is entitled to a deduction for the amount of estate taxes attributable to the benefits:
3. Generation Skipping Tax   Payments to an individual in a generation level lower than that of the deceased participant's children, may subject the benefits to the generation-skipping transfer tax. Grandchildren would have to pay an additional tax up to 55 percent.

Income taxes are charged on all withdrawals from qualified plans and traditional IRAs. The conventional wisdom dispensed is to let your money grow tax-free in your qualified plan as long as possible, spending down your other assets that are outside of your qualified plans. The problem with this advice is that, should you die with a large sum of money in your qualified plan or traditional IRA, your estate will pay confiscatory taxes on this money:

1. Federal estate tax 55 percent
2. Federal income tax 40 percent
3. State income and estate taxes
4. Generation-skipping taxes if you leave the plan money to a grandchild

For example, Mrs. Williams is a widow and has $2 million in a qualified plan. She wants to leave her $2 million to her only granddaughter. After taxes, her granddaughter will receive 7.6 percent of the $2 million ($153,290). *The federal and state governments take 92.4 percent of the qualified plan money.*

If Mrs. Williams had left her qualified plan money to one of her children, the taxes would have been less (the 55 percent generation-skipping transfer tax would not be charged). Mrs. Williams' daughter would receive a whopping 25 percent, *with 75 percent going to the federal and state governments in income and estate taxes.* Estate planning could have saved this family's inheritance. For those people who die with a large amount of money in their qualified retirement plans and IRAs, they can avoid these taxes and their loved ones can receive more of the assets with estate planning.

### Conventional Wisdom: Is It Best for You?

The other option you have is to reconsider the common strategy of accumulating large sums of money in your qualified plan account. Consider spending down your pension plan instead of spending your assets that are outside of your qualified plan. The assets outside of your qualified plan only pay estate taxes. Qualified plan assets, if they are required to come out of your plan at your death in a lump sum (plan that recalculates the minimum required distribution) may pay income taxes in the highest tax bracket and estate taxes. This is why so little qualified plan money is left for your loved ones. If you are planning to leave a large sum of money in your qualified plan accounts or traditional IRA, consult an estate planning attorney. There are ways to reduce taxes.

## INVESTMENT STRATEGIES FOR TAX-DEFERRED ACCOUNTS

The Department of Labor has statistics that show that three out of four employees with a retirement plan are not invested in any stocks; they are invested in GICs or other fixed-income investments. By this point in the book, you should realize that this is a loss of a golden opportunity and that there is a much better way.

Although there are tax-deferred retirement accounts that allow participants complete discretion as to their investments, more commonly, the participant is limited to a menu of investment options included in their employer provided plan. Your employer, in setting up a qualified plan, is required to provide for the diversification of plan investments "so as to minimize the risk of large losses." The plan administrators are required to administer the plan investments "with the care, skill, prudence, and diligence under the circumstances then prevailing that a prudent man acting in a like capacity and familiar with such matters would use in the conduct of an enterprise of a like character and with like aims." The advice that is generally given by the administrator of these qualified plans is to put some money in each investment option or each fund that is being offered. People frequently divide their plan

money into equal portions and a portion into each option offered because that is the advice they are given by the plan administrator. Now
you know why you get this advice. It is not necessarily well thought
out, nor is it coming from someone with any special knowledge; *it is
government mandated.*

Here are the facts about selecting investment vehicles in plans
where you have some discretion over how to invest your money. An
employer is required by law to offer several diverse investment choices
in the defined contribution plans, which typically include:

1. Stock or equity fund
2. Bond fund
3. Mixed stock and bond fund
4. GICs (guaranteed investment contracts)
5. Money-market fund

The employer has a fiduciary duty to provide funds with reasonable fees and comparatively reasonable returns. You can track the performance of your mutual funds by comparing their performance to the
performance of the Standard & Poor's 500 stock index and the Dow
Jones Industrial Average (thirty Dow stocks). Morningstar Inc. and Lip-
per also categorize the various types of mutual funds and provide comparison benchmarks.

The actively managed equity funds have a high stock turnover,
and, as discussed earlier, this turnover generates big tax bills for the
fund owners in taxable accounts. These funds, however, can be held in
a qualified retirement plan and the turnover or churn is not taxed annually.

Since the S&P 500 index funds beat all the other stock funds
80–90 percent of the time, hopefully you will be able to select one of
the equity index funds to grow your pension money. If you don't have
the choice of an equity index fund, look for a stock fund that has consistently beaten the S&P 500 benchmark and has low fees. This is difficult, however, because virtually no funds beat the S&P 500
consistently, year after year.

Louis Corigan wrote for the Motley Fool about the prospectus of
the mutual funds: "Sure, a prospectus looks daunting. It might be sim-
pler if there were just a single line at the top with a fill in the blank
structure. For example, '*The _____ Fund will jack you up for
about _____ percent of your assets every year in expenses
while growing those assets by _____ percent less than the
S&P 500 in an average year by investing in _____.'"*

Various retirement plans, whether through your employer or an
IRA, are called "taxed-deferred" plans. Up until now we have been dis-

cussing savings outside of these tax-deferred plans. There is a big difference in how these plans are taxed and regulated. Money grows in the plans tax-free until you take it out. When you take it out, you pay ordinary income taxes on every dollar, even on the capital gains that have occurred within the plan.

Mutual funds can be used in a tax-deferred retirement plan without paying income taxes on the turnover or churn at the end of each year as you do in an after-tax account or taxable account (your savings outside of your retirement plan). In the tax-deferred retirement plan you only have to pay the various management fees. John Bogle wrote about mutual fund fees in "The First Index Mutual Fund." Bogle has been a long-time proponent of passively managed equity index funds. Index funds mimicking the S&P 500 Index have historically outperformed most of the actively managed equity mutual funds in any given year by 80–90 percent. The management fees and other costs are also much lower in the index fund generally by about 2 percent. Bogle postulates the following:

What difference would an index fund make over fifty years? Well, let's postulate a 10 percent long-term annual return on stocks. . . . assume that actively managed mutual fund fees are 2 percent, giving the average mutual fund a return of 8 percent (give the average mutual fund the benefit of the doubt, that it performs the market average and the only difference between the actively managed fund and the passively managed index fund is the 2 percent fee). This 2 percent spread is very close to that of the past fifteen years, during which the Vanguard 500 Index Fund provided a 2.2 percent margin of return over the average equity fund. Over fifty years what does this mean to your $10,000 investment?

A $10,000 initial investment growing at market rates of 10 percent over fifty years would become $1,170,000. The actively managed mutual fund growing at 8 percent over the fifty years becomes $470,000.

$1,170,000 versus $470,000

This is a difference of $700,000, due to the 2 percent in annual fees turned over to the mutual fund industry. This is a 60–40 split between the fund industry and the mutual fund holder, with the mutual fund holder putting up 100 percent of the capital ($10,000). Just think what happens in a taxable account to further erode your earnings. This lends credence to the story of the stockbroker hearing about the year's results from his accountant: "You made money and the company made money. Two out of three ain't bad!" *The customer is the last one to benefit from these arrangements.*

## Conventional Wisdom Alert

The conventional wisdom is stated by Jonathan Clements in his *Wall Street Journal* column: "The typical stock fund is a fine choice for investors, despite its tax inefficiency, high cost, and indifferent performance." I beg to differ. *I would rather have the $1,170,000 nest egg than the $470,000 nest egg.*

The objective of this book is not to describe every detail about mutual fund selection: there are already many books written on the intimate details of mutual funds. My objective is to cover something that seems to be omitted or overlooked, and that is how *taxes and fees affect your returns over time.* The multitude of funds offered today are selling performance and returns, but the important facts to focus on are fees and taxes that destroy your returns. The average equity mutual fund does not even keep up with the benchmark S&P 500.

If you are selecting an actively managed equity fund for your qualified retirement plan money because that is all your employer offers, you must look at the fund manager's investment strategy. The investment strategy the fund uses will list investment objectives such as:

growth and income
growth
income
aggressive growth

You also need to look at the investment strategy used by the manager to achieve growth of your money; this reveals the amount of risk. You will want to know if the fund manager trades options and futures. The fund's prospectus will not detail the fund's actual holdings but will describe the fund's objective and game plan.

When you are fund shopping, compare the total return, which is the percent return for the given year assuming that all distributions had been reinvested. Keep in mind that the total return discounts the annual management fees but not the transaction charges (sales commissions and loads, sales charges to reinvest distributions, redemption fees, exchange fees to move money to another fund within the same family of funds). To compare apples to apples you need to find out what transaction costs you will be charged.

The S&P 500 over the last twenty years has had an average dividend yield of 3.9 percent per year and an average capital appreciation of 11 percent per year. This is why investing in a mutual fund tied to the S&P 500 index is so appealing. If you are going to go in this direction, I would like to point out another low-cost alternative, and other investing advantages that few people are aware of.

## Spiders and Diamonds

SPDR is an abbreviation for S&P Depository Receipts and are called "spiders." A "spider" is a single unit of ownership in the SPDR trust. Units of the trust are bought and sold like individual shares of stock traded on the American Stock Exchange, the trading symbol is SPY. The value of "spiders" conforms to the S&P 500 Index because the SPDR owns a representative sample of stocks in the S&P 500. Why buy spiders when an S&P 500 equity index fund will do the same thing? The SPDR trust is more tax efficient. The owner of a unit trust pays taxes on the capital gain when the stock is sold, the same as all other individual stock ownership. In other words, the stock is sold to other trust buyers throughout the day on the American Stock Exchange. The equity index funds can only be bought and sold at the end of each day, not during the trading day. The buying and selling of shares by one individual investor does not cause tax consequences to the other shareholders as it does in mutual funds. The administrative costs of the SPDR trust are less (.18 percent) than the costs of an S&P 500 Index fund (.30 percent to .50 percent). "Diamonds" are similar unit trusts that are indexed to the thirty stocks in the Dow Jones Industrial Average.

SPRDs are an investment option for those who want the diversification that the S&P 500 Index fund offers with minimal fees and expenses. It is a more tax efficient way to own a group of stocks that outperforms 80–90 percent of the actively managed mutual funds. These are suitable for either tax-deferred or taxable accounts.

## The Dividend Growth Investment Strategy and Tax-Deferred Accounts

Is it reasonable to use the Dividend Growth Investment Strategy in a tax-deferred account? For those plans that allow self-directed investments, *it is a very attractive alternative.* Your dividends and capital gains will grow the same way inside of these plans as they will in a taxable account. The Dividend Growth Investment Strategy will, using historic trends, outperform GICs, bond funds, and most actively managed mutual funds in the long run. Indexed funds, such as the Vanguard 500 Indexed Fund, are a good alternative in tax-deferred accounts. I don't know whether your self-directed Dividend Growth

Investment Strategy will outperform the S&P 500. The dividends in my strategy will aid you in falling, volatile, and recessionary markets.

## Social Security

This brings us to the third leg of your retirement income, after your taxable savings and your deferred savings accounts. This third leg is provided by your government in the form of the sacred cow: Social Security. Rather than show you what you can currently expect to receive in benefits from this program, I would like to show you what you could do with your payroll deductions if you were free to invest them yourself.

If you are a couple earning, together, $50,000, you are paying about $3,500 a year in Social Security and Medicare taxes directly. Your employer will also contribute $3,500 that would otherwise be available for your wages, giving a total contribution of $7,000. At retirement, this would entitle you to roughly $1,000 per month in Social Security and Medicare benefits. What would happen if you could take your Social Security contribution and, instead of giving it to the government, invest it in the stock market? Over your entire working life from twenty-five years of age to sixty-five years of age, you would have invested $280,000. If you assume that the market would grow at 10 percent per year, this is what you would accumulate:

Growth of $7,000 per year invested over your forty working years:

$3,101,000

This would pay for quite a retirement and for quite a lot of health insurance.

Assume you are single or a couple earning only $17,000 a year, which would mean that the contribution that you and your employer would make would total $2,500 a year or $100,000 over forty years.

Growth of $2,500 per year invested over your forty working years:

$1,107,500

Think about it. A worker earning $17,000 a year all of his life could be worth over a million dollars if he was free to invest his Social Security and Medicare contribution for himself. Even if he took this money at retirement ($1 million) and made the most conservative investment possible, buying 5 percent bonds, he would end up with over $50,000 a year in income, three times what he earned in his working life. Even more impressive, if this man had invested in stocks with a good record of dividend growth, he would have a dividend income of much greater than $50,000 per year and growing. Further, he would have an inheritance to pass on to his loved ones, rather than being a burden on his children in his old age. Under the current Social Security regime, he would be lucky to get back the $100,000 that he paid in.

Currently, the maximum payment into Social Security and Medicare is in the range of $10,500 per year from you and your employer for an income of $70,000 (this amount goes up every year). For the worst-case scenario, assume that both you and your husband are high earners, each paying in $10,500 (including your employers' contributions) for a grand total of $21,000 per year. We can even assume that, to reach this income level, you don't start working until your education is completed at age thirty, giving you thirty-five years to accumulate these funds. Over the thirty-five years you and your husband will have contributed $735,000 to the nonexistent Social Security trust fund. There is no way that you can recoup this sum in your retirement under the present system. But what if you had been free to invest this money for yourself, achieving the historic market rate of 10 percent per year.

Growth of $21,000 per year invested over your thirty-five working years: $5,691,000

## SUMMARY

There are many forms of tax-deferred savings plans, some offered by your employer, and some that you can set up for yourself. Because these plans are authorized by the government, they are subject to a myriad rules and restrictions. It is important to understand these rules, because they can cost you a lot of money if you run afoul of them. It is important to obtain professional advice from an expert in this area of the law. The tax bill that was passed May 26, 2001 makes extensive changes to retirement plan provisions, most of which are effective beginning in 2002. Many of the changes will be phased in over a period of years. Investing in these tax-deferred accounts is somewhat different than investing in a taxable account due to the differences in taxation. In spite of these differences, the Dividend Growth Investment Strategy is still a good strategy to use in these plans. Passively managed indexed mutual funds or unit trusts such as spiders are a reasonable alternative in tax-deferred plans. Social Security helps with your retirement, but it would help a lot more if it were in your hands instead of the government's.

# APPENDIX 1

## THE THIRTY THOROUGHBREDS (AND A FEW WORKHORSES): A SAMPLE PORTFOLIO

We have reached the point where, in the words of the old tire commercial, "the rubber meets the road." At some point, you need more than theory; you need to make a practical decision to act. You can't call your deep discount broker and say, "I want $1,000 of some stock that grows at 14 percent per year and raises its dividend 14 percent per year." You need to buy 100 shares of GE or 50 shares of Automatic Data Processing. You now have the tools to seek out the stocks that you want to put into your Dividend Growth Investment Strategy portfolio, but you may need a little push in the right direction. For this reason, I am including a portfolio to get you started. I am including a number of great companies that have been at the core of my portfolio and should be at the core of yours. These are companies that I am sure that you would discover on your own; it may be convenient, however, to see them compiled in one list. In addition to the core holdings, I have included as a second tier, a number of other companies that are good dividend raisers and may be at attractive prices at various times. I have also included some stocks that have a high current dividend payout for those of you who need immediate income.

In this chapter, I give my criteria for picking stocks for the Dividend Growth Investment Strategy. I include a section highlighting many of the core stocks, and discuss the prospects of future gains. Finally, for those of you that have extra cash that you want to invest outside of the Dividend Growth Investment Strategy, I include a section on the roller coaster of investing in high-tech companies.

## CRITERIA FOR INCLUSION IN THE
## DIVIDEND GROWTH PORTFOLIO

### Dividend Track Record

This is the core for a portfolio implementing the Dividend Growth Investment Strategy. The selected companies have to have an excellent record of rewarding their shareholders with consistent and increasing dividend payments. I included companies that have histories of increasing their dividend payments on average 14 percent per year. As discussed earlier, you need to diversify your portfolio, not only buying different companies, but buying companies from different industries. The thirty companies that I selected from the larger group diversify a portfolio across industries, and provide a historical average (1983–2000) of 14 percent dividend increases per year. Many of these companies have long histories of paying dividends, some going back to the turn of the century. They continued paying dividends through the Great Depression and both world wars. That is a persuasive track record.

### Companies Committed to Raising Dividends

Paying and increasing dividends is an unspoken/unwritten commitment that certain companies have to reward and retain shareholders. Dividend-paying companies are generally less volatile, because most of the companies' shareholders stick around when the market is melting down. One example of a company that is committed to raising its dividend is Cooper Tire. It has hit some earnings speed bumps in the last few years, as is reflected in the company's volatile and depressed share price. In spite of this, the company has continued to raise dividends significantly.

### Growth Potential

The various industries in the portfolio represent industries that should have a high potential for growth, based on demographics of the country. This may represent increasing demand for the same old products (Hillenbrand and Becton Dickinson, Wilmington Trust, Fannie Mae). Growth may occur through developing newer and better products, such as new drugs or razors (Pfizer, Merck, Schering-Plough, Gillette, Hewlett-Packard). Growth potential can also be realized through international growth (Coca-Cola and Pepsi, Wal-Mart, Home Depot, AFLAC, American International Group, Johnson & Johnson). Most companies in this portfolio are increasing their international business. Growth can also occur through mergers and acquisitions if it is done right (Heinz, General Electric, Illinois Tool Works). The food processors have acquired many companies with foreign brands of food, allowing, for example, Heinz to expand into foreign markets and sell food that appeals to the foreign palette. An American would not recognize some of the foods that Heinz is selling in foreign countries. Much of it is displayed in the Heinz annual report—it's interesting reading. All companies that are going to continue increasing their dividend payments must have some demonstrated way to continue growing.

## Recession Proof

No company is recession proof, but some do better than others in an economic downturn. These companies should continue to pay out dividends throughout a recession. Many of them sell inexpensive products that consumers buy habitually; these are the consumer nondurables such as food, beverage, drugs, toiletries. When a recession comes, these companies will still have decent earnings and can continue paying dividends. The car companies, however, dealing in large capital sales, may have to cut their dividends in a recession; they need to keep more cash just to survive the downturn in the business cycle. As I was researching this book I found one bank with a good track record for dividend growth and a long history of dividend payments, but it had to cut its dividend during the S&L banking crisis in the late 1980s, so I did not include it.

## Government Regulations

In *Fiddler on the Roof* the village rabbi is asked if there is a blessing for the czar. "Of course," he says. "May the Lord bless and keep the czar . . . far away from here." The government and lawyers are frequently bad for the well-being of shareholders. Admittedly, there is some good that they do, enforcing constant laws and upholding contracts. On balance, however, they produce more harm than good. Government regulations and controls are never put through the cost-benefit analysis test. Government regulations add costs to doing business. Can those costs be passed on or is the common shareholder going to pay for them? Probably both.

There are securities lawyers swarming over the high-tech companies waiting to sue on behalf of shareholders for any "misleading information." The argument the lawyers put forth in these so-called strike suits is that the company lies to the public, who then buy the shares and lose their shirts. In reality, the lawyers find one statement that, in retrospect, was inaccurate and use several shareholders to file a class-action suit on behalf of all the shareholders. Most of these cases are baseless, but are settled to avoid the costs of going to court. The majority of shareholders never see a nickel and the lawyers make millions, and the company is left in a weaker position (which, of course, hurts the shareholder even more). The high-tech companies have gotten wiser, and now routinely make pre-earnings announcements when earnings are not going to meet analyst expectations. These announcements are made weeks ahead of when earnings actually come out, so shareholders can sell; this is generally when the mutual fund managers sell off and the stock price takes a hit. Other types of litigation brought both by the government and lawyers against companies is very costly for companies (Microsoft is currently undergoing extensive anti-trust litigation). The common shareholders definitely pay for it.

The common shareholder is last and least when it comes to corporate distributions. The corporation has to pay its creditors, bondholders, and then its preferred shareholders before the common shareholder; we get what is left over. I weigh very carefully how much exposure a company may have to litigation and other burdens placed on companies by the government. Philip Morris is a great example. They have been a good dividend raiser for many years, but because of all the litigation from all sides (government and private citizens), a shareholder has little certainty about the company's ability to pay dividends in the future. The market abhors uncertainty and rewards certainty. This explains why Philip Morris has a P/E of 11 and a dividend yield of over 5 percent while Coca-Cola has a P/E of 44 and a dividend yield of 1.0 percent.

A further aspect of regulation includes the many direct and indirect mandates that the government places on companies. Electric utilities are highly regulated (although this is slowly changing) with their prices fixed and their pollution closely monitored. This is why many of these companies are trying to grow the unregulated portions of their business. My husband and I have seen the creeping regulation of the medical-care field. There are government regulators peering over your shoulder at every turn. File a bill or a report with a typographical error, or even an accurate report that is not understandable by the person reviewing it, and, if you are lucky, you just won't get paid. At worst, there are a host of federal agents snooping around trying to meet their quotas for fraud and abuse prosecutions. These guys make the IRS seem like a branch of Mother Teresa's corps. As a general rule, the more a society believes something is essential, such as health care or water quality, the more regulation you will see. There is no groundswell to regulate jewelry stores or hula hoop manufacturers. There will also be little impetus to regulate ketchup, cola, chewing gum, or Tootsie Pops.

## Fundamentals

The fundamentals of an individual company as well as the company's competitive position in the marketplace are paramount in evaluating a company as a core holding. A company's fundamentals determine the company's return on capital and shareholder equity. All the fundamentals have been discussed in the research section. The fundamental analysis is all based on historical data with a snapshot of what is going on currently and some projections that the analysts make about the future. Since none of us has a crystal ball, common sense, general knowledge, experience, and wisdom have to be applied to how you think this company is going to do in the future. How good is management at implementing its business plan? What is the quality of its cash flow?

All of these characteristics are important for the long-term shareholder. I also place great weight on the fact that a company has stayed in business for the last fifty to one hundred years and it is still a good company today. Most of the companies in the portfolio fit this profile; GE comes to mind as a real star. It is comforting to know that these corporations will probably outlive me. This is not to say that the company won't, at some point, slow down and rest. All companies experience business cycles, new product cycles, and even new CEO cycles. Business cycles are affected by the overall economic conditions in the world where the company does business. For example, people in Asia did not buy as many American products in 1998 because of the Asian recession, while Europe showed stronger sales.

The strength of the dollar also comes to bear on a company's earnings; when the dollar is strong, people overseas cannot afford our products as readily, especially if all the manufacturing occurs in the United States. The business cycle sometimes works in our favor and sometimes it works against us, but over time it evens out. When the business cycle is not favorable, we have to be prepared to wait it out.

Some of this happens in market sector rotation. For example, at the end of 1998 and beginning of 1999 the tech stocks were very strong and carried the markets higher, while the financials, food processing, oil, real-estate investment trusts (REITs), and utilities stocks were market laggards. This reversed dramatically in 2000. These stock prices do not necessarily move in tandem. Food stocks and utilities are defensive; when the fund managers are less optimistic, they move the fund's money into defensive stocks. This is part of the ebb and flow of the market, another reason to diversify into different industries.

The new product cycle is illustrated by analyzing the new drug pipelines, which have all been quite positive lately (Pfizer in particular). Gillette went through a new product cycle in 1998, and its share price rested at or near its fifty-two-week low most of the year. It was introducing its new Mach 3 razor and spending a lot of money advertising it. Many of the shareholders bailed out for the year, creating a buying opportunity for Dividend Growth investors. Now the Mach 3 razors are selling well but earnings have been under pressure from the strong dollar and unfavorable currency translations. You may want to take advantage of this volatility. There are many "momentum" fund managers that sell the fund's stake in a company whose earnings are not accelerating. This creates a great buying opportunity for the long-term individual investor, even in this very pricey market.

A stock that has rested for the past three years is Hewlett-Packard. It has had some new products that were not as well received as those of its competitors and the printer/PC market growth slowed down, causing the stock price to stagnate for several years. In 1999 market conditions improved. HP announced that its printer business was improving, especially in Asia. While it rested, it paid its shareholders a dividend. Now, in 2001, business is under pressure from a weakening economy and share prices of technology stocks are off markedly. In order to be a long-term investor for dividend growth, you cannot allow these market cycles to faze you; they are inevitable with every company. A diversified portfolio will always have some stocks that are in this resting phase, some with share prices that are trending down, and others that are going up. A good example: stocks of utilities and REITs move up as technology stocks move down.

## Competition

Warren Buffett said, "One of the secrets of life is weak competition." Competition is inevitable in capitalism, and is healthy. That is why we look to invest in the companies with the best management, best products, best delivery system, and the best prices. Does Wal-Mart ring a bell? Sam Walton accomplished all of these feats and catapulted Wal-Mart ahead of all of its competitors. Wal-Mart is now successfully expanding internationally, as well as finding new ways to expand domestically. The opposite end of the spectrum is the monopoly, which is usually blessed and controlled by the government. Electric utilities are an example of monopolies. Now utilities are being deregulated. The politicians have finally figured out that we could all get cheaper electricity and better service if competition is allowed.

Competition is a very healthy thing; it promotes the development of great products at great prices that we can sell to the rest of the world. I think about the poor Romanians who had government controlling everything, leaving them with virtually nothing that the rest of the world would want to buy. There was no competition. That is why the hat store we went into had hats of only one size and style. Central planning leads to bureaucrats making all the decisions; they could care less if it pleases anyone or sells—in a world of no competition, it doesn't matter. Who wants to buy shoes that were designed by a government bureaucrat?

This was a stark contrast to what is going on in the United States. This is why our companies are so successful at expanding overseas; people around the world love our products, services, and prices. Our companies are as good as they are because of competition. This can be a two-edged sword for an investor trying to chose between two companies. For example, in 1995 I looked at buying one of two Internet and networking hardware producers, Cisco and Cabletron. At that time, they were close to equal in market cap. Cisco was selling routers and Cabletron was selling hubs and cable, both for the networking of PCs, with some product overlap between the two. Their P/Es were different, with Cisco being more expensive. Cabletron had more sales and higher earnings and projected share price appreciation was supposed to be greater than that of Cisco. The analysts were wrong and Cisco won. Cisco pulled ahead of Cabletron because it had better management. The CEO of Cisco has very adroitly built a large-cap company mostly by very skillfully acquiring smaller technology companies that fit Cisco's business plan. The acquisitions went smoothly, and they rarely diluted earnings, but they were generally accretive (the new acquisition added to earnings). Cisco now has a market cap of $360 billion and Cabletron's Market Cap is $4.8 billion. The CEO of Cisco had the right vision, put the vision into a business plan, then implemented the business plan with no missteps.

While competition makes for good products, it can be a minefield for the investor who has to pick the winner. I learned from the Cisco-Cabletron comparison that excellent management is absolutely essential for a tech company to prosper. Another example illustrating this is Apple Computer. Apple has always had great products and has been a leader in developing these products, but they nearly went bankrupt due to some top-level management miscalculations and poor marketing. By 1998, with Steve Jobs back at the helm, Apple seemed to be turning around. An excellent CEO is the lifeblood of a tech company and a shareholder's best friend. A mediocre CEO will run a company into the ground and allow it to be cannibalized by its competition.

## Insider Ownership

Although not essential for inclusion, many of the companies in the portfolio have a high degree of inside ownership. When the officers and directors who are running the company have their fortunes and futures riding on the company's stock performance, this vested interest in the corporation gives its management great incentives to increase shareholder value. Many of the companies in the sample portfolio have relatively large amounts of inside ownership.

## Companies With High Income and Slow Growth

Many companies pay high dividends but are slow dividend growers. Utilities are the prototype of this kind of slow grower; they have grown even slower in these days of deregulation. Many of them are retaining more capital to try to increase the non-regulated parts of their businesses. I did not select any utilities for my core portfolio for these reasons. They would be more appropriate for your portfolio if you need immediate income. I have included a list of these companies for those of you who find yourself in this position. If you have time to grow dividends for a stream of income when you retire, buy stock in the companies where the dividend payment starts lower, but the dividend growth is more rapid. Take into account how long you have until retirement and how long you have to allow the dividend to grow. You may need to consider buying companies that start with a higher initial payout or yield.

## TECHS ARE THE ROLLER COASTER WITHOUT THE ESCALATOR

This is the time to talk to those of you that have some extra cash burning a hole in your pocket after having bought your core Dividend Growth portfolio. If you are looking for a little excitement, you may want to go fishing in the high-tech waters. If you do, minimize your risk by buying technology companies that are dominant in their industries. In order to become dominant and stay dominant, they have to have good management. When I first started buying technology companies, many of the companies were still in their emerging phase and it was hard to tell which ones would end up on top. The Cisco-Cabletron example illustrates this. Buying the dominant companies is the way to go if you plan to hold them for the long term.

You also have to know the trends in technology. Today, nothing has more impact than the Internet. "The Internet revolution will determine which companies survive and which get left behind," said John Chambers, president and chief executive of Cisco. "Increasingly, the Internet is recognized as the key driver in our global economy." About 80 percent of the traffic on the Internet travels through Cisco's switches, routers, and hubs.

Be prepared for volatility. The betas of technology companies far exceed the market average of 1.

In 1996 AT&T spun off Lucent Technologies Inc. This was done to placate disgruntled shareholders at AT&T, because AT&T had not been growing and its share price was languishing. When Lucent became a company that was no longer part of AT&T, it became a powerhouse. All of the phone companies that formerly were in direct competition with

AT&T now began ordering telecom equipment from Lucent. Telecom equipment makers were a growing industry, but Lucent started eating their lunch. Lucent is a large-cap company with a fabulous research and development division, Bell Labs. I was holding the stock of a company, DSC Communications, that had a good history of selling telecom equipment to the Baby Bells, until Lucent was unleashed. I finally sold DSC at a small loss and bought Lucent. Lucent grew fivefold through 1999. The year 2000 was, however, a downer for Lucent, cutting our profits in half. Remember the roller coaster and the fact that there is little dividend reward to cushion the dizzying drop. The problem with tech companies is that they are not very predictable. They need to constantly innovate and have the best technology at the best price; somehow management has to accomplish this either through constant innovation or acquisition.

If you are using the Dividend Growth Strategy and holding those recommended stocks as your core, you may want to add a few tech companies to your portfolio, not for reliable dividend growth, but for the potential growth and for further diversification of your portfolio. Frequently, when the tech stocks are rocketing up, the more defensive stocks are ignored and vice-versa.

## The Siren Call of the Techs

If you admire and use technology as much as I do, you may not be able to resist owning a few tech companies. Companies that have emerged as dominant technology companies are listed below. The problem with tech stocks is this: it is impossible to predict whether they will still be dominant companies five to ten years from now:

| Market Cap (in Billions) | |
| --- | --- |
| Lucent Technologies | $46.8 |
| Cisco Systems | $360 |
| Microsoft Corp. | $363 |
| Dell Computer | $60.2 |
| Intel Corp. | $235 |
| Sun Microsystems | $163 |
| EMC Corp. | $194 |
| America Online | $100 |
| Int'l Business Mach. | $197 |
| Hewlett-Packard | $86 |
| Compaq Computer | $41.5 |

These companies are all "large-cap" companies; that is, their market value is greater than $5 billion. The "mid-cap" companies have a value of $1 to $5 billion, and those with a market value of $1 billion or less are "small-caps." You may also want to consider the Nasdaq 100 (symbol QQQ), a spider-like investment trust that contains the one hundred Top NASDAQ stocks.

## Dividend-Paying Techs

For most high-tech companies, the dividends are small or nonexistent. Hewlett-Packard is the only one with a consistent track record. HP has not raised its dividend in the past two years. IBM cut its dividend payment in 1993 when it ran into earnings problems, earning a ticket out of the sample portfolio. IBM has turned around and has done well in recent years. It is now increasing its dividend again. Tech stocks should not be used for dividend growth; they are volatile, cyclical, and seasonal. They can be rewarding to own because they have tremendous growth potential (after all, the whole world needs technology). But owning tech stocks is a bumpy road, and a completely different ball game than holding blue-chip, dividend-raising stocks. Dollar cost averaging is less prudent. Tech stocks tend to sell off once or twice a year and that is the time to buy. As you can see, tech stocks take more time to follow, research, and stay on top of. You have to watch earnings closely; if the company's earnings do not match or exceed the analysts' consensus earnings (brokerage houses hire analysts to track and project earnings of companies in a sector that they specialize in following), the stock price will take a great hit. Then there are the "whisper numbers," the earnings expectations that even exceed the published projected earnings numbers. If the company does not meet or exceed these earnings, the fund managers dump the stock and the share price goes south. That is the stock market roller coaster, and most tech stocks have no escalator. A tech investor should have some understanding of the technology and some knowledge of where the technology trends are heading.

Many companies have conferences for analysts. These conferences are held by the company's officers to help guide the analysts on their earnings projections and the overall welfare and performance of the company. It is a time for the analysts to ask questions and you can join in. Notice of these conferences is posted on the Internet in various places (e.g., the company's web site or Motley Fool.) The time of the conference and the 800/888 phone number along with a pass number is all that is needed to participate. I find these conferences valuable if I have questions about a company that I am holding. Beware: they are time consuming. If you can't attend the live conference, it is usually replayed for several days after.

One caveat about evaluating the earnings of tech stocks. Frequently, earnings are not as good as you would think that they would be because many high-tech companies grant significant stock options to their employees. These stock options dilute earnings.

| Dividend Yields of Tech Stocks | | | |
| --- | --- | --- | --- |
| Company | Price | Dividend Yield | Payment (per share) |
| Lucent | $13 | 0.6% | $0.08 |
| Intel | $33 | 0.2% | $0.08 |
| HWP | $32 | 1.0% | $0.32 |
| IBM | $89 | 0.6% | $0.52 |
| Compaq Computer | $16 | 0.6% | $0.10 |

These stocks can all be researched in *Value Line*.

## NEVER MAKE A MISTAKE!

This is good advice for anyone, but, of course, it is impossible to follow. The only way never to make a mistake buying or selling stocks is to never buy or sell stocks. Warren Buffett, considered by many to be the world's top investor, freely admits to his mistakes. Let's see how he screwed up.

Buffett owned a large block of Disney stock that he sold in the 1960s and says, "Everything we've ever sold has gone up subsequently, but some of 'em have gone up more painfully than others. Certainly, the Disney sale in the sixties was a huge mistake. Forget about whether I should have continued holding it. I should have been buying it. That's happened many times." Buffett's company, Berkshire Hathaway, now owns Disney stock.

I have followed Buffett's investments and studied his investment philosophy over the years. I have wondered what great insight has kept Berkshire Hathaway from owning any drug companies. Buffett has said, "We just plain missed on pharmaceuticals. It was within our circle of competence to identify the industry as one likely to enjoy very high profits over time, but it wasn't [in our competence] to pick a single company. However, we probably should have recognized the fact that some sort of group purchase might have made sense." Buffett also does not invest in technology, but he admits to admiring Bill Gates

(Microsoft) and Andy Groves (Intel) and said, "I wish I'd translated that admiration into action by backing it up with money."

## PREDICTING THE FUTURE

Over the past twenty years, since 1982, the Dow and the S&P 500 have both had nearly tenfold increases. There have been large flows of money into the market, largely due to the increased realization of baby boomers that they need to start planning for their retirement. Most of this money has gone into mutual funds.

Annual returns, averaging seventeen percent the past few years, have far exceeded the historic market returns of 10 percent. What does this mean? No one knows, although the conventional wisdom and common sense tells us that this pace cannot continue. Warren Buffett was asked about this and he attributed these high returns to three factors:

1. Improved return of equity
2. Decline in interest rates
3. The market has created its own momentum

Buffett did not factor in technology, which has had a big impact on helping businesses become more efficient with higher productivity. The drug companies are an example of this. They are able to research new drugs in the lab using supercomputers to simulate experiments, rather than tedious hands-on, test-tube experiments. They can now screen thousands of new compounds in a fraction of the time it used to take to do a few. Saving large sums on research and development, with more bang for the buck, results in higher returns on shareholder equity.

Technology is being used to make almost every company more efficient. The oil services industry is another example; the use of computers has made finding and drilling for oil more efficient than ever. This has not only decreased their cost but has led to an oil glut that has brought oil prices down sharply in 1998 and 1999. Thus, technology in this sector has been a two-edged sword for the investor. Look at how Sam Walton used computers to inventory his Wal-Mart stores. Sam's "just in time" inventory approach kept Wal-Mart shelves well stocked and improved profit margins and returns on shareholder equity. Wal-Mart left its competition in the dust.

Buffett has been asked about the effects of the global economy on the stock market and this is what he has said, "We like our international businesses. Our three top holdings all have a major international aspect to them. Really, in aggregate, they are dominant internationally. And there is no question in my mind that Coke, Gillette, and American Express, for that matter will grow faster outside the United States. And that's built into our evaluation of those businesses." Buffett is optimistic about the continued growth prospects, globally, for both Coke and Gillette.

It has been his opinion that no one in the world is going to find a better way to deliver these products, which are craved by people around the world. I know this to be true from first-hand experience. We take all these beverages, toiletries, batteries, paper products like tissues and tampons for granted in the United States. Because of this, many people tend not to appreciate the investment opportunities. But there are millions of people around the world just beginning to earn a little money. These products are dear to them, and these simple products will be highly successful when they are made readily available. I was sharing some sweet and very sticky pastry with the Romanian woman who was taking me around Bucharest to get the paperwork done for my daughter's passport. There were no napkins in the restaurant where we were eating the pastry, so I took two tissues out of my purse. When I handed one to my Romanian friend, she tore it in half and handed the other half back to me, so as not to use up too much of this precious commodity. When Romanian orphanages were given disposable diapers, they washed them and hung them out to dry for reuse. Most people around the world are still wiping their noses on their sleeves. All of these low-cost items will be in high demand as the markets open up and people earn enough money to purchase them. This will be a slow, bumpy process, but one with an overall upward trend. This is bound to create growth for U.S. companies.

## LOOKING FORWARD FROM 1972

In the 1960s and 1970s, a popular list of stocks was dubbed the "Nifty Fifty": fifty surefire performers. Many of these companies, such as Kresge, Polaroid, Burroughs, and Digital Equipment Corp., have languished in recent years; some have matched the market and some have consistently outperformed the market over the intervening decades. Eight of the companies in my sample portfolio were listed in the "Nifty Fifty." These companies were among the best performers in this group, with strong annualized returns from the market peak, December 1972 to June 1997.

**Annualized Returns of Eight Stocks in the Thirty Thoroughbreds Sample Portfolio**

|  | *Annualized* | *1972 P/E* |
|---|---|---|
| Gillette Co. | 18.3% | 24.3 |
| Coca-Cola Co. | 17.2% | 46.6 |
| Pfizer Inc. | 16.9% | 28.4 |
| PepsiCo, Inc. | 16.7% | 27.6 |
| Merck & Co. | 16.1% | 43.0 |
| General Electric | 15.4% | 23.4 |
| Schering Corp.* | 13.7% | 48.1 |
| Johnson & Johnson | 12.9% | 57.1 |

*Schering-Plough Corp.

These statistics are from a study that Jeremy Siegel did on the "Nifty Fifty" stocks from 1972 to the present. At that time, these blue-chip stocks ran very high P/Es (the S&P 500 average P/E was 18.9; the Nifty Fifty P/E averaged 41.9), historically very high for the market. In 1973–74, a bear market hit that caused share prices to hemorrhage for nearly two years. When the bloodbath was over, the conventional wisdom was that investors would never again pay such dear prices for growth stocks. In retrospect, however, we can see that those investors who stayed put and did not sell were amply rewarded.

The lesson is: don't panic, stay invested. If you are patient while riding the stock market roller coaster, history says that you will come out on top. The stock that performed the best over this period (1972–97) was Philip Morris, returning 19.9 percent a year. These top stocks are still rewarding their shareholders and continue to be excellent companies and should be among your core holdings. Six of them have been paying dividends for more than sixty-four years (Johnson & Johnson, Merck, General Electric, Pfizer, Gillette, Coca-Cola). During this twenty-five-year period, 1972–97, the S&P 500 returned 12.9 percent per year.

Another lesson to be gleaned from this list is that you should buy what you want to hold forever; don't compromise by buying something that is of lesser quality but seems cheap. In the long run, like buying clothes or furniture, buying cheap only benefits you for the short run; the original purchase doesn't seem so cheap when you have to replace it in three years.

Unfortunately, there is no crystal ball that will tell you which stocks are going to perform the best. That is why my sample portfolio is large; it allows you to diversify. Charlie Munger, Warren Buffett's longtime partner, said about the Nifty Fifty stocks that, "there are huge advantages for an individual to get into the best five of the Nifty Fifty and just sit." Munger did not let us in on the secret of which were the best five.

| Seven Stocks That Are Still Going Strong | |
| --- | --- |
| | Dividend Growth Annual (1983–2000) |
| General Electric | 11% |
| Merck & Co. | 16% |
| Coca-Cola Co. | 11% |
| Schering-Plough Corp. | 14% |
| Gillette Co. | 13% |
| Johnson & Johnson | 13% |
| Pfizer Inc. | 12% |

These seven companies, with the same dollar amount invested in each company, in aggregate, have an average dividend growth of 13 percent.

These seven stocks, however great, are not sufficient for your core portfolio. They are too heavily weighted with drug companies and need more diversification. My sample portfolio of thirty blue-chip stocks has companies from other industries to allow for this diversification. The companies in the portfolio are at different phases in their business cycles. Some are resting with their stock prices trending down after this long bull market; the Asian recession has taken a toll on some; and other global travails are affecting others. These problems will bring share prices back in line, closer to historic norms.

## THE SAMPLE PORTFOLIO

We have finally reached the list that you have been waiting for with bated breath. I have broken down the portfolio into thirty core stocks that I believe should form a basis for a Dividend Growth Investment Strategy portfolio. I have also included a further group of companies that are good dividend raisers and may be suitable for further diversification at the right price. I will start out with a summary of each of the thirty core stocks, organized by industry, followed by a graphic presentation of the entire portfolio. *The figures used for calculations go through November of 2000.* These figures are meant as a guide for general trends, not as precise investment statistics. All figures are corrected for splits that occurred prior to November of 2000. Stocks that have split in 2001 are not split adjusted (Duke Energy, ExxonMobil, AFLAC, Jefferson-Pilot, Johnson & Johnson, and State Street).

---

### The Core Thirty: Sample Portfolio

Abbott Laboratories
AFLAC, Inc.
American International Group
Automatic Data Processing
Avery Dennison Corporation
Cintas Corporation
Coca-Cola Company
ConAgra Foods, Inc.
Eaton Vance Corporation
Fannie Mae
General Electric Company
Gillette
Hillenbrand Industries
Heinz (H.J.) Co.
Home Depot, Inc.
Illinois Tool Works, Inc.
Johnson & Johnson
Merck & Co., Inc.
Medtronic, Inc.
Pall Corporation
PepsiCo, Inc.
Philip Morris Companies, Inc.
Pfizer, Inc.
Schering-Plough Corp.
Sysco Corp.
State Street Corp.
Tootsie Roll Industries, Inc.
Wal-Mart Stores
Wilmington Trust Corporation
Wrigley (Wm.) Jr. Company

---

## Financial Sector

*Fannie Mae*

Fannie Mae is the nation's largest provider of residential mortgage funds and provides the secondary market for residential mortgages.

Fannie Mae has increased dividends on average 30 percent annually (1983–2000).

### Eaton Vance Corp.

The company manages and markets mutual funds and provides management and advisory services to institutions and individuals. A diverse number of equity, bond, and cash funds are offered by Eaton Vance. Eaton also specializes in tax managed equity funds that are favored by investors concerned with higher returns after taxes. Eaton Vance has provided shareholders with a high return on equity, 45.5 percent. A dollar invested in Eaton Vance in 1985 had a low dividend yield of 1.3 percent. The dividend payment grew at a rate of 21 percent annually. The yield on the dollar invested in 1985 climbed to 27 percent in the year 2000. Eaton Vance has raised its dividend every year for the past sixteen years.

### State Street Corp.

State Street has favorable demographics, foremost of which is the privatization of government pension plans. Many countries are shifting away from government-run retirement plans toward privately run pension plans, providing State Street with growth opportunities. Overseas investors are also pouring money into mutual funds and State Street is the market leader in servicing off-shore funds. State Street is a leader in mutual fund administration and is benefiting from the growing outsourcing trend. With $4.3 trillion in assets under custody and $422 billion under management, State Street Corporation is the world's leading specialist in serving institutional investors. Offices are located in the United States, Canada, Chile, Cayman Islands, Netherlands Antilles, Ireland, United Kingdom, Netherlands, France, Belgium, Luxembourg, Switzerland, Germany, Czech Republic, Austria, United Arab Emirates, Russia, People's Republic of China, Taiwan, South Korea, Japan, Singapore, Australia, and New Zealand. State Street has paid dividends since 1910. Dividends have been increased 14 percent every year for the past eighteen years. State Street has raised its dividend every year for the past twenty years. The company splits its shares two for one in early 2001.

### Wilmington Trust Corp.

Wilmington Trust Corp. is the largest banking company in Delaware. It is the eighth largest personal trust institution in the United States. The demographics are favorable; trust business is growing with the aging population. Officers and directors own 7.5 percent of common stock.

WL has raised dividend payouts on average 13 percent every year for the past eighteen years, and has a high dividend payout ($1.77 a share in 2000). Dividends have been paid since 1914.

## Insurance Sector

*AFLAC*

AFLAC is an international insurance provider (life, Medicare supplement, accident, disability, and long-term convalescent care policies). AFLAC is the world's largest underwriter of supplemental cancer insurance, most of which is sold through trade and employee organizations in Japan. Japanese operations, consisting primarily of cancer insurance, account for 80 percent of revenues. AFLAC has sizable inside ownership with officers and directors owning 6 percent of stock. AFLAC has had good dividend growth, raising its dividend on average 15 percent every year for the past eighteen years.

*American International Group*

AIG is a large and well run international insurance holding company engaged in a broad range of insurance and insurance-related products. The domestic property and casualty insurance operations rank fourth in the United States. It also sells group life and health insurance policies, provides risk management and agency services, and financial services. The company recently bought Sun America to expand its operations into the lucrative and growing annuities markets. Officers and directors control 6.7 percent of the company's stock. AIG has raised its dividend 12 percent on average every year for the past eighteen years. The dividend payout is low, $0.15 per share (yield starts below 1 percent at a share price of $97). The company has had 25 percent average annual share price appreciation.

## Technology Sector

*Automatic Data Processing*

Automatic Data Processing, Inc. has three segments: the nation's largest payroll and tax filing processor; brokerage services that include quotation workstations, record keeping, order entry, and proxy services; and services for truck and auto dealers including accounting, inventory, leasing, and parts ordering. These are outsourcing tasks, and outsourcing is an increasing trend in our new economy. ADP is also adapting to growing Internet commerce. ADP has had 149 consecutive quarters of double-digit, year-over-year revenue and share net growth. This is thirty-seven years of continuous growth (a smooth ride). ADP has raised its dividend 15 percent every year (1983–2000). It has raised its dividend payment every year for the last twenty-three years. This company should be a core portfolio holding.

## Beverage Sector

*PepsiCo, Inc.*

PepsiCo is a beverage and snack food business. Its two trade names, Pepsi and Frito-Lay, are two of the strongest names in the world. Pepsi is also in the process of acquiring Quaker Oats and its strong Gatorade brand. Pepsi has been restructuring, spinning off the slow-growing restaurants and its U.S. bottling operations. Coke is strong competition for PepsiCo's beverage business, which is 36 percent of Pepsi's sales and 34 percent of profits. PepsiCo's snack-food business, Frito-Lay, is 64 percent of sales and 66 percent of Pepsi's profits. Most companies experience a learning curve when they start expanding overseas. Pepsi's international sales are 32 percent of total sales. Pepsi's return on shareholder equity has been trending up: it was 30 percent in 2000. Pepsi has increased dividend payments every year for the past twenty-seven years. Over the most recent eighteen years dividends were raised on average of 11 percent a year.

*Coca-Cola Co.*

Coca-Cola Co. is one of the world's most-admired companies. Coke is a Dow company and a company that has most of the characteristics that make an investment rewarding. In contrast to Pepsi, Coke's international business is more profitable than its domestic business. International business accounted for 62 percent of net sales and 68 percent of profits in 1999. Coke has international expansion down to a science that other companies should study. They have been at it for years. Coke typically builds the bottling facility in the market where they want entry. Once their soft drinks are distributed and they are established in the region, they sell the bottling facility and take their capital to open another one. While Coke does have some fractional ownership in bottlers, its main business consists of manufacturing and selling a concentrate or syrup that is sold to bottlers who combine the concentrate with the other ingredients and distribute it. This way they can have local management and they don't become a capital-intensive business. Coke has had some hard times; e.g., the decade of the 1970s was dismal for Coke. They had disputes with bottlers, accusations of mistreatment from workers at its Minute Maid groves, environmentalists charged Coke with polluting the earth with its containers, and the federal government charged them with antitrust violations. If that was not enough to keep its stock on the roller coaster, there was an Arab boycott of Coke because Coke put a franchise in Israel, and Japanese consumers were protesting Coke's use of coal-tar for coloring Fanta Grape.

Coke's CEO of the seventies started diversifying the company into fragmented low-profit-margin businesses. In those days Coke had 20 percent return on equity. Coke got a new and effective CEO, Roberto Goizueta, in 1980, who set out to divest Coke of all the businesses that had low profit margins. The money was used instead to grow Coke's high-margin business of selling syrup. Goizueta had a mission for Coke: to bring refreshments to every corner of the world. Coke started to improve under Goizueta's direction.

These facts demonstrate how difficult it can be to be a long-term investor. The shareholders that stayed invested in Coke have done very well. The typical institutional or professional money manager would have been panicked by each of these tales and would have been in and out of this stock a dozen times, paying taxes all the way. Coke's return on equity is 38 percent. It is Coke's goal to achieve 8–10 percent annual growth outside the United States. This goal has been momentarily thwarted with actual slowing of growth. Coke's stock has been trending sideways for the past four years (the stock became overpriced). Coke's sales fell; first Asia took a toll, then Russia and Brazil. After falling sales and earnings in 1998 and 1999, the company's earnings are again rising in 2000. Analysts are expecting profits to continue rising through 2001. Worldwide soft drink demand is expected to grow at 5–6 percent a year.

Coke started paying dividends in 1883 and has raised them every year for the last thirty-six years. Dividends have been raised on average of 11 percent a year (1983–1998). Even when the company's sales and earnings were down in 1998 and 1999, the company raised its dividends.

## Food-Processing Sector

*ConAgra Foods Inc.*

ConAgra is the nation's second-largest food processor. It operates three divisions: packaged foods, refrigerated foods, and agricultural products. Its famous name brands include Healthy Choice, Armour, and Butterball. The company has been in the process of restructuring and introducing new products. The dividend payout has been raised the past eighteen years at an average of 14 percent a year. ConAgra has raised its dividend every year for twenty-three years. The company's share price has appreciated on average 11 percent a year for the past 18 years. ConAgra's return on shareholder equity in 2000 was 27 percent.

## H. J. Heinz Co.

With sales approaching $10 billion, Heinz is one of the world's leading food processors and purveyors of nutritional services. Its fifty affiliates operate in some 200 countries, offering more than 5,000 varieties. Among the company's famous brands are Heinz, StarKist, Ore-Ida, 9-Lives, Weight Watchers, Wattie's, Plasmon, Farley's, The Budget Gourmet, Rosetto, Bagel Bites, John West, Petit Navire, Earth's Best, Ken-LRation, Kibbles 'n Bits, Pup-Peroni, Nature's Recipe, Orlando, Olivine, and Pudliszki. One-half of Heinz's sales are international. Officers and directors own 6 percent of the stock. Heinz started paying dividends in 1911. As is typical of food stocks, the dividend payout is high, $1.58 per share in 2000 (yield is 3.4 percent currently). If Heinz continues to raise its dividend payment 11 percent a year, the yield will double every 6.5 years. It will take 6.5 years to yield 6.8 percent, that is more than treasuries are yielding today. Heinz has raised its dividend payments every year for the past thirty-seven years.

## Tootsie Roll Industries, Inc.

Tootsie Roll makes candy, the kind of candy that kids love. Some of its name brands include: Tootsie Roll, Tootsie Pop, Junior Mints, Sugar Babies, Charms, and Blow Pops. If the kids in the rest of the world are like American kids, Tootsie Roll has an extensive international expansion opportunity. Tootsie Roll's operations are doing well in Canada and Mexico. International sales are 8 percent of TR's total sales. The company's earnings increased 10 percent in 2000. The market has recognized this opportunity and the share price is dear. The stock price of Tootsie Roll has a median P/E of 20 and a trailing P/E of 25, which is expensive for a food processor. Officers control 68 percent of the voting shares. This company has a good dividend history. It has raised its dividend for thirty-seven consecutive years and for the past eighteen years has raised the dividend 16 percent a year. In addition, the company traditionally has rewarded shareholders with a 3 percent stock dividend annually.

## Wm. Wrigley Jr. Co.

Wrigley is the world's largest manufacturer and seller of gum, specialty gum, and gum products. International sales and profits are 59 percent of the total. The president and CEO, William Wrigley, owns 21 percent of common and 55 percent of class B shares. Wrigley rewards its shareholders with its longstanding dividend payout of 50 percent of net profit. Wrigley has no debt. WWY has paid dividends since 1913. Dividends have been raised on average 14 percent a year (1983–2000). The company has increased dividend payouts every year for the past twenty years. Wrigley's share price has trended sideways for the past three years. Its revenues and earnings have continued to increase. Overseas revenues advanced 15 percent in 2000 and earnings advanced 10 percent year over year. Analysts anticipate that Wrigley's earnings will be driven higher by overseas growth and new product introductions.

## Tobacco Industry Sector

*Philip Morris Companies, Inc.*

Philip Morris is primarily a tobacco and foods company. Its name brands include Marlboro, Benson & Hedges, Virginia Slims, Merit, Lark, Post cereals, Jell-O, Kool-Aid, Oscar Mayer, Kraft, Velveeta, and Miracle Whip. Philip Morris is acquiring Nabisco. It plans to combine it with its Kraft Foods division and spin them off as a separate entity in early 2001 to shareholders. This should increase the value of the food division, which has been weighed down by tobacco. The tobacco division is 60 percent of revenues and 66 percent of operating profits. Some analysts believe that Philip Morris will remain profitable and continue to sell tobacco products to a certain segment of the population worldwide despite all the bad press and litigation costs. Philip Morris has been a good dividend raiser, averaging 17 percent annually for the past eighteen years (1983–2000). The company has raised its dividend every year for the past thirty-two years. It is currently yielding 4.9 percent at a share price of $43. Using the current figures, its yield will double in 4.2 years if the company continues to raise its dividend at 17 percent annually. Prospective shareholders will have to decide if this company will remain viable and prosper or if the litigation and regulation will sink it. Philip Morris is a Dow component.

## Medical Supply Sector

*Abbott Laboratories*

Abbott Laboratories is a global, diversified health care company devoted to the discovery, development, manufacture, and marketing of pharmaceuticals, diagnostic, nutritional, and hospital products. Abbott's revenues and earnings accelerated in 2000 due to the introduction of new pharmaceuticals. Abbott is a large-cap company and employs 54,000 people. Its products are marketed in more than 130 countries. International business is over 46 percent of Abbott's sales. Abbott has been paying dividends since 1926, and raising them for twenty-nine consecutive years. The past eighteen years Abbott raised its dividend 15 percent a year. Abbott's record of paying dividends, seventy-seven years of consecutive quarterly dividends, demonstrates its ability to deliver long-term, consistent results to shareholders.

*Medtronic, Inc.*

Medtronic is the leading manufacturer of implantable biomedical devices (pacemakers and prosthetic heart valves) and surgical equipment, including oxygenators, and blood pumps. Medtronic has been aggressively acquiring complementary businesses, which will give it the ability to offer group purchasing packages that include pacemakers, internal and external defibrillators, as well as vascular, neurological, and spinal surgery products. Medtronic also has a new product cycle that will contribute to internal growth. These are products that an aging world population will need and should keep Medtronic's top and bottom lines growing. International business is over 35 percent of sales and 33 percent of profits. Medtronic has been raising dividends every year for twenty-three years and raising them on average 18 percent a year for the past eighteen years. The dividend payout and yield starts out low, but if it maintains its 18 percent annual increases, the dividend payout will double every four years.

*Johnson & Johnson*

JNJ is a leading manufacturer of health care products, organized into three divisions. Consumer products include toiletries, first aid, hygiene, and baby care. Band-Aid, Stayfree, Neutrogena, Modess, and Reach are among their familiar brands. Professional products include medical equipment, surgical, orthopedic, and dental products. Pharmaceutical division includes Tyenol, Aciphex for decreasing gastric acidity, antibiotics, antifungals, dermatologic preparations, and contraceptives. In 1999, about 44 percent of the company's total sales are from international sources. Earnings are affected by the strength of the dollar and currency fluctuations, sometimes creating a buying opportunity for this Dow company. Johnson & Johnson has raised dividend payments every year for the past thirty-six years. Dividends have been paid since 1905 and have increased 13 percent a year over the past eighteen years.

## Drug Sector

*Merck & Co., Inc.*

Merck is one of America's leading drug companies. In 2000, Merck's drug sales were driven by five drugs (Vioxx, Zocor, Cozaar/Hyzaar, Fosamax, and Singular). These five drugs accounted for 58% of Merck's total sales. The patents of some of Merck's key drugs will be expiring in the next few years (Vasotec, Pepcid, Mevacor, Prinivil). These drugs will be exposed to generic competition. There is some question at this time as to whether the new drugs Merck has introduced can replace the lost sales of drugs going off patent. This pipeline problem relates back to the days (1992–1994) when Hillary Clinton was bashing the drug companies and pushing her health-care-reform project. Top management at Merck became jittery and slowed down R&D on new drugs. Instead, they used their capital to buy Medco, a drug benefits management company, in an attempt to have some future pricing control. In contrast, top management at Pfizer kept pumping R&D money into new drugs, producing a currently superior pipeline. Some of this is already discounted by the market as Merck's P/E has not expanded as much as its industry competitors.

Merck is a Dow stock. It has been paying dividends since 1935 and has raised its dividend payout 16 percent a year for the past eighteen years. American drug companies have been very innovative and have given us many drugs that have made our lives better in untold ways, including the lives of investors. One problem with investing in them is that every time a politician starts bashing them and promulgates controlling drug prices, their share prices drop as investors bail out. If drug prices are controlled by the government, research and development will dry up and so will dividends. This is why it is important to diversify and support politicians who believe in capitalism and free markets.

*Schering-Plough Corp.*

Schering-Plough Corp. is a worldwide manufacturer of prescription drugs, over-the-counter drugs, animal healthcare products, vision care products, sun care and foot care lines. Important brand names include Claritin, Proventil, Vancenase, Afrin, Eulexin, Intron A, Scholl's, and Coppertone. Sales of Claritin, the world's favorite antihistamine, are boosting earnings. Schering-Plough has several new drugs that should keep earnings rising: Intron A/Rebetron for treatment of hepatitis C, Nasonex for hay fever symptoms, Vasomax for impotence, and Asmanex for asthma. It is also introducing a second generation Claritin. Schering-Plough has return on equity of 44.5 percent. International sales account for 36 percent of total sales. The company has raised annual dividend payments on average 14 percent from 1983 to 2000.

### Pfizer Inc.

Pfizer Inc. is the global pharmaceutical company that everyone knows as the creator of Viagra. Pfizer is in the process of merging with Warner-Lambert. This merger has created a giant drug company with a market cap of $278 billion. The company has a blockbuster-laden portfolio of drugs. Pfizer has eight drugs that are billion dollar plus sellers. Pfizer has launched new drugs that are selling well: Celebra (arthritis and pain); Tikosyn (atrial fibrillation); Relpax (migraines); Zoloft (antidepressant); Zithromax (antibiotic); Norvasc (cardiovascular); Viagra (impotence); Diflucan (antifungal); Trovan (broad spectrum antibiotic). Pfizer has a very rewarding pipeline of new drugs that should keep shareholders healthy and wealthy. Pfizer has paid dividends since 1901. Dividends have been raised on average 12 percent annually for the past eighteen years. The year 2000 marked the thirty-third consecutive year of quarterly dividend increases for Pfizer shareholders. The board of directors declared a three-for-one stock split in 1999. The company is confident of its prospects.

## Retail Sector

### Home Depot

The Home Depot was added to the Dow in 1999. It operates a chain of retail building supply and home improvement stores across the U.S. and Canada. They recently opened a South America division with a store in Argentina. This retailing giant has a market cap of $130 billion. Home Depot is continuing to expand in the United States with a new high-end store format, Expo Design Center, and a new format that reaches out to the professional customer through its Pro Initiative. It is also opening new smaller stores, Villager's Hardware, which are suitable for downtown and residential areas. These new formats complement rather than complete with the original stores. Home Depot has grown from fifty stores in 1985 to one thousand stores in July of 2000. The company is in the process of rolling out its e-commerce site, which provides online shopping that is integrated with its store base. Home Depot continues to implement improvements. Officers and directors own 5.6 percent of the stock. Home Depot has raised its dividend 26 percent every year for the last twelve years. Home Depot started paying dividends in 1989.

### Wal-Mart

Wal-Mart has been on a roll after four years of having its share price trend sideways (1993–1996). Wal-Mart has proven that it can expand into foreign markets and is going over well with international bargain shoppers. I had some doubts about the success of the big-box stores outside of the United States, but I am now a believer. Wal-Mart has become the world's largest retailer and has expanded into Latin America, Canada, Europe, and South America (1,045 foreign stores). Wal-Mart's international prospects are bright. The company is accelerating growth in China, Korea, and Mexico. Wal-Mart is also introducing its supercenter format in the United Kingdom. Wal-Mart has stepped up the pace of expansion of its supercenter stores in the United States. It currently operates 1,723 discount stores, 866 supercenters, and 469 Sam's Clubs. Wal-Mart has improved its operating margins by expanding its private-label grocery items and by introducing higher-margined services. Officers and directors own 40.1 percent of shares. Wal-Mart is a good dividend raiser, 24 percent a year over the past eighteen years, although the payout and thus the yield starts out low.

## Toiletries/Cosmetics Sector

### Gillette Co.

Gillette is a leading producer of grooming products and batteries. King Gillette started the company on the advice that he market a product that people need to buy over and over again: thus, he invented the safety razor. The company's major divisions include razors, toiletries, small household appliances, oral care products, and batteries. Blades and razors represent 30 percent of the company's total sales. Sales have continued to increase, but earnings fell in 1998 and 1999, due primarily to currency translations. Despite the decrease in earnings, the company raised its dividend. Foreign operations account for 60 percent of operations. Warren Buffett's company, Berkshire Hathaway, owns 9.1 percent of Gillette's common stock. Gillette has paid dividends since 1906; raising them every year for the past twenty-three years (13 percent average annual dividend increases, 1983–2000).

## Chemical (Specialty) Sector

### Avery Dennison Corp.

Avery Dennison Corp. is a global manufacturer of self-adhesive base materials, labels, tapes, office products, and specialty chemical adhesives. It does business in over thirty countries and foreign sales are 37 percent of total sales. Its return on equity has been trending up and is up to 26 percent. Analysts are projecting 2001 revenue growth for Avery in the 6 percent range and a share net increase of 10 percent. Avery is implementing a cost-reduction program combined with enhancing manufacturing efficiencies. Avery has increased dividend payments on average 13 percent a year (1983–2000) and has increased dividends every year for the past twenty-five years.

## Metal-Fabricating Sector

*Illinois Tool Works Inc.*

Illinois Tool Works manufactures components and fasteners for automotive, construction, and general industrial applications. Analysts are predicting continued double digit share net growth for Illinois Tool Works out to 2003–2005. This growth will be fueled by acquisitions and ongoing improvements in productivity. It has subsidiaries and affiliates in forty countries and on six continents. International sales are 33.6 percent of the total sales. Officers and directors own 13.5 percent of this company (worth $2.5 billion). They run this company well and have rewarded the shareholders with 14 percent-a-year dividend increases (1983–2000). The company has raised dividends every year for the past thirty-eight years.

## Diversified Sector

*General Electric Co.*

General Electric is an all-star blue-chip company that everyone should have as a core holding in their portfolio. GE is the only remaining original Dow stock, and has been paying dividends since 1899. The company has edged out Microsoft for having the largest market cap, $562 billion. GE is a conglomerate whose businesses include light bulbs, jet engines, appliances, power-generation equipment, medical equipment, broadcasting, and financial services. Trends remain strong at nearly all of these businesses. Services account for the majority of GE's revenue. One-third of the company's profits comes from its financial services division. GE raised its dividend on average 11 percent annually over the past eighteen years (1983–2000).

*Hillenbrand Industries*

Hillenbrand is a family-owned-and-operated business with good demographics. They make adjustable hospital beds, stretchers, and other hospital and nursing home equipment and furniture. Once we aging baby boomers are done with this equipment, we can buy Hillenbrand funeral planning products, caskets, and cremation receptacles. This is a recession-proof business, but the company's health care division has been hurt recently by government cuts in Medicare reimbursement. The funeral division has also been hurt by slower death rates, broader acceptance of cremation, and casket discounting. HB has been responding by cutting costs and increasing efficiencies. Analysts are forecasting a 10 percent earnings gain in 2001, with good prospects out to 2003–2005. HB has raised dividends at 12 percent a year the last eighteen years and has raised its dividend every year for the last thirty years.

## Industrial Services Industry

*Cintas Corporation*

Cintas designs, manufacturers, and distributes uniforms through its rental division. It also rents mops, dust cloths, and entrance mats. The company also sells uniforms to its large national accounts through catalogs. Seventy-five percent of revenues come from uniform rental and cleaning services. The company's earnings have grown steadily and analysts are forecasting an 18 percent increase in earnings for 2001. Cintas has accomplished this growth through its ability to win new accounts (first-time users of uniform services), and then leverage its new accounts by providing additional supplies such as entrance mats, soap dispensers, etc. This low-tech growth company commands a high P/E. Buy this one on the dips. Cintas has raised its dividend on average 21 percent annually (1983–2000).

## Food Wholesalers Industry

*Sysco Corporation*

Sysco (not to be confused with Cisco) is a leading distributor of food and other products used by the food-service industry in the United States and Canada. The company serves 356,000 customers (restaurants, hotels, motels, hospitals, schools, and nursing homes) from its centrally located distribution centers. Demographics are good for Sysco. People are eating out more, and the food-service industry now commands more than half of the food dollar. Sysco has an advantage over its competitors because its size gives it more buying power and efficiencies. Sysco has plenty of room to grow. It has only 11 percent of the food-distribution market, with the top fifty distributors accounting for less than 30 percent of total industry sales. Sysco has raised its dividend on average 19 percent annually (1983–2000). The company has raised its dividend payment annually for the past twenty-four years.

## Chemical (Diversified) Industry

*Pall Corporation*

Pall Corporation is a leading manufacturer of fluid filters and fluid-filtering equipment. Its filters and equipment remove solid, liquid, and gaseous contaminants from a variety of liquids and gases. Sales growth in the micro-electronic, bio-pharmaceutical, and water filtration markets is expected to improve due to new products and a more profitable mix of products. Pall has raised its dividend on average 14 percent annually (1983–2000). The company has raised its dividend every year for the past twenty years.

## THE GRAPHS

A picture is worth a thousand words, so I have included a lot of pictures. These charts of the dividend and stock price performance of the companies in my portfolio should be of help in visualizing the actual course that these companies have taken over the last eighteen years.

All of the graphs in my portfolio look similar, with steadily rising dividend payouts. If they didn't have this appearance, they wouldn't have been picked for this book. In order to disabuse you of the notion that *all* large-cap stocks have dividend increases that look like an escalator, I have included charts of two Dow stocks, Caterpillar and General Motors, for comparison. These companies are very cyclical, going up and down with the economy. The comparison with the charts in my portfolio is striking. This is the reason that you must go back many years to establish a dividend history.

Also, as you view these graphs, think of the tumultuous year 2000 in the stock market. The stock price of nearly all of the companies in my portfolio showed much volatility. In 1999, large amounts of money went into technology and out of defensive stocks (REITs, utilities, old economy blue-chips, etc.). In 2000 the reverse happened, and the NASDAQ (heavily weighted in technology) had its worst year ever. This is the stock-price roller coaster. The escalator remained intact. The dividends, while perhaps not rising quite as much as in previous years, still went up. The comparison between the graph for the stock price and the dividend payout is often dramatic.

# The Thirty Thoroughbreds

*Low initial yield, but fast dividend growth*

## ABBOTT LABORATORIES
## ABT (NY)

| | |
|---|---|
| *Share Price: $47* | *Yield: 1.6%* |
| *P/E: 27* | *Dividend Payment per Share: $0.76* |
| *Market Cap: $67 Billion* | *Industry: Medical Supplies* |
| *(Large Cap)* | |
| *Return on Share Equity: 31%* | *Operating Margin: 30.5%* |

In 1971, when my husband was graduating medical school, we took a train to north Chicago to visit Abbott Laboratories' main plant. We were mightily impressed at that time; the intervening years have given us only more room for optimism. Note Abbott's return on equity and the operating margin, 31 percent and 30.5 percent respectively. Abbott experienced revenue and earnings acceleration in 2000 due to new drugs they brought to market.

Abbott Laboratories is a diversified medical supply company. Pharmaceuticals account for about 30 percent of Abbott's business. Nutritional products account for another 30 percent. Hospital and laboratory products such as i.v. solutions and diagnostic tests and equipment account for 35 percent. The remainder is made up by chemicals and agricultural products. Isomil, Similac, Murine, and Selsun Blue are some of the consumer products. Abbott is increasing efforts to sell its infant formulas and adult nutritionals overseas. Abbott is benefiting from an increasing demand for its high-margin products such as hospital pharmaceuticals, including new anesthetics, injectable drugs, drug-delivery system, and contrast agents for diagnostic imaging (procedures in the radiology departments, such as GI studies, CAT scans, etc.). Abbott introduced a number of new products in 2000. These are products used in hospital laboratories for diagnostic studies on body fluids including clinical chemistry and hematology systems, immunoassay analyzers and blood screening devices. The FDA recently approved Abbott's new diabetes product, Sof-Tact. It is the first automated glucose monitor that offers lancing, blood collection, and glucose testing all in one press of a button. Abbott also has received approval and has released a migraine medication, Depakote ER, and an HIV drug, Kaletra. These new drugs are expected to contribute to Abbott's earnings acceleration in 2001.

Abbott Labs is a large-cap company with a recent market capitalization of $67 billion. Of Abbott's sales 46 percent are international.

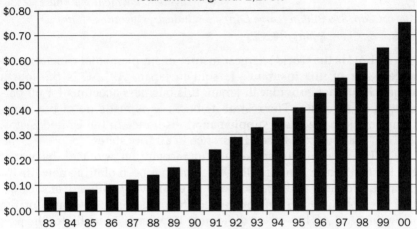

## Annual Dividend Payment Per Share 1983–2000

Current yield on original 1983 investment 30%
Average annual dividend growth 15%
Total dividend growth 1,170%

In 1983 one share of Abbott Laboratories cost $2.50 and the dividend payment was $0.06 a share. By 2000 the dividend payment had risen to $0.76 a share; that is a 30 percent yield on the dollars invested in Abbott Laboratories in 1983. The yield went from 2.4 percent to 30 percent over eighteen years.

## Annual Share Price 1983–2000

Average annual share price appreciation 19%
Total share price appreciation 2,140%

■ year's high
■ year's low

The share price of Abbott Laboratories went from $2.50 in 1983 to $56 in 2000. The dollars invested in Abbott Laboratories in 1983 appreciated 2,140 percent in eighteen years.

# AFLAC, INC.
# AFL (NY)

*Share Price: $70*                          *Yield: 0.5%*
*P/E: 31*                                    *Dividend Payment per Share: $0.36*
*Market Cap: $16 Billion (Large Cap)*        *Industry: Insurance (Life)*
*Return on Share Equity: 14.5%*

AFLAC is the world's largest insurer of supplemental cancer insurance. Most of this insurance is sold in Japan. AFLAC is the fourth largest insurance provider in Japan; this business accounts for 80 percent of its revenues. The rest of its business is made up of life, long-term-care, and Medicare supplemental insurance in the United States. AFLAC is authorized to sell insurance in all fifty states.

AFLAC is receiving some overdue recognition as one of the best of the life and health insurers. The company has been offering new life insurance products that should keep sales growing. Officers and directors own about 6 percent of the outstanding common shares of the company. AFLAC has raised dividends 15 percent annually for the past eighteen years.

### Annual Dividend Payment Per Share 1983–2000

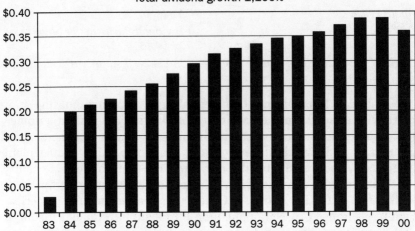

Current yield on original 1983 investment 48%
Annual dividend growth 15%
Total dividend growth 1,100%

In 1983 one share of AFLAC, Inc. cost $0.75 and the dividend payment was $0.03 a share. By 2000 the dividend payment had risen to $0.36 a share; that is a 48 percent yield on the dollars invested in AFLAC in 1983. The yield went from 4 percent to 48 percent over eighteen years.

### Annual Share Price 1983–2000

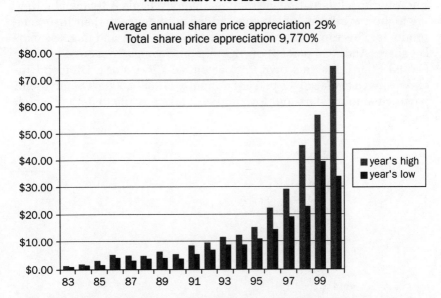

Average annual share price appreciation 29%
Total share price appreciation 9,770%

The share price of AFLAC, Inc. went from $0.75 in 1983 to $74 in 2000. The dollars invested in AFLAC in 1983 appreciated 9,770 percent in eighteen years.

## AMERICAN INTERNATIONAL GROUP
## AIG (NY)

*Share Price: $97*                    *Yield: 0.2%*

*P/E: 42*                             *Dividend Payment per Share:*
                                      *$0.15*

*Market Cap: $220 Billion (Large Cap)*   *Industry: Insurance (Diversified)*

*Return on Share Equity: 15.5%*

American International Group is a large insurance holding company with a broad range of insurance products. These include domestic casualty insurance, accident insurance, cancer insurance, and group and individual life and health insurance. Risk management, agency services, and financial services expand their interests. Recently, AIG merged with Sun America, a large variable-annuity company, to further diversify its business. Other subsidiaries include American Home Assurance Co., National Union Fire Insurance Co. of Pittsburgh, and New Hampshire Insurance Company. AIG has been a model for prudent financial management and remains one of the top-performing financial stocks. The company is primarily a low-cost player with a broad array of businesses, diversified both geographically and across business lines. Analysts are predicting a faster growth rate for AIG because it is shifting into faster growing businesses with lower capital requirements.

American International Group maintains a triple A financial rating, the highest available, which gives added confidence to their insurance products. This top rating has allowed AIG to prosper and increase market share. About 50 percent of AIG's income comes from outside of the United States. Insiders own 6.7 percent of AIG's stock. Dividend increases have averaged 12 percent annually (1983–2000). The dividend payment amount starts out low, and will take a while to deliver a high yield.

**Annual Dividend Payment Per Share 1983–2000**

Current yield on original 1983 investment 7.5%
Annual dividend growth 12%
Total dividend growth 700%

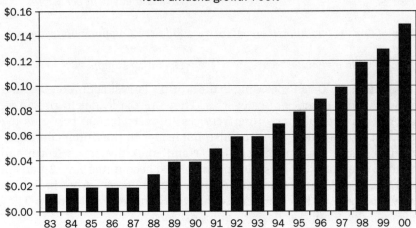

In 1983 one share of American International Group cost $2 and the dividend payment was $0.02 a share. By 2000 the dividend payment had risen to $0.15 a share; that is a 7.5 percent yield on the dollars invested in American International Group in 1983. The yield went from .7 percent to 7.5 percent over eighteen years.

**Annual Share Price 1983–2000**

Average annual share price appreciation 25%
Total share price appreciation 5,050%

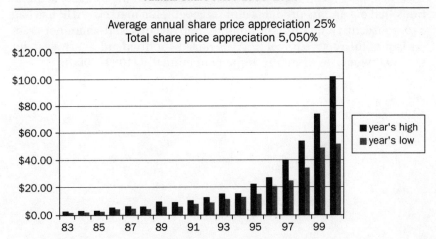

The share price of American International Group went from $2 in 1983 to $103 in 2000. The dollars invested in American International Group in 1983 appreciated 5,050 percent in eighteen years.

## AUTOMATIC DATA PROCESSING
## ADP (NY)

*Share Price: $59*

*Yield: 0.7%*

*P/E: 44*

*Dividend Payment per Share:
$0.34*

*Market Cap: $42.9 Billion (Large Cap)*

*Industry: Computer Software and
Services*

*Return on Share Equity: 18.3%*

*Operating Margin: 26%*

Automatic Data Processing is the world's largest computer-services provider in a number of categories. They are the leader in providing payroll services and tax-filing services to over 500,000 accounts (57 percent of revenues). They are also the leader in providing computerized data and backup services to car and truck dealers in North and South America as well as Europe and Asia, accounting for 12 percent of revenues. About 24 percent of their income comes from brokerage services, helping stockbrokers with quotes and record keeping. They also handle claims services for auto insurers.

Due to their long history and vast experience, the services provided by Automatic Data Processing are highly suited for the upward trend in outsourcing that is sweeping the world's industries. There is an increasing trend to outsource nonstrategic tasks. There is plenty of room for growth in this area, since only half of companies with over one hundred employees outsource their payrolls, and only 20 percent of companies with under one hundred employees outsource their payrolls. ADP has used its strong balance sheet and cash flow to make acquisitions that expand its products and its geographic markets. ADP has had 149 consecutive quarters of double-digit revenue and share-net comparisons (thirty-seven years). ADP raised its dividend every year for the past twenty-five, and by 15 percent annually (1983–2000).

**Annual Dividend Payment Per Share 1983–2000**

Current yield on original 1983 investment 17%
Average annual dividend growth 15%
Total dividend growth 1,030%

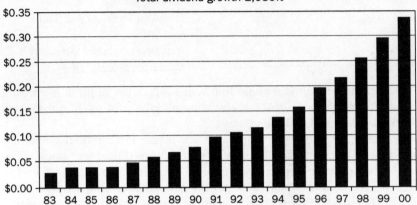

In 1983 one share of Automatic Data Processing cost $2 and the dividend payment was $0.03 a share. By 2000 the dividend payment had risen to $0.34 a share; that is a 17 percent yield on the dollars invested in Automatic Data Processing in 1983. The yield went from 1.5 percent to 17 percent over eighteen years.

**Annual Share Price 1983–2000**

Average annual share price appreciation 22%
Total share price appreciation 3,350%

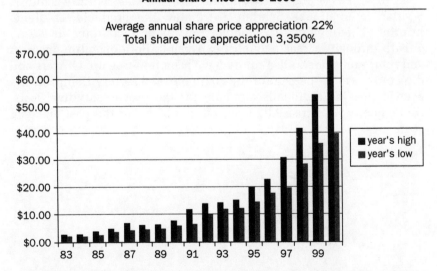

The share price of Automatic Data Processing went from $2 in 1983 to $69 in 2000. The dollars invested in Automatic Data Processing in 1983 appreciated 3,350 percent in eighteen years.

## AVERY DENNISON CORP.
## AVY (NY)

| | |
|---|---|
| *Share Price: $51* | *Yield: 2.4%* |
| *P/E: 18* | *Dividend Payment per Share: $1.08* |
| *Market Cap: $5.2 Billion (Large Cap)* | *Industry: Chemical (Specialty)* |
| *Return on Share Equity: 26%* | *Operating Margin: 15.5%* |

Avery Dennison is a name that will keep popping up at home and at work, on labels, glues, fasteners, notebooks, and even star-shaped stickers for your daughter's charts.

Avery Dennison's business extends much farther than consumer products. Office and industrial glues, stamps and peel-and-stick adhesives, fasteners, and specialty chemical adhesives are manufactured in thirty-three countries. Office products such as three-ring binders, notebooks, organizational systems, business forms, tickets, and imprinting equipment comprise the nonadhesive portion of their business. One of Avery's most ubiquitous products is peel-and-stick postage stamps. Pressure-sensitive material products account for 50 percent of the company's sales.

Avery Dennison realizes over two-thirds of its income from U.S. sales. In order to increase international sales AVY has formed a joint venture with a German office-supplies firm, and has recently acquired Spartan International. Spartan distributes film products for digital printing. This high-quality company has room to continue its steady growth through increasing global expansion. Both operating margins and return on shareholder equity have been trending up. Officers and directors own 1.9 percent of the common stock. Avery Dennison has been increasing dividends annually for the past twenty-five years. Dividends have increased 13 percent annually for the past eighteen years.

**Annual Dividend Payment Per Share 1983–2000**

Current yield on original 1983 investment 25%
Average annual dividend growth 13%
Total dividend growth 800%

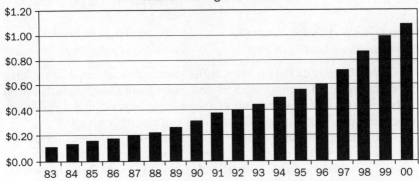

In 1983 one share of Avery Dennison cost $4.30 and the dividend payment was $0.12 a share. By 2000 the dividend payment had risen to $1.08 a share; that is a 25 percent yield on the dollars invested in Avery Dennison in 1983. The yield went from 2.7 percent to 25 percent over eighteen years.

**Annual Share Price 1983–2000**

Average annual share price appreciation 18%
Total share price appreciation 1,710%

The share price of Avery Dennison went from $4.30 in 1983 to $78 in 2000. The dollars invested in Avery Dennison in 1983 appreciated 1,710 percent in eighteen years.

## CINTAS CORPORATION
## CTAS (NDQ)

*Share Price: $52*                          *Yield: 0.4%*

*P/E: 42*                                   *Dividend Payment per Share:*
                                            *$0.19*

*Market Cap: $8.1 Billion (Large Cap)*      *Industry: Industrial Services*

*Return on Share Equity: 18.5%*             *Operating Margin: 21.2%*

Cintas Corporation is a low-profile company that most of us have not come in direct contact with. If you guess from the high-tech sound of its name that it is a computer software company, a biomed producer, or an aerospace company, you would be only partly correct.

Cintas Corporation is at the low-tech end of all of these industries and many more. It is one of the largest producers of uniforms for corporations, with corporate identification, and it rents them to various companies. They also rent dust mops, wiping cloths, and entrance mats. Cintas cleans and services all of these products with 17,000 employees and a fleet of over 27,000 vehicles. Catalogue sales and sales of first-aid equipment account for a quarter of its revenues. Most of Cintas's business is domestic. Cintas sells at a premium for its ability to deliver strong and consistent earnings. Over the years Cintas has been adept at opening new markets for its services. Cintas now has nineteen plants under construction, which may pressure margins. This could lead to a buying opportunity.

Insiders own 31.9 percent of the common stock, including 21.6 percent owned by the CEO. Cintas has raised dividends on average 21 percent a year (1983–2000).

---

**Annual Dividend Payment Per Share 1983–2000**

---

Current yield on original 1983 investment 20%
Average annual dividend growth 21%
Total dividend growth 3,070%

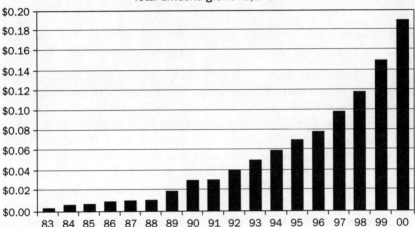

In 1983 one share of Cintas Corp. cost $0.93 and the dividend payment was $0.006 a share. By 2000 the dividend payment had risen to $0.19 a share; that is a 20 percent yield on the dollars invested in Cintas Corp. in 1983. The yield went from 0.7 percent to 20 percent over eighteen years.

---

**Annual Share Price 1983–2000**

---

Average annual share price appreciation 25%
Total share price appreciation 5,490%

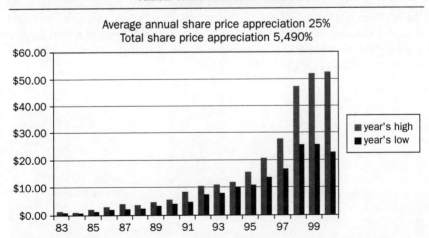

The share price of Cintas Corp. went from $0.93 in 1983 to $52 in 2000. The dollars invested in Cintas in 1983 appreciated 5,490 percent in eighteen years.

## THE COCA-COLA COMPANY
## KO (NY)

*Share Price: $58*

*P/E: 77*

*Market Cap: $150 Billion (Large Cap)*

*Return on Share Equity: 38%*

*Yield: 1.2%*

*Dividend Payment per Share:
$0.68*

*Industry: Beverage (Soft Drinks)*

*Operating Margin: 28.5%*

The Coca-Cola Company is one of the world's most admired companies. Coke, in addition to being the world's largest distributor of soft drinks, is the world's largest distributor of juices such as Minute Maid, Five Alive, and Hi-C. Coke has provided its shareholders with steady earnings, until 1998. The economic turmoil in Asia, Japan, South America, and Russia hurt Coke's sales and then their earnings in 1999. The strong dollar reduced reported U.S. earnings by up to 10 percent. Coke has historically tried to grow its volume sales at 8–10 percent. Coke has been expanding into new markets such as China, India, Russia, and the Ukraine. Their markets in India and China are performing well and have been accounting for above-average gains. Coke's earnings are rising again, and worldwide demand for soft drinks is growing again. Coke recently acquired the Cadbury Schweppes brands to sell outside the United States. Coke also distributes Coca-Cola, Sprite, Fanta, and TAB through bottlers throughout the world. International sales accounted for 62 percent of net sales and 68 percent of the company's profits.

Warren Buffett's company Berkshire Hathaway owns 8.1 percent of the common stock. Coke has raised dividends annually for the last thirty-six years. Dividend payments have risen 11 percent a year for the past eighteen years. Even more remarkable is that the company started paying dividends in 1883.

## Annual Dividend Payment Per Share 1983–2000

Current yield on original 1983 investment 36%
Average annual dividend growth 11%
Total dividend growth 520%

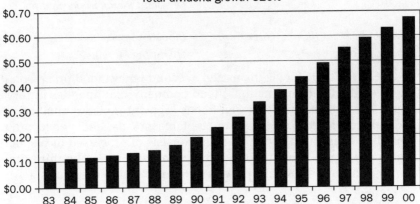

In 1983 one share of Coca-Cola Co. cost $1.90 and the dividend payment was $0.11 a share. By 2000 the dividend payment had risen to $0.68 a share; that is a 36 percent yield on the dollars invested in Coca-Cola Co. in 1983. The yield went from 5 percent to 36 percent over eighteen years.

## Annual Share Price 1983–2000

Average annual share price appreciation 22%
Total share price appreciation 3,370%

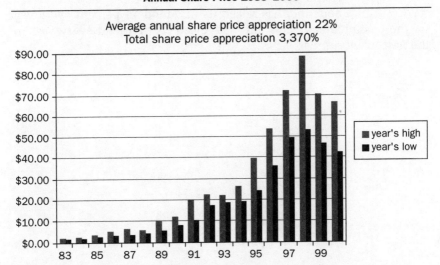

The share price of Coca-Cola Co. went from $1.90 in 1983 to $66 in 2000. The dollars invested in Coca-Cola Co. in 1983 appreciated 3,370 percent in eighteen years.

## CONAGRA FOODS INC.
## CAG (NY)

*Share Price: $25*                          *Yield: 3.5%*

*P/E: 22*                                   *Dividend Payment per Share:*
                                            *$0.79*

*Market Cap: $11.4 Billion (Large Cap)*     *Industry: Food Processing*

*Return on Share Equity: 27%*               *Operating Margin: 7.2%*

ConAgra Foods Inc. is the nation's second largest food processor. It is a diversified and international food company that operates in three industry segments. The Packaged Foods segment includes shelf-stable foods, frozen foods, cheese products, tablespreads, and potato products. The Refrigerated Foods segment consists of processed meats, deli meats, beef, pork, lamb, turkey, and chicken products. The third division, Agricultural Products, provides crop protection chemicals, fertilizers, and seeds.

ConAgra Foods Inc. brand names include Healthy Choice, Armour, and Butterball. Sales are growing in the single digits and earnings advanced 11 percent in 2000. The company's earnings growth has been driven by cost reductions and restructuring. The company's restructuring plan, "Operation Overdrive," has created an annual projected cost savings of $600 million. These savings will be used to make acquisitions and for new product development. The company has announced nineteen new products.

ConAgra Foods Inc. has raised its dividend 14 percent every year for the past eighteen years and has raised its dividend every year for the past twenty-three years.

**Annual Dividend Payment Per Share 1983–2000**

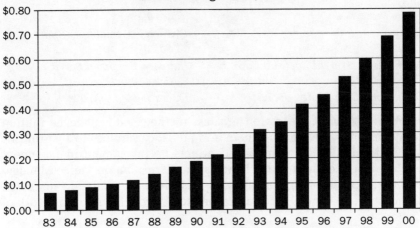

Current yield on original 1983 investment 20%
Average annual dividend growth 14%
Total dividend growth 1,029%

In 1983 one share of ConAgra cost $4 and the dividend payment was $0.07 a share. By 2000 the dividend payment had risen to $0.79 a share; that is a 20 percent yield on the dollars invested in ConAgra in 1983. The yield went from 2 percent to 20 percent over eighteen years.

**Annual Share Price 1983–2000**

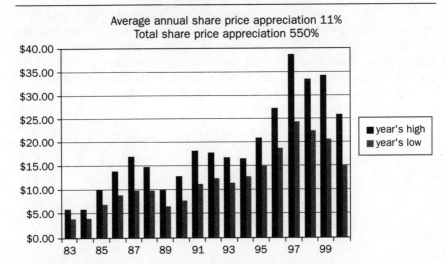

Average annual share price appreciation 11%
Total share price appreciation 550%

The share price of ConAgra went from $4 in 1983 to $26 in 2000. The dollars invested in ConAgra in 1983 appreciated 550 percent in eighteen years.

## EATON VANCE CORP.
## EV (NY)

*Share Price: $29*

*P/E: 19*

*Market Cap: $1.6 Billion (Mid Cap)*

*Return on Share Equity: 45.5%*

*Yield: 0.8%*

*Dividend Payment per Share: $0.20*

*Industry: Financial Services (Diversified)*

*Operating Margin: 62%*

Eaton Vance Corporation creates, markets, and manages mutual funds and provides management and advisory services to institutions and individuals. The company conducts its investment management and advisory services through two subsidiaries, Eaton Vance Management and Boston Management and Research. Its funds are marketed through Eaton Vance Distributors and sold through a retail network of dealers.

The diversity of assets under management serves Eaton Vance well in a volatile equity market. In stock market declines money flows into Eaton's cash funds, bank funds, and fixed income funds. The company is expanding its floating-rate bank loan-funds line. Eaton is one of the leaders in this asset class and manages $10 billion in bank loan assets. These funds offer daily liquidity for investors. Most competitors' bank-loan funds feature limited liquidity, which makes them less appealing to investors.

Eaton is introducing new funds across all product lines, and they should contribute to future growth of assets under management. Eaton has the majority of its equity assets in tax-managed funds. This tax-managed product line gives the company an advantage over its competitors by attracting investors seeking a higher return after taxes.

Officers and directors control 100 percent of the voting stock and own 10 percent of the common stock.

## Annual Dividend Payment Per Share 1985–2000

Current yield on original 1985 investment 27%
Average annual dividend growth 21%
Total dividend growth 1,900%

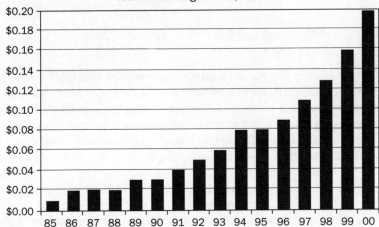

In 1985 one share of Eaton Vance Corp. cost $0.75 and the dividend payment was $0.01 a share. By 2000 the dividend payment had risen to $0.20 a share; that is a 27 percent yield on the dollars invested in Eaton Vance Corp. in 1985. The yield went from 1.3 percent to 27 percent over sixteen years.

## Annual Share Price 1985–2000

Average annual share price appreciation 25.8%
Total share price appreciation 3,820%

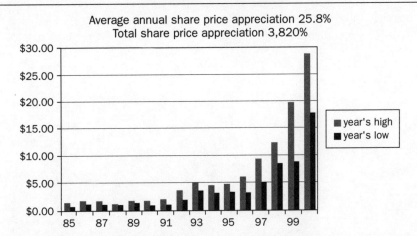

The share price of Eaton Vance Corp. went from $0.75 in 1985 to $29 in 2000. The dollars invested in Eaton Vance Corp. in 1985 appreciated 3,820 percent in sixteen years.

# FANNIE MAE
# FNM (NY)

*Share Price: $81*

*P/E: 20*

*Market Cap: $80 Billion (Large Cap)*

*Return on Share Equity: 21%*

*Yield: 1.4%*

*Dividend Payment per Share: $1.12*

*Industry: Thrift*

Fannie Mae is the nation's largest provider of residential mortgage funds. It was formerly known as the Federal National Mortgage Association, set up in 1983 to stabilize the home mortgage market. This company was originally a government agency, but recently has become partly privatized. It is still, however, under government regulation, and the president of the United States appoints five out of eighteen members of the board.

Fannie Mae has the largest reserves of mortgage money in the United States. The main function of this company is to buy and sell mortgages from primary lenders and to provide guarantees for the mortgages. This stabilizes the market by freeing up money from primary lenders for new mortgages. Debt enjoys favorable government agency status, but no explicit federal guarantee. This business has become very profitable, especially in times of a strong housing market. This is a pure-play housing stock; its fortunes are tied to those of the housing market. The company has been an excellent dividend raiser, averaging 30 percent annually over the past eighteen years.

### Annual Dividend Payment Per Share 1983–2000

Current yield on original 1983 investment 70%
Average annual dividend growth 30%
Total dividend growth 11,100%

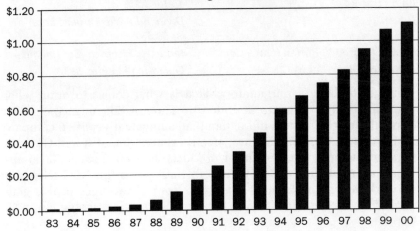

In 1983 one share of Fannie Mae cost $1.60 and the dividend payment was $0.01 a share. By 2000 the dividend payment had risen to $1.12 a share; that is a 70 percent yield on the dollars invested in Fannie Mae in 1983. The yield went from 0.6 percent to 70 percent over eighteen years.

### Annual Share Price 1983–2000

Average annual share price appreciation 24.7%
Total share price appreciation 5,213%

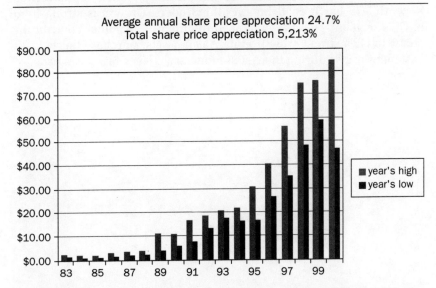

The share price of Fannie Mae went from $1.60 in 1983 to $85 in 2000. The dollars invested in Fannie Mae in 1983 appreciated 5,213 percent in eighteen years.

# GENERAL ELECTRIC CO.
## GE (NY)

| | |
|---|---|
| *Share Price: $48* | *Yield: 1.3%* |
| *P/E: 40* | *Dividend Payment per Share: $0.55* |
| *Market Cap: $562 Billion (Large Cap)* | *Industry: Electrical Equipment* |
| *Return on Share Equity: 25.5%* | *Operating Margin: 22%* |

Light bulbs and refrigerators: That is what comes to mind when you think of the company founded by Thomas Edison in the 1800s. General Electric is much more than that, a hugely diversified company that produces airplane engines, electric generators, MRI and CT scanners for medical use, industrial products, and chemicals. GE is also broadcasting, owning RCA which, in turn, owns the NBC television network. Most surprising is that 37 percent of revenues of this giant come from, not manufacturing, but financial services embodied in GE Capital.

GE is the only company that has been on the Dow Jones Industrial Average since its inception. It has been run by CEO Jack Welch since 1980. He has been extremely successful in cutting costs and improving quality control to increase shareholder value. Unfortunately, he has announced that he is retiring in 2001.

Depending on the day, GE and Microsoft seesaw back and forth as the world's largest corporation as measured by market capitalization. Recently, GE has been firing on all cylinders. Growth is strong in all of GE's segments. GE has embraced the Internet. Another contributing factor to GE's strong growth is its Asian assets, purchased at bargain-basement prices during the Asian monetary crisis a few years back.

### Annual Dividend Payment Per Share 1983–2000

Current yield on original 1983 investment 30%
Average annual dividend growth 11%
Total dividend growth 590%

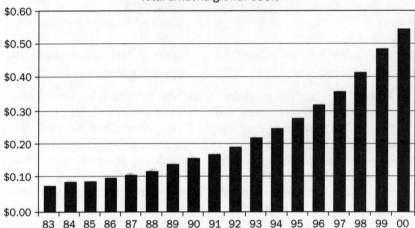

In 1983 one share of General Electric cost $1.85 and the dividend payment was $0.08 a share. By 2000 the dividend payment had risen to $0.55 a share; that is a 30 percent yield on the dollars invested in General Electric in 1983. The yield went from 4 percent to 30 percent over eighteen years.

### Annual Share Price 1983–2000

Average annual share price appreciation 21%
Total share price appreciation 3,140%

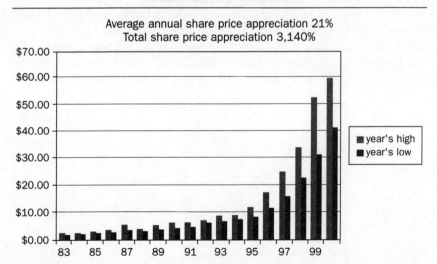

The share price of General Electric went from $1.85 in 1983 to $60 in 2000. The dollars invested in General Electric in 1983 appreciated 3,140 percent in eighteen years.

## GILLETTE
## G (NY)

*Share Price: $33*                              *Yield: 1.9%*

*P/E: 44*                                       *Dividend Payment per Share:*
                                                *$0.65*

*Market Cap: $31.6 Billion (Large Cap)*         *Industry: Toiletries and Cosmetics*

*Return on Share Equity: 44%*                   *Operating Margin: 26.6%*

Gillette is a leading producer of razors, toiletries, stationery products, batteries, and other personal care products. The brand names include MACH3, Sensor, SensorExcel, TracII, Atra, Good News, Gillette Series, Adorn, Right Guard, Soft and Dri, Foamy, Dry Idea, Paper Mate, Parker, Waterman, Braun small household appliances and electric shavers, Oral-B mouth care products, and Duracell batteries. Gillette's international operations account for 63 percent of its total sales. Gillette's earnings slowed in 1998 due to the turmoil and weak currency translations in Asia, Latin America, and Russia. These lower earnings depressed Gillette's share price. MACH3 is selling well in the United States and Europe. The company completed its rollout of MACH3 in its remaining international markets in 1999. The company is anticipating an improvement in margins due to its global cost-cutting and drop in start-up costs associated with MACH3. Gillette has many new products in its pipeline which will drive future growth. It is launching a new line of Duracell Ultra alkaline batteries. Gillette has recently agreed to sell its stationery-products business, which should enable Gillette to focus more on its top-line performers.

Gillette has raised dividends 13 percent on average annually for the past eighteen years. Gillette has increased dividends annually for the past twenty-three years. Gillette started paying dividends in 1906.

### Annual Dividend Payment Per Share 1983–2000

Current yield on original 1983 investment 50%
Average annual dividend growth 13%
Total dividend growth 830%

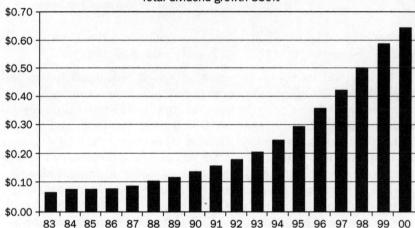

In 1983 one share of Gillette cost $1.30 and the dividend payment was $0.07 a share. By 2000 the dividend payment had risen to $0.65 a share; that is a 50 percent yield on the dollars invested in Gillette in 1983. The yield went from 5 percent to 50 percent over eighteen years.

### Annual Share Price 1983–2000

Average annual share price appreciation 22%
Total share price appreciation 3,210%

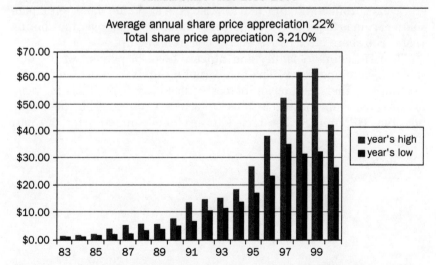

The share price of Gillette went from $1.30 in 1983 to $43 in 2000. The dollars invested in Gillette in 1983 appreciated 3,210 percent in eighteen years.

## HILLENBRAND INDUSTRIES, INC.
## HB (NY)

| | |
|---|---|
| *Share Price: $50* | *Yield: 1.6%* |
| *P/E: 25* | *Dividend Payment per Share:* |
| | *$0.80* |
| *Market Cap: $2 Billion (Mid Cap)* | *Industry: Diversified Company* |
| *Return on Share Equity: 15%* | *Operating Margin: 16%* |

Hillenbrand Industries is particularly well positioned for the demographics of the aging baby boom generation. This company has two main divisions. The first is the hospital supply division that makes adjustable hospital beds, stretchers, patient room furniture, and designs for hospital rooms. The second division takes care of the next step after the hospital and nursing home. Over 40 percent of their business takes place in the funeral industry, providing caskets and funeral planning services. Hillenbrand has had several difficult years. Medicare has cut its reimbursements, which hurt the revenue for Hillenbrand's health care rental business, Hill-Rom. Hillenbrand's revenues will be increased, however, by an exclusive contract with the nation's largest funeral home operator, Service Corporation, to provide caskets. This contract will increase revenues, but decrease profit margins because of the low pricing provisions in the contract. Hillenbrand also has a problem in Europe where they have excess manufacturing capacity and are restructuring. There were increased charges and expenses related to restructuring in 1999. The share price has been on a roller coaster for several years, reflecting this news. Analysts at *Value Line* anticipate share-earnings to grow at a 10 percent annualized rate over the coming years. The share price has recently been trending up.

The Hillenbrand family and officers own 28 percent of the outstanding common stock. The demographics are very positive for Hillenbrand, as there will be an increasing need for its products for years to come. Hillenbrand has as close to a recession-proof business as is possible. Hillenbrand has raised its dividend annually for the past thirty years.

**Annual Dividend Payment Per Share 1983–2000**

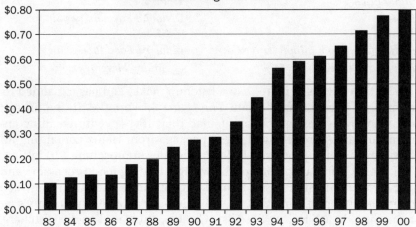

Current yield on original 1983 investment 18%
Average annual dividend growth 12%
Total dividend growth 630%

In 1983 one share of Hillenbrand Industries cost $4.50 and the dividend payment was $0.11 a share. By 2000 the dividend payment had risen to $0.80 a share; that is an 18 percent yield on the dollars invested in Hillenbrand in 1983. The yield went from 2.4 percent to 18 percent over eighteen years.

**Annual Share Price 1983–2000**

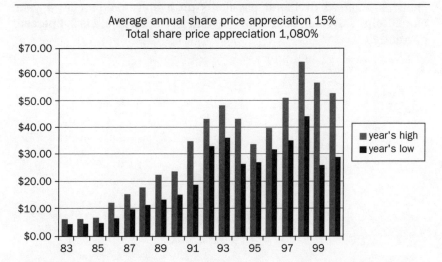

Average annual share price appreciation 15%
Total share price appreciation 1,080%

The share price of Hillenbrand Industries went from $4.50 in 1983 to $53 in 2000. The dollars invested in Hillenbrand in 1983 appreciated 1,080 percent in eighteen years.

# H. J. HEINZ CO.
## HNZ (NY)

| | |
|---|---|
| *Share Price: $46* | *Yield: 3.4%* |
| *P/E: 25* | *Dividend Payment per Share: $1.58* |
| *Market Cap: $14.9 Billion (Large Cap)* | *Industry: Food Processing* |
| *Return on Share Equity: 51%* | *Operating Margin: 21.5%* |

H. J. Heinz Co. is more than a ketchup maker and has expanded its number of products far beyond *The Heinz 57 Varieties.* In the fifties I remember when my grandparents had their fifty-seventh wedding anniversary and they received a gift package from Heinz containing all Fifty seven Heinz products. Today, with sales approaching $10 billion, H. J. Heinz Company is one of the world's leading food processors and purveyors of nutritional services. Its fifty affiliates operate in some 200 countries, offering more than 5,000 varieties. Among the company's famous brands are Heinz, StarKist, Ore-Ida, 9-Lives, Weight Watchers, Wattie's, Plasmon, Farley's, The Budget Gourmet, Rosetto, Bagel Bites, John West, Petit Navire, Earth's Best, Ken-LRation, Kibbles 'n Bits, Pup-Peroni, Nature's Recipe, Orlando, Olivine, and Pudliszki. One-half of Heinz's sales are international.

Officers and directors own 4.4 percent of the stock. Heinz started paying dividends in 1911. It has raised dividend payments every year for the past thirty-seven consecutive years. The past eighteen years Heinz has raised dividend payments on average 11 percent a year. Note: Heinz's dividend starts with a high payment. (Yield is 3.4 percent currently.)

## Annual Dividend Payment Per Share 1983–2000

Current yield on original 1983 investment 40%
Average annual dividend growth 11%
Total dividend growth 590%

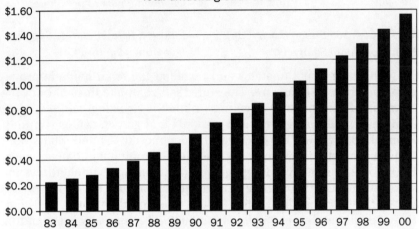

In 1983 one share of Heinz cost $4 and the dividend payment was $0.23 a share. By 2000 the dividend payment had risen to $1.58 a share; that is a 40 percent yield on the dollars invested in Heinz in 1983. The yield went from 5.7 percent to 40 percent over eighteen years.

## Annual Share Price 1983–2000

Average annual share price appreciation 15%
Total share price appreciation 1,080%

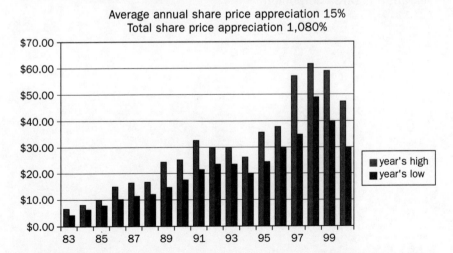

The share price of Heinz went from $4 in 1983 to $47 in 2000. The dollars invested in Heinz in 1983 appreciated 1,080 percent in eighteen years.

# HOME DEPOT (THE), INC.
## HD (NY)

| | |
|---|---|
| Share Price: $42 | Yield: 0.4% |
| P/E: 36 | Dividend Payment per Share: $0.16 |
| Market Cap: $65 Billion (Large Cap) | Industry: Retail Building Supply |
| Return on Share Equity: 20% | Operating Margin: 11.4% |

The Home Depot operates and invented the retail home-improvement warehouse superstore. The stores sell complete lines of building materials; floor and wall coverings; plumbing, heating, and electrical equipment; paint and furniture; seasonal and garden center supplies. Home Depot Stores are located throughout the United States and Canada. The stores are built for one-stop shopping and convenience. Home Depot's size gives it a large buying advantage, which allows the store to pass on their pricing power to customers. Home Depot has grown from 50 stores in 1985 to 1,000 stores in July of 2000. The company's earnings grew at 25 percent in 2000. The company is expanding overseas and in the United States. It is opening new stores with different formats. One of the new formats is the Expo design center, which sells high-margin kitchen renovations. Home Depot has opened an e-commerce site with online shopping integrated with its stores. The company's operating margins are improving due to lower costs.

Officers and directors own 5.6 percent of the stock. The company started paying dividends in 1989, raising them on average 26 percent a year for this Dow component.

## Annual Dividend Payment Per Share 1989–2000

Current yield on original 1989 investment 18%
Average annual dividend growth 26%
Total dividend growth 1,500%

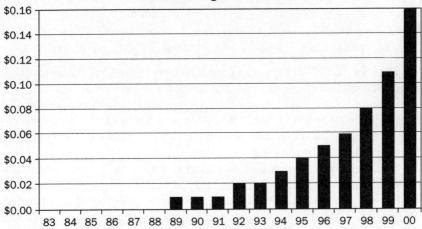

In 1989 one share of Home Depot cost $0.90 and the dividend payment was $0.01 a share. By 2000 the dividend payment had risen to $0.16 a share; that is an 18 percent yield on the dollars invested in Home Depot in 1989. The yield went from 1.1 percent to 18 percent over twelve years.

## Annual Share Price 1983–2000

Average annual share price appreciation 54%
Total share price appreciation 26,820%

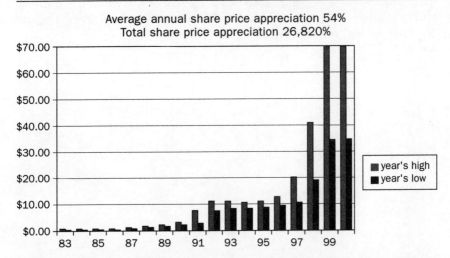

The share price of Home Depot went from $0.26 in 1983 to $70 in 2000. The dollars invested in Home Depot in 1983 appreciated 26,820 percent in eighteen years.

# ILLINOIS TOOL WORKS, INC.
## ITW (NY)

*Share Price: $57*                    *Yield: 1.4%*

*P/E: 19*                             *Dividend Payment per Share:*
                                     *$0.76*

*Market Cap: $16 Billion (Large Cap)*   *Industry: Metal Fabricating*

*Return on Share Equity: 18%*         *Operating Margin: 20.5%*

Illinois Tool Works, Inc. is an old-line industrial company that manufactures components and fasteners for many industries, such as automobiles, construction, machinery, bottling, food processing, and many specialty applications. No matter how computerized society becomes, these solid metal components will be needed and likely will be supplied by this company.

Illinois Tool has subsidiaries and affiliates in thirty-four countries. International sales account for 34 percent of the company's total sales. This wide geographic diversification and product-line diversification will serve ITW well. Northern Trust (another company in this sample portfolio) owns slightly less than 14% of Illinois Tool. Insiders own a little over 13.5 percent of the common stock, a good sign for us outsiders. ITW's operating margin has been improving the past ten years and is now at 20.5 percent. The company uses its cash to acquire new companies, which adds to revenues and will eventually expand margins once cost-cutting measures are implemented. Through these small- to medium-sized acquisitions ITW has maintained a steady rate of growth. The company has raised its dividend annually the past thirty-eight years. Dividend increases have averaged 14 percent a year for the past eighteen years.

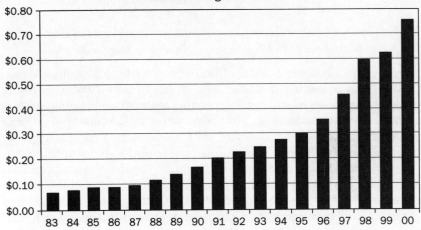

### Annual Dividend Payment Per Share 1983–2000

Current yield on original 1983 investment 32%
Average annual dividend growth 14%
Total dividend growth 990%

In 1983 one share of Illinois Tool Works cost $2.40 and the dividend payment was $0.07 a share. By 2000 the dividend payment had risen to $0.76 a share; that is a 32 percent yield on the dollars invested in Illinois Tool Works in 1983. The yield went from 3 percent to 32 percent over eighteen years.

### Annual Share Price 1983–2000

Average annual share price appreciation 21%
Total share price appreciation 2,780%

The share price of Illinois Tool Works went from $2.40 in 1983 to $69 in 2000. The dollars invested in Illinois Tool Works in 1983 appreciated 2,780 percent in eighteen years.

## JOHNSON & JOHNSON
## JNJ (NY)

*Share Price: $101*              *Yield: 1.3%*

*P/E: 31*                        *Dividend Payment per Share:*
                                 *$1.24*

*Market Cap: $139 Billion (Large Cap)*    *Industry: Medical Supplies*

*Return on Share Equity: 25.5%*  *Operating Margin: 28.5%*

You don't become a $139 billion company by just selling Band-Aids. JNJ is a leading manufacturer of health care products. JNJ is divided into three, roughly equal, product segments: consumer, professional, and pharmaceutical. The most visible to the public is its consumer division, which makes and sells products for first aid, hygiene, baby care, and toiletries. The professional supplies division sells dental supplies, surgical dressings and supplies, wound closure products, angiography catheters, monitoring equipment, etc. to medical professionals. JNJ recently acquired a company, DePuy, which manufactures products used by surgeons to reconstruct joints, correct spinal deformities, and repair bone fractures. With an aging world population this acquisition should contribute to JNJ's growth prospects. In the near term this acquisition is going to dilute JNJ's earnings. Their third division produces and manufactures pharmaceuticals, such as antibiotics, antifungals, contraceptives, dermatologic preparations, and veterinary preparations. The pharmaceutical division has helped to improve JNJ's operating margins (28.5 percent). This division is introducing a new drug, Aciphex, for suppressing the buildup of acid in the stomach. This is a $2 billion gastrointestinal market and Aciphex will capture a part of this market. JNJ's familiar brands include Tylenol, Band-Aid, Neutrogena, Modess, Stayfree, Reach, and Benecol Spread.

Johnson & Johnson is a true blue-chip company and Dow component that has been growing steadily for years, with excellent prospects for the future. In 1999, foreign sales were about 44 percent of their total.

### Annual Dividend Payment Per Share 1983–2000

Current yield on original 1983 investment 25%
Average annual dividend growth 13%
Total dividend growth 790%

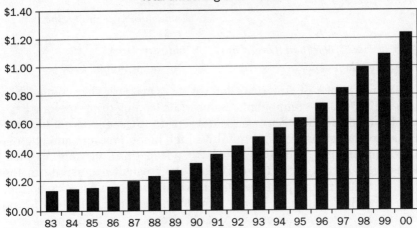

In 1983 one share of Johnson & Johnson cost $5 and the dividend payment was $0.14 a share. By 2000 the dividend payment had risen to $1.24 a share; that is a 25 percent yield on the dollars invested in Johnson & Johnson in 1983. The yield went from 2.8 percent to 25 percent over eighteen years.

### Annual Share Price 1983–2000

Average annual share price appreciation 18%
Total share price appreciation 1,960%

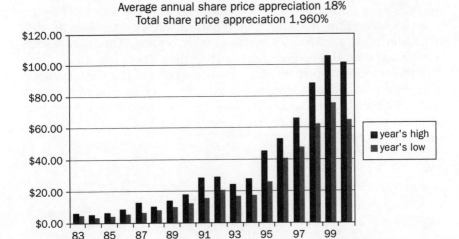

The share price of Johnson & Johnson went from $5 in 1983 to $103 in 2000. The dollars invested in Johnson & Johnson in 1983 appreciated 1,960 percent in eighteen years.

## MERCK & CO., INC.
## MRK (NY)

*Share Price: $90*

*P/E: 32*

*Market Cap: $159 Billion (Large Cap)*

*Return on Share Equity: 49%*

*Yield: 1.5%*

*Dividend Payment per Share:*
*$1.21*

*Industry: Drug*

*Operating Margin: 27%*

Merck is one of America's largest drug makers. This company is one of the 30 Dow components. Some of its leading drugs include Pepsid for ulcer disease, Zocor and Mevacor to lower blood cholesterol, Fosamax for osteoporosis, Prinivil for high blood pressure and angina, Crixivan for AIDS, and Recombivax HB, a Hepatitis B vaccine. Vasotec, Pepsid, Mevacor, and Prinivil all lose their patent exclusivity in the United States in the next few years, which will hurt Merck's bottom line. The five drugs that Merck brought to market in 1998 are lifting revenues (Aggrastat, Singulair, Maxalt, Propecia, and Cosopt). Merck received FDA approval in 1999 of Vioxx for arthritis. This drug is supposed to have greatly reduced gastrointestinal side effects and will probably replace the nonsteroidal anti-inflammatory drugs (NSAIDs). In 2000 Merck's drug sales have been driven by five drugs—Vioxx, Zocor, Cozaar/Hyzaar, Fosamax, and Singulair—which now account for 58 percent of Merck's total sales.

In 1993, during the Clinton health care scare, Merck bought Medco Containment Services, Inc., a pharmacy benefits management company. Medco distributes drugs to HMOs and large institutional buyers. Merck's ownership of Medco should help get Merck drugs into the distribution pipeline. Medco's business is expanding. This year Medco contracted with United Healthcare's 10 million lives program.

Merck does 22 percent of its business outside the United States, sales and profits. Merck's operating margins and return on equity have been climbing back up since their lows in 1993–1996. Merck has raised dividends on average 16 percent a year (1983–2000) and has paid dividends since 1935.

## Annual Dividend Payment Per Share 1983–2000

Current yield on original 1983 investment 54%
Average annual dividend growth 16%
Total dividend growth 1,410%

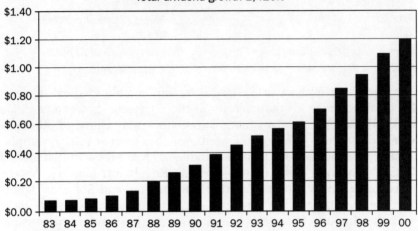

In 1983 one share of Merck cost $2.25 and the dividend payment was $0.08 a share. By 2000 the dividend payment had risen to $1.21 a share; that is a 54 percent yield on the dollars invested in Merck in 1983. The yield went from 3.5 percent to 54 percent over eighteen years.

## Annual Share Price 1983–2000

Average annual share price appreciation 23%
Total share price appreciation 4,170%

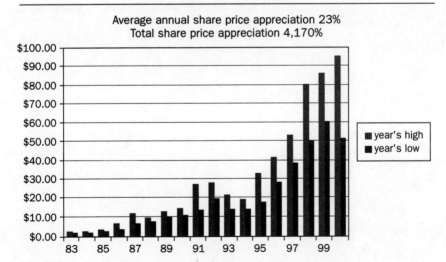

The share price of Merck went from $2.25 in 1983 to $96 in 2000. The dollars invested in Merck in 1983 appreciated 4,170 percent in eighteen years.

## MEDTRONIC, INC.
## MDT (NY)

*Share Price: $58*

*P/E: 59*

*Market Cap: $65 Billion (Large Cap)*

*Return on Share Equity: 23%*

*Yield: 0.3%*

*Dividend Payment per Share: $0.19*

*Industry: Medical Supplies*

*Operating Margin: 37.5%*

Medtronic is the world's leader in implantable medical devices. Pacemakers make up the majority of these devices; however, cardiac defibrillators, heart valves, neurostimulators, and a host of other devices add to their product mix. Medtronic has been acquiring complementary companies to expand its products. They have acquired Physio Control (external defibrillators), Midas Rex (neurosurgery), Avecor (cardiac surgery), Arterial Vascular Engineering, and Sofamor Danek. Medtronic will have the ability to offer group-purchasing plan packages that include pacemakers, internal and external defibrillators, as well as vascular and neurological surgical products. This business plan, in light of cost containment that prevails in all countries today, has produced superior profit momentum and share price appreciation for Medtronic. It has given Medtronic the competitive edge in selling more of its products, as part of a package.

Medtronic sells devices in 120 countries. International sales account for over 35 percent (33 percent of profits) of their business. The aging world population will increasingly need Medtronic's products; this can only be positive for Medtronic's bottom line.

### Annual Dividend Payment Per Share 1983–2000

Current yield on original 1983 investment 32%
Average annual dividend growth 18%
Total dividend growth 1,800%

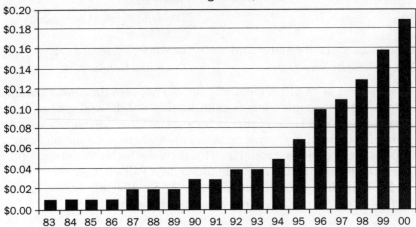

In 1983 one share of Medtronic cost $0.60 and the dividend payment was $0.01 a share. By 2000 the dividend payment had risen to $0.19 a share; that is a 32 percent yield on the dollars invested in Medtronic in 1983. The yield went from 1.6 percent to 32 percent over eighteen years.

### Annual Share Price 1983–2000

Average annual share price appreciation 29%
Total share price appreciation 9,730%

The share price of Medtronic went from $0.60 in 1983 to $59 in 2000. The dollars invested in Medtronic in 1983 appreciated 9,730 percent in eighteen years.

# PALL CORPORATION
## PLL (NY)

*Share Price: $20*                    *Yield: 3.3%*

*P/E: 17*                             *Dividend Payment per Share:*
                                      *$0.66*

*Market Cap: $2.6 Billion (Mid Cap)*    *Industry: Industrial Supply*

*Return on Share Equity: 19%*          *Operating Margin: 27%*

Pall Corp. is an old economy industrial concern that manufactures filters to remove contaminants from liquids, solids, and gasses. It is, however, part of the new economy because its filters are widely used in the manufacture of electronic components and magnetic media as well as filtration for blood products. The increase in biotechnology produced drugs needing filtration should benefit Pall's bottom line.

Pall has raised its dividend annually for the last twenty years. Fifty-four percent of Pall's business is international.

**Annual Dividend Payment Per Share 1983–2000**

Current yield on original 1983 investment 29%
Average annual dividend growth 14%
Total dividend growth 1,000%

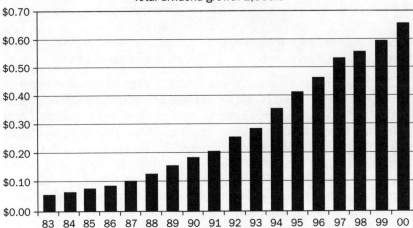

In 1983 one share of Pall cost $5.00 and the dividend payment was $0.06 a share. By 2000 the dividend payment had risen to $0.66 a share; that is a 29 percent yield on the dollars invested in Pall Corp. in 1983. The yield went from 1.2 percent to 29 percent over eighteen years.

**Annual Share Price 1983–2000**

Average annual share price appreciation 9%
Total share price appreciation 400%

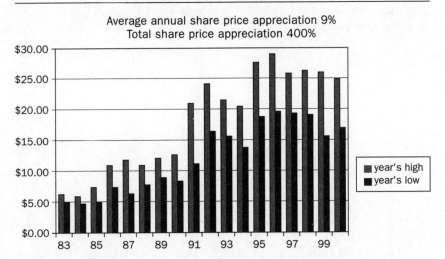

The share price of Pall Corp. went from $5.00 in 1983 to $25.00 in 2000. The dollars invested in Pall in 1983 appreciated 400 percent in eighteen years.

# PEPSICO, INC.
## PEP (NY)

Share Price: $45

P/E: 38

Market Cap: $69 Billion (Large Cap)

Return on Share Equity: 30%

Yield: 1.2%

Dividend Payment per Share: $0.56

Industry: Beverage (Soft Drinks)

Operating Margin: 20%

PepsiCo, Inc. is a beverage and snack food business. Beverages are 36 percent of Pepsi's sales and 34 percent of profits; snack foods are 64 percent of sales and 66 percent of profits. Beverages include Pepsi-Cola, Diet Pepsi, Mountain Dew, and Pepsi-One. PepsiCo recently acquired Tropicana. Snack foods produced by Frito-Lay include Doritos, Ruffles, Lay's, and the new Wow! chips. Walker Crisps and Smiths Crisps are also part of PepsiCo's snack foods division. PepsiCo has been restructuring; it recently spun off its slower growing three restaurant chains. The company sold a majority interest in its Pepsi Bottling Group, which will free up capital for acquisitions and debt reduction.

PepsiCo's international sales are 32 percent of total sales. The company's two trade names are two of the strongest in the world: Pepsi and Frito-Lay. Pepsi's share price went sideways for four years (1996–1999) while the company's restructuring was underway. In 2000 the share price trended up. Analysts are optimistic about PepsiCo's long-term growth prospects.

PepsiCo has been raising its dividend payments annually for the past twenty-nine years. The past eighteen years PepsiCo has raised its dividend on average 11 percent a year.

## Annual Dividend Payment Per Share 1983–2000

Current yield on original 1983 investment 47%
Average annual dividend growth 11%
Total dividend growth 520%

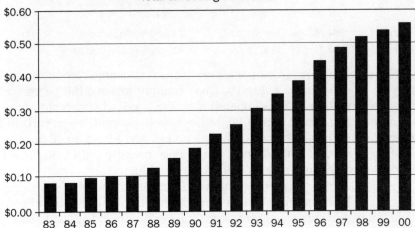

In 1983 one share of PepsiCo cost $1.20 and the dividend payment was $0.09 a share. By 2000 the dividend payment had risen to $0.56 a share; that is a 47 percent yield on the dollars invested in PepsiCo in 1983. The yield went from 7 percent to 47 percent over eighteen years.

## Annual Share Price 1983–2000

Average annual share price appreciation 23%
Total share price appreciation 3,980%

■ year's high
■ year's low

The share price of PepsiCo went from $1.20 in 1983 to $49 in 2000. The dollars invested in PepsiCo in 1983 appreciated 3,980 percent in eighteen years.

## PHILIP MORRIS COMPANIES INC.
## MO (NY)

*Share Price: $43*

*P/E: 12*

*Market Cap: $84 Billion (Large Cap)*

*Return on Share Equity: 48%*

*Yield: 4.9%*

*Dividend Payment per Share:*
*$1.97*

*Industry: Tobacco*

*Operating Margin: 20%*

The Philip Morris Companies is a leading consumer products company with four major segments. They include tobacco (60 percent of revenues and 66 percent of operating profits), foods (34 percent of revenues and 29 percent of profits), Miller beer (5 percent, 3 percent), and financial services. The major brand names are Marlboro, Benson & Hedges, Virginia Slims, Merit, Lark, Post cereals, Jell-O, Kool-Aid, Oscar Mayer, Kraft, Velveeta, and Miracle Whip.

Philip Morris is in the process of acquiring the Nabisco Group Holding. The company plans to combine Nabisco with its Kraft Foods subsidiary and spin them off as a separate entity in early 2001 to shareholders. This should increase the value of the food segment, which has been dragged down by the tobacco segment.

Despite the litigation and restrictions placed on tobacco, Philip Morris is still posting solid results. Operating margins continue to improve. The company dominates 50 percent of the U.S. cigarette market and has 60 percent market share of premium cigarettes. Philip Morris will remain under a litigation cloud which may give investors cause for concern. This company is a Dow component.

**Annual Dividend Payment Per Share 1983–2000**

Current yield on original 1983 investment 99%
Average annual dividend growth 17%
Total dividend growth 1,540%

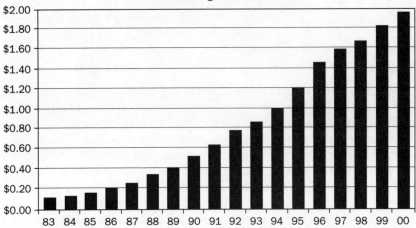

In 1983 one share of Philip Morris cost $2 and the dividend payment was $0.12 a share. By 2000 the dividend payment had risen to $1.97 a share; that is a 99 percent yield on the dollars invested in Philip Morris in 1983. The yield went from 6 percent to 99 percent over eighteen years.

**Annual Share Price 1983–2000**

Average annual share price appreciation 19%
Total share price appreciation 2,150%

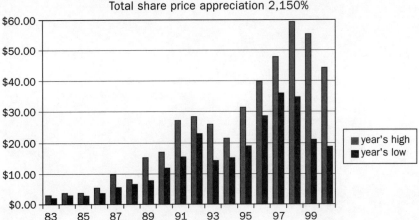

The share price of Philip Morris went from $2 in 1983 to $45 in 2000. The dollars invested in Philip Morris in 1983 appreciated 2,150 percent in eighteen years.

# PFIZER INC.
# PFE (NY)

*Share Price: $44*  *Yield: 1%*

*P/E: 47*  *Dividend Payment per Share: $0.36*

*Market Cap: $278 Billion (Large Cap)*  *Industry: Drug*

*Return on Share Equity: 38.5%*  *Operating Margin: 33.5%*

Pfizer is one of the world's premier pharmaceutical companies. The company is in the process of merging with Warner-Lambert. The combined companies have a blockbuster-laden product portfolio. Pfizer has eight drugs that are billion-dollar-plus sellers. These drugs include Lipitor, Norvasc, Viagra, Neurontin, and Celebrex. Other drugs in their armamentarium include the antibiotic Zithromax, Aricept for Alzheimer's disease, Zoloft for depression, Diflucan as an antifungal agent, the antihistamine Zyrtec, and Ben-Gay for rub-on pain relief. Pfizer also has a new broadspectrum antibiotic, Trovan, that is off to a promising start. Pfizer recently launched drugs for treatment of atrial fibrillation (Tikosyn) and migraines (Relpax), and an antipsychotic drug (Zeldox). Pfizer probably has the most visible and healthiest pipeline in the industry. Pfizer also has an active animal health division.

About 39 percent of Pfizer's sales and operating profits are from 150 foreign countries, mostly in Europe, Asia, and Latin America. Pfizer has been raising dividends for the last thirty-three years. Dividends were raised on average 12 percent a year (1983–2000).

### Annual Dividend Payment Per Share 1983–2000

Current yield on original 1983 investment 27%
Average annual dividend growth 12%
Total dividend growth 620%

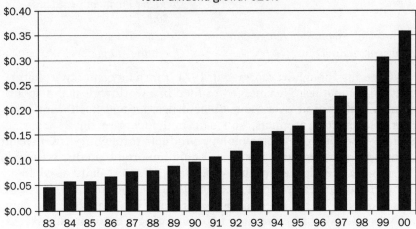

In 1983 one share of Pfizer cost $1.34 and the dividend payment was $0.05 a share. By 2000 the dividend payment had risen to $0.36 a share; that is a 27 percent yield on the dollars invested in Pfizer in 1983. The yield went from 1 percent to 27 percent over eighteen years.

### Annual Share Price 1983–2000

Average annual share price appreciation 22%
Total share price appreciation 3,560%

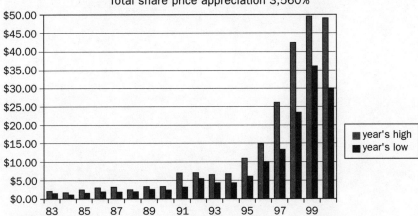

The share price of Pfizer went from $1.34 in 1983 to $49 in 2000. The dollars invested in Pfizer in 1983 appreciated 3,560 percent in eighteen years.

## SCHERING-PLOUGH CORP.
## SGP (NY)

*Share Price: $56*

*P/E: 36*

*Market Cap: $64 Billion (Large Cap)*

*Return on Share Equity: 40.5%*

*Yield: 1%*

*Dividend Payment per Share: $0.55*

*Industry: Drug*

*Operating Margin: 34.5%*

Schering-Plough was formed in 1971 from a merger of two pharmaceutical companies. This merger resulted in a worldwide manufacturer of prescription and over-the-counter drugs, animal healthcare products, vision care products, sun care and foot care lines. Schering-Plough manufactures biotechnology products through its 100 percent owned DNAX Research Institute. Their important products include Claritin for allergies, Proventil, Vancenase, Nasonex daily nasal spray, Coppertone sunscreens, and Dr. Scholl's foot-care products. Rebetron was approved for treatment of hepatitis C and is a big seller. The company is planning to introduce two new drugs, one for asthma, Asmanex, and a second-generation Claritin.

Foreign business accounts for about 36 percent of Schering-Plough's total sales. Schering-Plough has raised its dividend on average 14 percent annually (1983–2000).

## Annual Dividend Payment Per Share 1983–2000

Current yield on original 1983 investment 46%
Average annual dividend growth 14%
Total dividend growth 1,000%

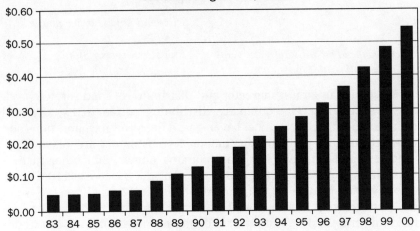

In 1983 one share of Schering-Plough cost $1.20 and the dividend payment was $0.05 a share. By 2000 the dividend payment had risen to $0.55 a share; that is a 46 percent yield on the dollars invested in Schering-Plough in 1983. The yield went from 4 percent to 46 percent over eighteen years.

## Annual Share Price 1983–2000

Average annual share price appreciation 24%
Total share price appreciation 4,730%

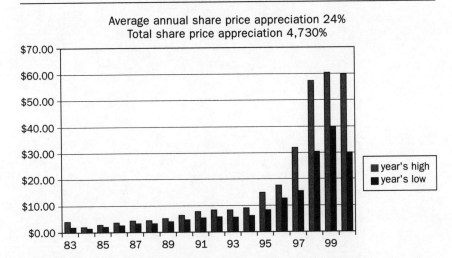

The share price of Schering-Plough went from $1.20 in 1983 to $60 in 2000. The dollars invested in Schering-Plough in 1983 appreciated 4,730 percent in eighteen years.

# SYSCO CORPORATION
## SYY (NY)

Share Price: $28                        Yield: 0.5%

P/E: 38                                 Dividend Payment per Share:
                                        $0.24

Market Cap: $17.2 Billion (Large Cap)   Industry: Grocery Store

Return on Share Equity: 25.8%           Operating Margin: 6%

Sysco is the largest marketer and distributor of food-service products in America. The company distributes entrée items, dry and
canned foods, fresh produce, beverages, dairy products, and non-food
products to over 300,000 customers. Its customers are restaurants,
schools, hotels, motels, hospitals, nursing homes, and other institutions throughout the United States and Canada. Sysco has 118 distribution service centers in the United States and 7 in Canada. Sysco's
sales are growing. Sysco has an extensive infrastructure (service centers and semi-trucks), and they are enlarging and improving their sales
force to boost sales and margins.

Sysco has raised its dividend payments annually for twenty-four
consecutive years. Dividend payments have been increased on average
19 percent a year (1983–2000). If Sysco continues to raise its dividend
at about 20 percent annually, the dividend yield will double every 3.8
years.

**Annual Dividend Payment Per Share 1983–2000**

Current yield on original 1983 investment 25%
Average annual dividend growth 19%
Total dividend growth 2,300%

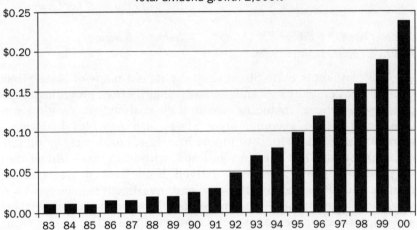

In 1983 one share of Sysco cost $0.95 and the dividend payment was $0.01 a share. By 2000 the dividend payment had risen to $0.24 a share; that is a 25 percent yield on the dollars invested in Sysco in 1983. The yield went from 1 percent to 25 percent over eighteen years.

**Annual Share Price 1983–2000**

Average annual share price appreciation 21%
Total share price appreciation 2,850%

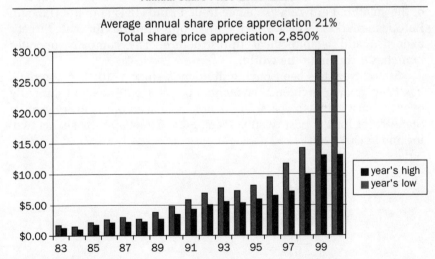

The share price of Sysco went from $0.95 in 1983 to $28 in 2000. The dollars invested in Sysco in 1983 appreciated 2,850 percent in eighteen years.

## STATE STREET CORP.
## STT (NY)

Share Price: $121                                Yield: 0.6%

P/E: 29                                          Dividend Payment per Share:
                                                 $0.66

Market Cap: $19.5 Billion (Large Cap)            Industry: Banking

Return on Share Equity: 19.5%

You may know State Street Corp. by its old name of State Street Boston. The company's revenues come primarily from providing financial asset services, including accounting, custody, information services, and record keeping. State Street also provides investment management services to institutional investors, businesses, and financial institutions. The company has $6.2 trillion in assets under custody. State Street's income is derived from fees on assets under management. Fees from institutional and investment management services now account for 76 percent of State Street's noninterest income and 55 percent of the company's revenues. State Street is benefiting from new trends that are sweeping through the new global economy. Many countries are privatizing their government retirement plans and State Street is managing those funds. Overseas investors are increasingly contributing to mutual funds, and mutual funds are turning to State Street for outsourcing services. State Street handles the back office administrative duties for asset management firms, including PIMCO, Merrill Lynch, and Scottish Widows. STT manages $30 billion of the small but growing exchange-traded funds (ETFs) in the U.S. and European markets. These are all growth opportunities for State Street's expertise and technological infrastructure. The company operates branches throughout the world.

State Street has been paying dividends since 1910. The company has been raising dividend payments on average 14 percent annually over the past eighteen years. Dividends have been raised every year by State Street for the past twenty years. State Street split its shares two-for-one in early 2001.

**Annual Dividend Payment Per Share 1983–2000**

Current yield on original 1983 investment 41%
Average annual dividend growth 14%
Total dividend growth 1,000%

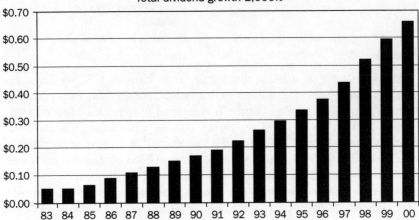

In 1983 one share of State Street cost $1.60 and the dividend payment was $0.06 a share. By 2000 the dividend payment had risen to $0.66 a share; that is a 41 percent yield on the dollars invested in State Street in 1983. The yield went from 3.7 percent 41 percent over eighteen years.

**Annual Share Price 1983–2000**

Average annual share price appreciation 28%
Total share price appreciation 8,400%

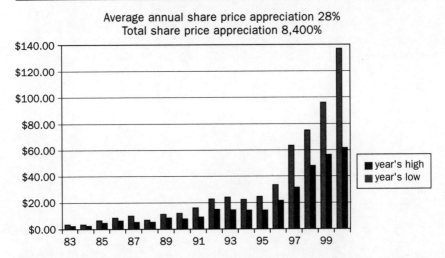

The share price of State Street went from $1.60 in 1983 to $136 in 2000. The dollars invested in State Street in 1983 appreciated 8,400 percent in eighteen years.

## TOOTSIE ROLL INDUSTRIES, INC.
## TR (NY)

*Share Price: $46*

*P/E: 30*

*Market Cap: $1.9 Billion (Mid Cap)*

*Return on Share Equity: 17%*

*Yield: 0.6%*

*Dividend Payment per Share: $0.27*

*Industry: Food Processing*

*Operating Margin: 30%*

Tootsie Roll is still making candy that kids love. They have expanded their line of products to include: Tootsie Roll Pops, Tootsie Bubble Pops, Tootsie Pop Drops, Tootsie Roll Flavor Rolls, Mason Dots, Junior Mints, Sugar Daddies, Sugar Babies, Charleston Chews, Pom Poms, Charms, and Blow Pops. TR has started selling in international markets, primarily in Canada and Mexico, which accounted for 8 percent of sales and 3 percent of profits. TR has had double-digit growth due to its well-received products, sales promotions, and cost controls. The company's operating margin has been improving steadily over the past ten years.

Officers and directors control 70 percent of the voting stock. TR has raised its dividend annually for the past thirty-seven years. The past eighteen years the company raised its dividend an average 16 percent every year.

---

**Annual Dividend Payment Per Share 1983–2000**

---

Current yield on original 1983 investment 36%
Average annual dividend growth 16%
Total dividend growth 1,250%

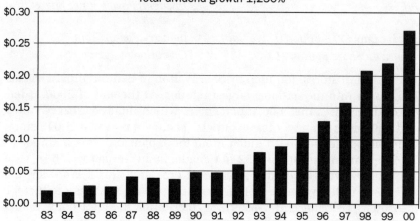

In 1983 one share of Tootsie Roll Industries cost $0.75 and the dividend payment was $0.02 a share. By 2000 the dividend payment had risen to $0.27 a share; that is a 36 percent yield on the dollars invested in Tootsie Roll in 1983. The yield went from 2.6 percent to 36 percent over eighteen years.

---

**Annual Share Price 1983–2000**

---

Average annual share price appreciation 25%
Total share price appreciation 5,500%

■ year's high
■ year's low

The share price of Tootsie Roll Industries went from $0.75 in 1983 to $42 in 2000. The dollars invested in Tootsie Roll in 1983 appreciated 5,500 percent in eighteen years.

# WAL-MART STORES
## WMT (NY)

*Share Price: $53*                    *Yield: 0.5%*

*P/E: 30*                             *Dividend Payment per Share:*
                                      *$0.23*

*Market Cap: $218 Billion (Large Cap)*   *Industry: Retail Store*

*Return on Share Equity: 21%*         *Operating Margin: 6.6%*

Wal-Mart stores, founded by Sam Walton in Bentonville, Arkansas, has grown into the nation's largest retailer. At the end of 2000, it had 1,723 discount stores, 866 supercenters which include grocery stores, and 469 Sam's Club wholesale outlets. There are now over 1,045 stores in foreign countries, with much room for expansion. This includes 13 in Argentina, 14 in Brazil, 152 in Canada, 95 in Germany, 416 in Mexico, 14 in Puerto Rico, and 4 each in Korea and China. Wal-Mart has about 380 million square feet of floor space to fill with its products. It also owns McLane and Western, a distributor to small convenience stores and groceries. Wal-Mart is planning to open 150 new supercenters a year, outpacing its domestic competition.

Wal-Mart owes much of its success to the distribution system set up by Sam Walton. All stores are within 450 miles of one of Wal-Mart's distribution centers, which use computers to keep inventories up to date. Officers and directors own 40 percent of the common stock, a great benefit for the rest of the shareholders. Return on shareholder equity is on the rise again; it bottomed out at 17 percent in 1996. Wal-Mart appears to have its supercenter and international expansion learning curve behind it. Wal-Mart has raised its dividend an average 24 percent annually over the past eighteen years. This company is a recent addition to the Dow.

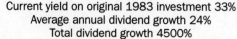

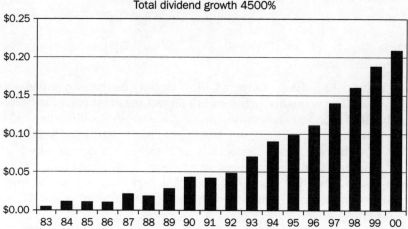

In 1983 one share of Wal-Mart cost $0.70 and the dividend payment was $0.005 a share. By 2000 the dividend payment had risen to $0.23 a share; that is a 33 percent yield on the dollars invested in Wal-Mart in 1983. The yield went from 0.7 percent to 33 percent over eighteen years.

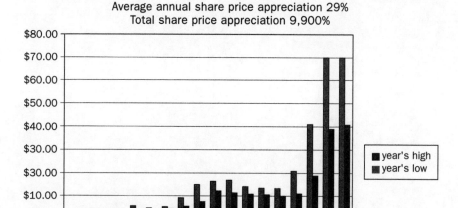

The share price of Wal-Mart went from $0.70 in 1983 to $70 in 2000. The dollars invested in Wal-Mart in 1983 appreciated 9,900 percent in eighteen years.

# WILMINGTON TRUST CORP.
## WL (NY)

*Share Price: $60*

*P/E: 18*

*Market Cap: $1.7 Billion (Mid Cap)*

*Return on Share Equity: 22%*

*Yield: 3.0%*

*Dividend Payment per Share: $1.77*

*Industry: Banking*

Wilmington Trust Corp. is the largest banking company in Delaware. The company is the eighth largest personal trust institution with $26 billion in assets under custody in sixty-five offices located in five eastern states. Wilmington Trust Corp. has recently affiliated with two investment advisory firms in New York and California which are contributing to its asset management income. Noninterest income (fees from individual and corporate financial services) is growing more rapidly than income from interest income, now accounting for 47 percent of revenues.

Officers and directors own 7.5 percent of the common stock. The company started paying dividends in 1914. Dividend payments were raised on average 13 percent a year (1983–2000).

### Annual Dividend Payment Per Share 1983–2000

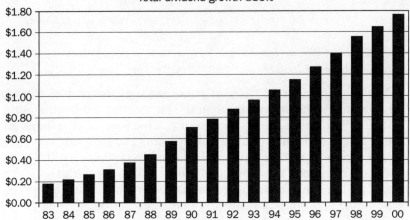

Current yield on original 1983 investment 44%
Average annual dividend growth 13%
Total dividend growth 830%

In 1983 one share of Wilmington Trust cost $4 and the dividend payment was $0.19 a share. By 2000 the dividend payment had risen to $1.77 a share; that is a 44 percent yield on the dollars invested in Wilmington trust in 1983. The yield went from 4 percent to 44 percent over eighteen years.

### Annual Share Price 1983–2000

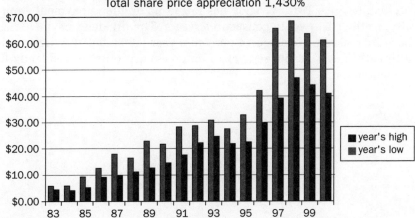

Average annual share price appreciation 16%
Total share price appreciation 1,430%

The share price of Wilmington Trust went from $4 in 1983 to $61 in 2000. The dollars invested in Wilmington Trust in 1983 appreciated 1,430 percent in eighteen years.

## WM. WRIGLEY JR. COMPANY
## WWY (NY)

Share Price: $93                        Yield: 1.5%

P/E: 33                                 Dividend Payment per Share:
                                        $1.40

Market Cap: $91 Billion (Large Cap)     Industry: Food Processing

Return on Share Equity: 27%             Operating Margin: 24.5%

Wrigley is the world's largest gum manufacturer and distributor. The company's name brands include Doublemint, Spearmint, Juicy Fruit, Big Red, Winterfresh, Extra, Orbit, Freedent, Bubble Tape, Big League Chew, and Hubba Bubba bubble gum. The company is gaining revenues from its new products Eclipse and Extra Polar Ice. The company has announced the formation of a new division, Wrigley Healthcare. It will produce chewing gums that have a medicinal effect. The first product is Surpass, an antacid in pellet gum form.

This company has no debt. International sales and profits account for 59 percent of the company's total. International business has been mixed, sales have been strong in Eastern and Central Europe, and China. Combined sales in Europe and the Asia/Pacific region advanced 15 percent in year over year comparison. A significant dependence on foreign sales makes revenue projections difficult due to volatile currency-translation effects.

The president and CEO, William Wrigley, owns 21 percent of common and 55 percent of Class B stock. The Offield Family owns 4 percent of common and 13 percent of Class B stock. Wrigley has paid dividends since 1913. Wrigley has raised its dividend payment annually for the past twenty consecutive years. The dividend payment has been increased on average 14 percent a year (1983–2000). Wrigley traditionally pays out 50 percent of annual net profits in dividends to shareholders.

### Annual Dividend Payment Per Share 1983–2000

Current yield on original 1983 investment 64%
Average annual dividend growth 14%
Total dividend growth 900%

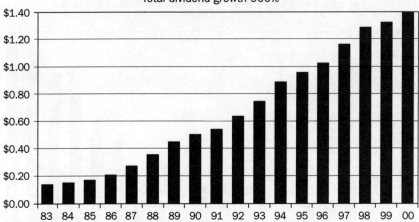

In 1983 one share of Wrigley cost $2.20 and the dividend payment was $0.14 a share. By 2000 the dividend payment had risen to $1.40 a share; that is a 64 percent yield on the dollars invested in Wrigley in 1983. The yield went from 7 percent to 64 percent over eighteen years.

### Annual Share Price 1983–2000

Average annual share price appreciation 23%
Total share price appreciation 4,080%

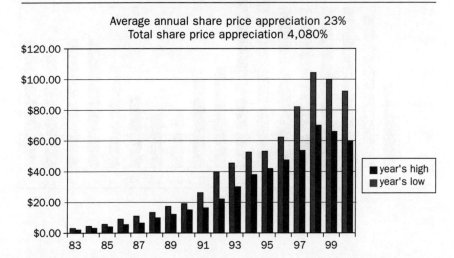

The share price of Wrigley went from $2.20 in 1983 to $94 in 2000. The dollars invested in Wrigley in 1983 appreciated 4,080 percent in eighteen years.

Dividend histories of two companies, Caterpillar, Inc. and General Motors, which have *not* shown steady dividend increase.

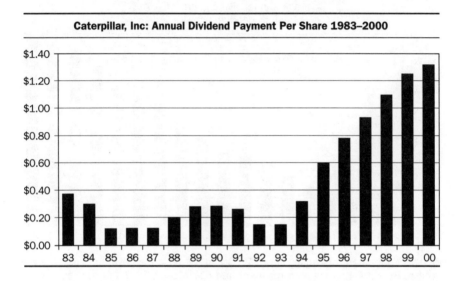

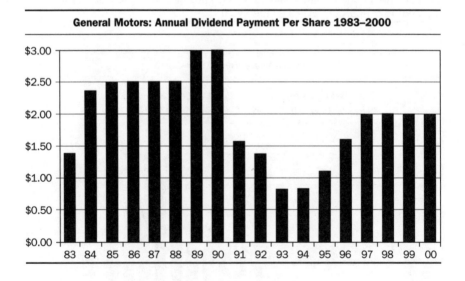

# Additional Work Horses

*Low Initial Yield, but Fast-Growing Dividends*

# ALBERTSON'S, INC.
## ABS (NY)

*Share Price: 25*

*P/E: 13*

*Market Cap: $10 Billion (Large Cap)*

*Return on Share Equity: 15.5%*

*Yield: 3.3%*

*Dividend Payment per Share: $0.76*

*Industry: Grocery Store*

*Operating Margin: 7.7%*

Albertson's is one of the largest retail food-drug chain in the U.S. The company operates over 2,500 retail grocery stores and drug stores in 36 states. Albertson's has been expanding rapidly through acquisitions: Seesel's (10 stores); Smitty's (10 stores); Bruno's (14 stores); Buttrey (29 stores); and a mega-merger with American Stores that created an industry of 1,800 grocery stores and 750 drug stores. This mega-merger has more than doubled sales, which approach $37 billion a year. These mergers have created some upheaval with Albertson's earnings and share price. Albertson's share price has tumbled from its 1998 highs of $66 a share, creating a value stock. The grocery industry has become a very competitive business. The company operates stores in three different formats: combination food and drug; conventional; warehouse. The combination food and drug stores contain grocery, general merchandise, meat and produce, pharmacy, bakery, and lobby floral and video. The warehouse stores are full-line, mass merchandise markets. All retail stores are supported by twenty-two distribution centers.

Officers and directors own 2.3 percent of stock. Albertson's has raised its dividend annually for the past consecutive twenty-seven years. Albertson's has raised dividend payments on average 13 percent a year (1983–2000).

## Annual Dividend Payment Per Share 1983–2000

Current yield on original 1983 investment 30%
Average annual dividend growth 13%
Total dividend growth 850%

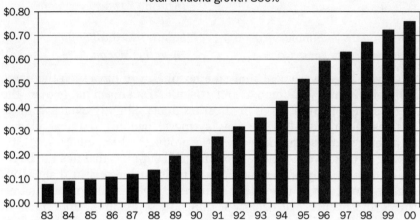

In 1983 one share of Albertson's cost $2.50 and the dividend payment was $0.08 a share. By 2000 the dividend payment had risen to $0.76 a share; that is a 30 percent yield on the dollars invested in Albertson's in 1983. The yield went from 3 percent to 30 percent over eighteen years.

## Annual Share Price 1983–2000

Average annual share price appreciation 17%
Total share price appreciation 1,460%

| | year's high |
| | year's low |

The share price of Albertson's went from $2.50 in 1983 to $39 in 2000. The dollars invested in Albertson's in 1983 appreciated 1,460 percent in eighteen years.

## BECTON, DICKINSON & COMPANY
## BDX (NY)

*Share Price: $32*

*P/E: 22*

*Market Cap: $8.6 Billion (Large Cap)*

*Return on Share Equity: 20%*

*Yield: 1.2%*

*Dividend Payment per Share: $0.37*

*Industry: Medical Supplies*

*Operating Margin: 22%*

If you have ever spent time in a hospital, you have seen the name BD ubiquitously scattered about. Becton, Dickinson is one of the world's largest suppliers of medical products. Slightly over half of its business is in supplies such as syringes, needles, surgical blades, catheters, suction equipment, elastic products, thermometers, elastic gloves; in other words, the numerous small supplies that need to be re-ordered constantly. The remainder of their business is in diagnostics such as blood and microbiology analysis. BD is focusing on making syringes and needles with safety features; these features add value and contribute to wider operating margins. I can confirm that health care professionals will pay a premium for those safety features to avoid exposure to hepatitis, HIV, and other diseases carried in body fluids.

Becton, Dickinson has almost half of its sales in foreign markets. There should be tremendous potential growth for BD's products in emerging markets. Many of these countries do not have disposable needles, surgical blades, and other medical supplies. They have used and reused these items over and over.

Officers and directors own 6.2 percent of common shares, a healthy percentage for a large-cap company.

**Annual Dividend Payment Per Share 1983–2000**

Current yield on original 1983 investment 18%
Average annual dividend growth 10%
Total dividend growth 430%

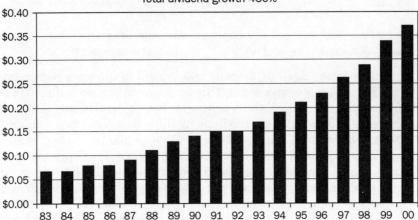

In 1983 one share of Becton, Dickinson cost $2.10 and the dividend payment was $0.07 a share. By 2000 the dividend payment had risen to $0.37 a share; that is an 18 percent yield on the dollars invested in Becton, Dickinson in 1983. The yield went from 3 percent to 18 percent over eighteen years.

**Annual Share Price 1983–2000**

Average annual share price appreciation 17%
Total share price appreciation 1,520%

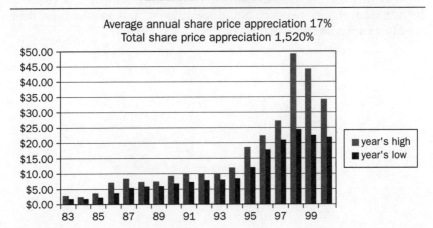

The share price of Becton, Dickinson went from $2.10 in 1983 to $34 in 2000. The dollars invested in Becton, Dickinson in 1983 appreciated 1,520 percent in eighteen years.

## BRISTOL-MYERS SQUIBB COMPANY
## BMY (NY)

*Share Price: $68*                              *Yield: 1.6%*

*P/E: 30*                                        *Dividend Payment per Share:*
                                                 *$0.98*

*Market Cap: $102 Billion (Large Cap)*           *Industry: Drug*

*Return on Share Equity: 49.5%*                  *Operating Margin: 35.5%*

Bristol-Myers Squibb Company was formed in 1989 by a merger between its two large components. This company sells a wide line of prescription pharmaceuticals and consumer health care, beauty aid, and nutritional products. These products include: Ban deodorant, Bufferin aspirin compounds, Clairol and Herbal Essence hair products, Exedrin for pain relief, Isovue intravenous X-Ray contrast agent. Drugs showing promise are Lanoteplase for blood clot dissolution, Omapatirlat for high blood pressure, Pravachol for lowering cholesterol, Glucophage for diabetes. Other drugs include BuSpar, Capoten, Comtrex, Taxol, VePesid, Videx. Bristol-Myers has signed an agreement with Dura Pharmaceuticals to distribute its Maxipime and Azaxtam drugs, which are for combating infectious disease.

Bristol-Myers Squibb does about 31 percent of its business in foreign markets. In November 1998 the company announced that, after spending $3 billion on breast-implant litigation and settlements over eight years, its liability had finally ended. This is good news for shareholders in many ways. This will free up cash for raising dividends, buying back shares, research and development, and acquisitions. Bristol-Myers split its stock two for one March 1, 1999.

### Annual Dividend Payment Per Share 1983–2000

Current yield on original 1983 investment 20%
Average annual dividend growth 10%
Total dividend growth 480%

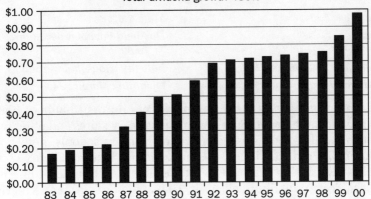

In 1983 one share of Bristol-Myers Squibb cost $5 and the dividend payment was $0.17 a share. By 2000 the dividend payment had risen to $0.98 a share; that is a 20 percent yield on the dollars invested in Bristol-Myers in 1983. The yield went from 4 percent to 20 percent over eighteen years.

### Annual Share Price 1983–2000

Average annual share price appreciation 16%
Total share price appreciation 1,340%

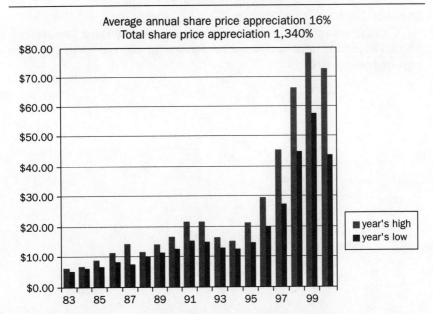

The share price of Bristol-Myers Squibb Co. went from $5 in 1983 to $72 in 2000. The dollars invested in Bristol-Myers in 1983 appreciated 1,340 percent over eighteen years.

# CLOROX CO.
# CLX (NY)

| | |
|---|---|
| *Share Price: $32* | *Yield 2.6%* |
| *P/E: 19* | *Dividend Payment per Share: $0.80* |
| *Market Cap: $9.2 Billion (Large Cap)* | *Industry: Household Products* |
| *Return on Share Equity: 23.4%* | *Operating Margin: 24%* |

Clorox Company is a leading producer and distributor of household products. Their products are sold to grocery stores and other retail outlets as well as food service customers such as schools, hotels, and restaurants. Products include Clorox liquid bleach, Clorox 2 dry bleach, Clorox Pre-Wash, Clorox Detergent, Formula 409 spray cleanser, Soft Scrub liquid cleanser, Tilex, Pine-Sol cleaners, Kingsford charcoal briquets, Match Light, BBQ Bag Charcoal, Hidden Valley Ranch salad dressing, Fresh Step cat litter, Combat and Black Flag insecticides, Liquid-Plumber, K.C. Masterpiece barbecue sauce, Brita water filtration systems, and Armor All auto appearance products. Clorox has recently acquired First Brands, which will increase its annual sales by over a billion dollars, making Clorox a market leader in cat litter, automotive treatment products, and plastic bags. Consumer demand is strong for Clorox products and it has recently launched new products (Rain Clean Pine-Sol, Lemon Fresh Pine-Sol, Tilex Fresh Shower).

Clorox has raised its dividend annually for the past twenty-four years. Dividends have increased on average 11 percent a year over the past eighteen years.

**Annual Dividend Payment Per Share 1983–2000**

Current yield on original 1983 investment 31%
Average annual dividend growth 11%
Total dividend growth 570%

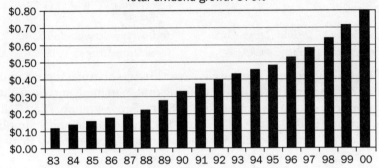

In 1983 one share of Clorox cost $2.55 and the dividend payment was $0.12 a share. By 2000 the dividend payment had risen to $0.80 a share; that is a 31 percent yield on the dollars invested in Clorox in 1983. The yield went from 4.7 percent to 31 percent over eighteen years.

**Annual Share Price 1983–2000**

Average annual share price appreciation 19%
Total share price appreciation 2,100%

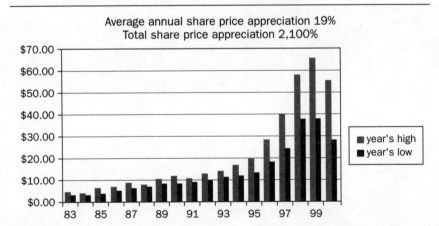

The share price of Clorox went from $2.55 in 1983 to $56 in 2000. The dollars invested in Clorox in 1983 appreciated 2,100 percent in eighteen years.

## COLGATE-PALMOLIVE COMPANY
## CL (NY)

*Share Price: $60*                           *Yield: 1.1%*
*P/E: 36*                                     *Dividend Payment per Share:*
                                             *$0.59*
*Market Cap: $27 Billion (Large Cap)*        *Industry: Household Products*
*Return on Share Equity: 51.5%*              *Operating Margin: 22.5%*

Colgate-Palmolive Company is a worldwide manufacturer and distributor of consumer products, including oral, personal, and household care products. Brand names are Fresh Start, Fab, Dynamo, Ajax, Palmolive, Colgate and Ultra Brite toothpastes, Irish Spring and Palmolive soaps, Colgate shave cream, Hill's and Science Diet pet food, Princess House crystal, and Mennen deodorant products.

International sales account for 72 percent of the company's sales and profits. Colgate's strong domestic performance has offset revenue declines in Latin America, Europe, Asia, and Africa. Colgate continues to grow market share in emerging markets.

Colgate-Palmolive has raised dividends on average 8 percent a year for the past eighteen years. The company has raised dividends for the past thirty-eight consecutive years. Colgate-Palmolive has paid dividends since 1895.

### Annual Dividend Payment Per Share 1983–2000

Current yield on original 1983 investment 25%
Average annual dividend growth 8%
Total dividend growth 270%

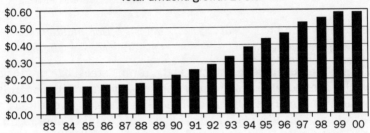

In 1983 one share of Colgate-Palmolive cost $2.35 and the dividend payment was $0.16 a share. By 2000 the dividend payment had risen to $0.59 a share; that is a 25 percent yield on the dollars invested in Colgate-Palmolive in 1983. The yield went from 6 percent to 25 percent over eighteen years.

### Annual Share Price 1983–2000

Average annual share price appreciation 20%
Total share price appreciation 2,710%

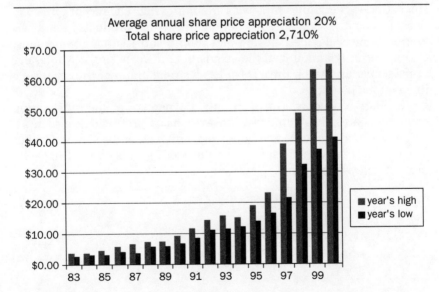

The share price of Colgate-Palmolive went from $2.35 in 1983 to $66 in 2000. The dollars invested in Colgate-Palmolive in 1983 appreciated 2,710 percent in eighteen years.

## COOPER TIRE & RUBBER COMPANY
## CTB (NY)

| | |
|---|---|
| *Share Price: $11* | *Yield: 4%* |
| *P/E: 6* | *Dividend Payment per Share: $0.42* |
| *Market Cap: $700 Million (Small Cap)* | *Industry: Tires and Rubber* |
| *Return on Share Equity: 11.5%* | *Operating Margin: 13.5%* |

Cooper Tire & Rubber Company is the ninth-largest tire producer in the world. Most of its revenues are derived from tire sales, mainly in the replacement market. One half of the tires are sold under their own name and the Falls tire name. The rest are sold to other manufacturers to market under their private brand names; about half are sold to GM. One of Cooper's largest customers is Sears. Cooper Tire has had several rough years with earnings down, contracting operating margins and return on equity. Sears reduced its orders of replacement tires in 1998, and the GM strike hurt Cooper's revenues. Cooper Tire, despite its recent earnings set back, has continued to raise its dividends on average 14 percent a year. Cooper's shareholders have continued to benefit from growing dividends, even though the share price has declined significantly. Cooper has bought back nearly 3 million shares of common stock. Cooper's earnings prospects are improving. The recent Firestone debacle may help Cooper Tire's bottom line. Other products include vibration control devices, hosing and tubing and seating components. Cooper recently announced the acquisition of Dean Tire, a wholesaler of passenger and truck tires. Dean has a strong brand of tires that sells in about ten countries.

Insiders of Cooper Tire own only 1.5 percent of the outstanding common shares. The company, however, has a profit-sharing plan for employees that accounts for about 9 percent of all of the shares. Cooper Tire may currently be considered a value stock as it is now selling at 30 percent below book value.

### Annual Dividend Payment Per Share 1983–2000

Current yield on original 1983 investment 28%
Average annual dividend growth 14%
Total dividend growth 950%

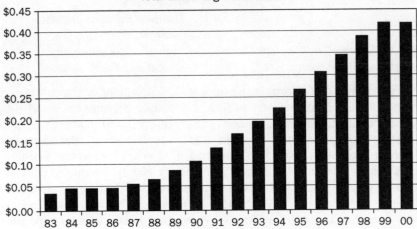

In 1983 one share of Cooper Tire cost $1.50 and the dividend payment was $0.04 a share. By 2000 the dividend payment had risen to $0.42 a share; that is a 28 percent yield on the dollars invested in Cooper Tire in 1983. The yield went from 2.6 percent to 28 percent over eighteen years.

### Annual Share Price 1983–2000

Average annual share price appreciation 14%
Total share price appreciation 970%

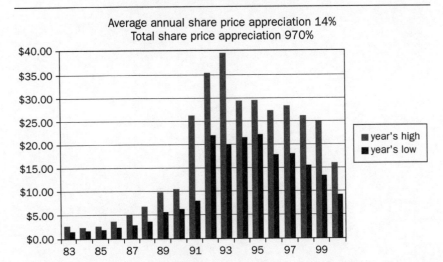

The share price of Cooper Tire went from $1.50 in 1983 to $16 in 2000. The dollars invested in Cooper Tire in 1983 appreciated 970 percent in eighteen years.

## HERSHEY FOODS CORPORATION
## HSY (NY)

| | |
|---|---|
| *Share Price: $62* | *Yield: 1.8%* |
| *P/E: 27* | *Dividend Payment per Share: $1.08* |
| *Market Cap: $7.5 Billion (Large Cap)* | *Industry: Food Processing* |
| *Return on Share Equity: 27%* | *Operating Margin: 18%* |

Hershey Foods Corp. is the largest U.S. producer of chocolate and nonchocolate confectionery products. Hershey produces a broad line of chocolate, confectionery, and pasta products that includes chocolate candies, cocoa, baking chocolate, and chocolate syrup. Brand names include Hershey's, Reese's, Peter Paul, Luden's, Life Savers, Planters, San Giorgio, Ronzoni, and American Beauty. Hershey acquired the U.S. confectionery business of Cadbury Schweppes. Hershey's chocolate business is growing faster than the confectionery business, due to Hershey's ability to come out with new products (Taste Tations hard candies and Hershey's Sweet Escapes, reduced fat and calorie chocolate bars).

Hershey Trust Co. owns 11.4 percent of common stock and 99.5 percent of class B shares. Hershey has raised dividend payments annually for twenty-six consecutive years. Dividend payments have been raised on average 11 percent a year (1983–2000).

### Annual Dividend Payment Per Share 1983–2000

Current yield on original 1983 investment 27%
Average annual dividend growth 11%
Total dividend growth 500%

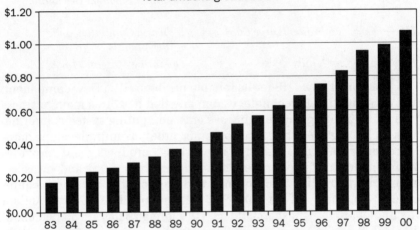

In 1983 one share of Hershey cost $4 and the dividend payment was $0.18 a share. By 2000 the dividend payment had risen to $1.08 a share; that is a 27 percent yield on the dollars invested in Hershey in 1983. The yield went from 4.5 percent to 27 percent over eighteen years.

### Annual Share Price 1983–2000

Average annual share price appreciation 17%
Total share price appreciation 1,530%

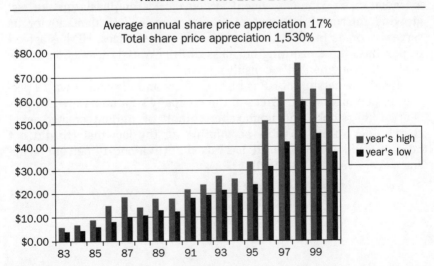

The share price of Hershey went from $4 in 1983 to $65 in 2000. The dollars invested in Hershey in 1983 appreciated 1,530 percent in eighteen years.

## HEWLETT-PACKARD COMPANY
## HWP (NY)

*Share Price: $32*

*P/E: 18*

*Market Cap: $86 Billion (Large Cap)*

*Return on Share Equity: 23%*

*Yield: 1.0%*

*Dividend Payment per Share: $0.32*

*Industry: Computers and Peripherals*

*Operating Margin: 11.5%*

Everyone knows HP for its reliable printers. HP, a Dow component, is a diversified high technology company that has three main business segments: printing and imaging systems; computing systems; information technology services. The computer products unit, develops hardware and software systems, networking products, and provides maintenance and support services. The electronic test and measurement unit providing maintenance and support for electronic equipment was spun off in 2000 as an independent entity, Agilent Technologies, to HP's shareholders. HP's foreign sales are 55 percent of its total. Sales in Asia were climbing rapidly, until the 1998 turmoil in that area caused a sharp drop in sales. At the same time, European operations were doing well. HP has recently entered into a cost-cutting program. On the bright side, HP has a large base of installed printers and is selling its very profitable printer supplies to this base. HP's UNIX-based servers and Window's NT are selling well. The company is branching into electronic commerce through its purchase of VeriFone, a leader in electronic payment systems. HP's emphasis on the fast growing internet infrastructure market may lead to demand for its servers, storage products, and consulting and services. HP has agreed to purchase the consulting business of PriceWaterhouseCoopers. The deal will strengthen HP's consulting arm.

Inside ownership of HP is high. Officers and directors own 19 percent of common stock. Trusts of the company's founders own 16 percent of the stock. The nontaxable spinoff of Agilent created great shareholder value, possibly accounting for the fact that HP did not raise its dividend in 2000. HP has raised its dividend 17 percent on average every year (1983–2000).

## Annual Dividend Payment Per Share 1983–2000

Current yield on original 1983 investment 8%
Average annual dividend growth 17%
Total dividend growth 1,500%

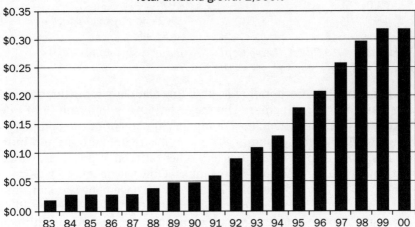

In 1983 one share of Hewlett-Packard cost $4.25 and the dividend payment was $0.02 a share. By 2000 the dividend payment had risen to $0.32 a share; that is a 8 percent yield on the dollars invested in Hewlett-Packard in 1983. The yield went from 0.4 percent to 8 percent over eighteen years.

## Annual Share Price 1983–2000

Average annual share price appreciation 17%
Total share price appreciation 1,500%

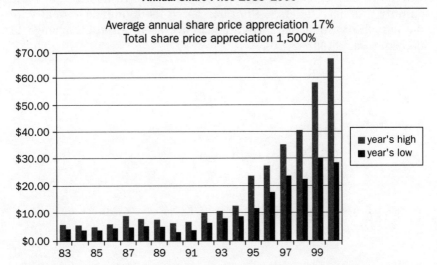

The share price of Hewlett-Packard went from $4.25 in 1983 to $68 in 2000. The dollars invested in Hewlett-Packard in 1983 appreciated 1,500 percent in eighteen years.

# JEFFERSON-PILOT CORP.
## JP (NY)

*Share Price: $72*                  *Yield: 2.1%*

*P/E: 15*                           *Dividend Payment per Share:*
                                    *$1.44*

*Market Cap: $6.3 Billion (Large Cap)*    *Industry: Insurance (Life)*

*Return on Share Equity: 15.5%*

Jefferson-Pilot Corporation is a holding company for insurance and communications companies. The major holding is Jefferson-Pilot Life Insurance Company, which accounts for 50 percent of the company's revenues. They sell life and health insurance to both groups and individuals. They also sell annuities and other retirement products, which accounts for 20 percent of JP's revenues. Other segments of Jefferson-Pilot provide fire and casualty insurance. Management services, mutual funds, and title insurance complete the mix. Jefferson-Pilot Communications Company, which owns three television and thirteen radio stations, contributes slightly under 10 percent of the corporation's business.

Jefferson-Pilot hopes to realize increased profits from equity-indexed annuities, a subject that you will recall from the annuities chapter. These accounted for 40 percent of annuities sales in early 1998. JP has also been expanding its distribution network; it recently entered into an agreement with twelve banks to sell its insurance and annuity products. Jefferson-Pilot has raised its dividends annually for the past thirty-three years. Dividends have been raised on average 11 percent a year (1983–2000).

## Annual Dividend Payment Per Share 1983–2000

Current yield on original 1983 investment 41%
Average annual dividend growth 11%
Total dividend growth 530%

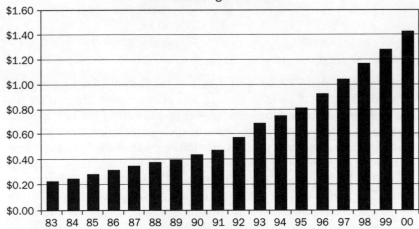

In 1983 one share of Jefferson-Pilot cost $3.50 and the dividend payment was $0.23 a share. By 2000 the dividend payment had risen to $1.44 a share; that is a 41 percent yield on the dollars invested in Jefferson-Pilot in 1983. The yield went from 6.5 percent to 41 percent over eighteen years.

## Annual Share Price 1983–2000

Average annual share price appreciation 19%
Total share price appreciation 2,010%

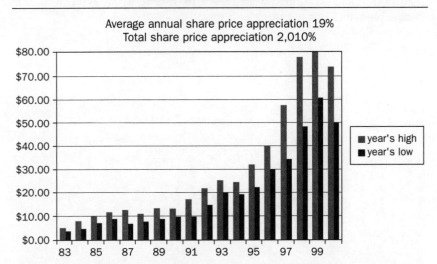

The share price of Jefferson-Pilot went from $3.50 in 1983 to $74 in 2000. The dollars invested in Jefferson-Pilot in 1983 appreciated 2,010 percent in eighteen years.

## NORTHERN TRUST CORPORATION
## NTRS (NDQ)

*Share Price: $82*                      *Yield: 0.8%*

*P/E: 41*                               *Dividend Payment per Share:*
                                        *$0.54*

*Market Cap: $18.4 Billion (Large Cap)*   *Industry: Banking*

*Return on Share Equity: 19%*

Northern Trust Corporation is one of the nation's leading individual and corporate financial fiduciaries, operating in nine states and five foreign countries. Northern Trust provides all of the services that banks usually provide such as loans and clearing house functions. Fee based services, however, are driving their growth. Fees from trust management are growing at 15 percent a year. At Northern Trust, trust fees accounted for 52 percent of revenues and 77 percent of non-interest income. The personal trust fee revenues are growing in Arizona, California, Texas, Illinois, and Florida. Business on the corporate side is also growing, with increasing custody, retirement, and advisory services.

As the name "trust" implies, this company is concentrating its resources in the direction of personal financial consulting and management of trusts. This business is financially rewarding and will increase logarithmically as the baby boom generation approaches retirement.

Insiders own about 11.5 percent of the common stock, and one of its competitors, U.S. Trust, owns about 6 percent of Northern Trust's common stock. Northern Trust raised its dividend on average 12 percent a year over the past eighteen years.

### Annual Dividend Payment Per Share 1983–2000

Current yield on original 1983 investment 43%
Average annual dividend growth 12%
Total dividend growth 620%

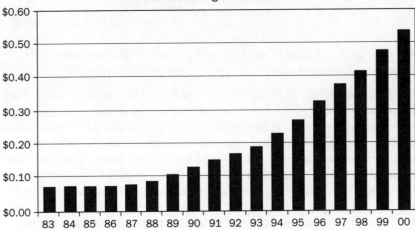

In 1983 one share of Northern Trust cost $1.25 and the dividend payment was $0.075 a share. By 2000 the dividend payment had risen to $0.54 a share; that is a 43 percent yield on the dollars invested in Northern Trust in 1983. The yield went from 6 percent to 44 percent over eighteen years.

### Annual Share Price 1983–2000

Average annual share price appreciation 27%
Total share price appreciation 7,260%

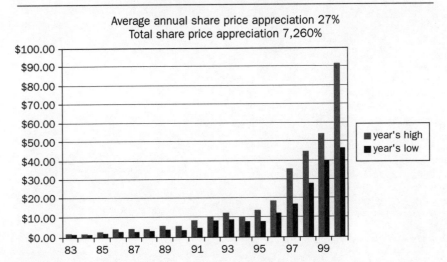

The share price of Northern Trust went from $1.25 in 1983 to $92 in 2000. The dollars invested in Northern Trust in 1983 appreciated 7,260 percent in eighteen years.

# PPG INDUSTRIES
# PPG (NY)

*Share Price: $45*                                    *Yield: 3.5%*

*P/E: 12*                                             *Dividend Payment per Share:*
                                                      *$1.60*

*Market Cap: $7.6 Billion (Large Cap)*                *Industry: Chemical Manufacturing*

*Return on Share Equity: 21%*                         *Operating Margin: 20%*

PPG Industries (known in my younger years as Pittsburgh Plate Glass) is a dominant manufacturer of coatings, glass products, specialty chemicals, and resins. It is the world's largest producer of automobile and industrial coatings and the second largest manufacturer of fiberglass products. It has 110 plants in 22 countries: international business accounts for 33 percent of its revenues. Officers own 1 percent of stock, but an ESOP (employee ownership) owns another 9 percent. This company has strong growth prospects, but its bottom line is dependent on the price and supply of oil and gas, which may have a negative effect in the future.

At current prices, PPG is well below its cash flow line and has an attractive dividend yield. Value investors should consider this "old economy" manufacturing giant. PPG has raised its dividend every year for the past twenty-nine years. It has raised dividend payment on average 10 percent annually for the past eighteen years.

### Annual Dividend Payment Per Share 1983–2000

Current yield on original 1983 investment 23%
Average annual dividend growth 10%
Total dividend growth 450%

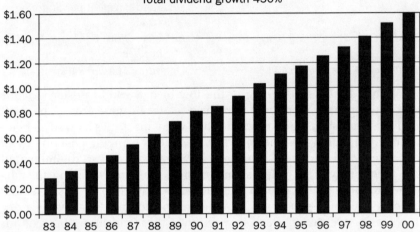

In 1983 one share of PPG cost $7 and the dividend payment was $0.29 a share. By 2000 the dividend payment had risen to $1.60 a share; that is a 23 percent yield on the dollars invested in PPG in 1983. The yield went from 4.1 percent to 23 percent over eighteen years.

### Annual Share Price 1983–2000

Average annual share price appreciation 13%
Total share price appreciation 830%

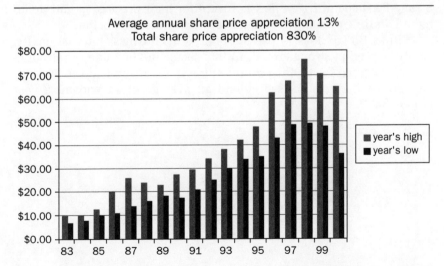

The share price of PPG went from $7 in 1983 to $65 in 2000. The dollars invested in PPG in 1983 appreciated 830 percent in eighteen years.

# PITNEY BOWES, INC.
## PBI (NY)

| | |
|---|---|
| *Share Price: $31* | *Yield: 3.7%* |
| *P/E: 12* | *Dividend Payment per Share: $1.14* |
| *Market Cap: $7.1 Billion (Large Cap)* | *Industry: Office Equipment and Supplies* |
| *Return on Share Equity: 38.5%* | *Operating Margin: 34%* |

Pitney Bowes is the king of the low-tech world of postage meters and mailing equipment. It is the world leader in these areas. The company also sells facsimile machines and copy machines as well as management, financing, and leasing services. PB is bringing post offices all over the world into the digital age with its state-of-the-art digital metering technology. These digital meter machines are replacing the mechanical ones. PB has also introduced a new line of systems that automate all mail-processing functions. The company receives service fees for the maintenance and inspection of these machines. Inspections can be done remotely through modems. PB's Business Services segment is filling an outsourcing demand for administrative tasks such as mail-room operations at large corporations. With the advent of the euro, Pitney Bowes sees opportunities to sell its postal equipment and services in Europe. This company had a disappointing year 2000 due to deferred sales of high-end mailing systems and weakness of the euro. Their earnings increased, but not as much as analysts expected. Strong R&D spending on new software for mail processing and document handling systems should make their future look better.

Pitney Bowes does 14 percent of all of its business internationally. Analysts predict strong growth in this sector in 2001 due to introduction of Personal Post Office product line in Germany and the UK. Pitney Bowes has raised its dividend an average of 14 percent a year (1983–2000).

### Annual Dividend Payment Per Share 1983–2000

Current yield on original 1983 investment 44%
Average annual dividend growth 14%
Total dividend growth 940%

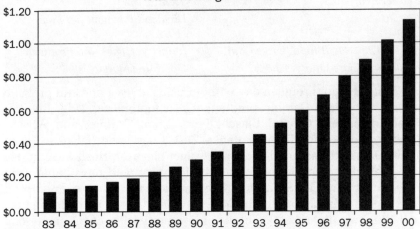

In 1983 one share of Pitney Bowes cost $2.60 and the dividend payment was $0.11 a share. By 2000 the dividend payment had risen to $1.14 a share; that is a 44 percent yield on the dollars invested in Pitney Bowes in 1983. The yield went from 4 percent to 44 percent over eighteen years.

### Annual Share Price 1983–2000

Average annual share price appreciation 18%
Total share price appreciation 1,980%

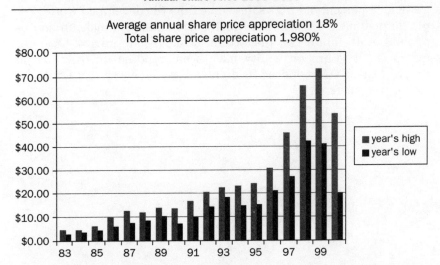

The share price of Pitney Bowes went from $2.60 in 1983 to $54 in 2000. The dollars invested in Pitney Bowes in 1983 appreciated 1,980 percent in eighteen years.

## PROCTER & GAMBLE CORP.
## PG (NY)

*Share Price: $73.8*  
*P/E: 30*

*Yield: 1.9%*  
*Dividend Payment per Share: $1.28*

*Market Cap: $91 Billion (Large Cap)*  
*Return on Share Equity: 28.8%*

*Industry: Household Products*  
*Operating Margin: 23.5%*

You can't go through a day without using at least one and probably several Procter & Gamble products: Crest toothpaste, Tide, Era, and Cheer detergent, Oxydol bleach, Ivory soap, Tampax and Always, Downy and Bounce fabric softener, Zest, Coast, and Safeguard soap, Dawn, Joy, and Cascade for dishes, Comet cleanser, Head & Shoulders and Prell shampoo, Bounty, Charmin, Pampers, and Luvs paper products, Cover Girl, Old Spice, and Noxema for personal care. Food products include Hawaiian Punch, Folgers Coffee, Crisco, and Olestra (new substitute for dietary fat). This is only a partial list of the many consumer products produced by the 110,000 employees of this corporation. P&G is launching some new products, one that is doing better than expected is Febreze, a fabric deodorizer that was introduced last spring and may become a $100 million a year product.

Proctor & Gamble does about one-third of its business in foreign countries. P&G's sales are growing in Latin America, especially Mexico. There is long term growth potential in the emerging economies, at present 75 percent of P&G's sales come from the developed world. People throughout the world need toothpaste and soap; makeup and deodorant will follow as the world economy improves. Operating margins and return on equity have been trending up over the last twelve years. P&G has raised its dividend payout every year for the last forty-seven years.

### Annual Dividend Payment Per Share 1983–2000

Current yield on original 1983 investment 16%
Average annual dividend growth 9%
Total dividend growth 360%

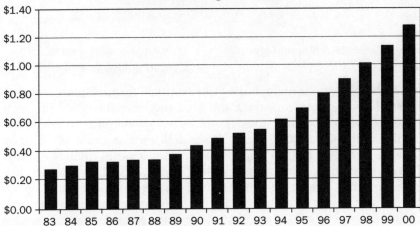

In 1983 one share of Procter & Gamble cost $8 and the dividend payment was $0.28 a share. By 2000 the dividend payment had risen to $1.28 a share; that is a 16 percent yield on the dollars invested in Procter & Gamble in 1983. The yield went from 3.5 percent to 16 percent over eighteen years.

### Annual Share Price 1983–2000

Average annual share price appreciation 16%
Total share price appreciation 1,380%

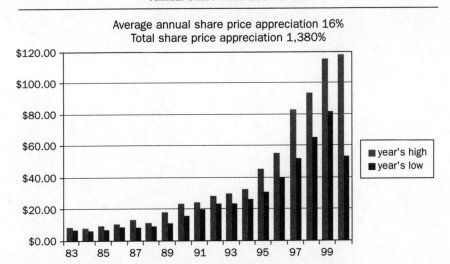

The share price of Procter & Gamble went from $8 in 1983 to $118 in 2000. The dollars invested in Procter & Gamble in 1983 appreciated 1,380 percent in eighteen years.

# SARA LEE CORP.
# SLE (NY)

*Share Price: 25*

*P/E: 18*

*Market Cap: $18.5 Billion (Large Cap)*

*Yield: 2.4%*

*Dividend Payment per Share:*
*$0.53*

*Industry: Food Processing*

*Operating Margin: 13.4%*

Sara Lee Corp. is a diversified international manufacturer and marketer of brand-name consumer and food products. The food products include coffee, specialty meats, and baked goods with name brands such as Hillshire Farms, Jimmy Dean, Ball Park, Kahn's, Mr. Turkey, Egberts, and Sara Lee. The consumer products group includes Hanes, L'eggs, Kiwi, Bali, Champion, Playtex, Coach, and Dim. International sales account for over 40 percent of total company sales. Sara Lee has been restructuring, which is widening gross margins. The company is in the process of divesting assets with low return on capital, selling non-core businesses, and increasing use of outsourcing. The savings from reduced capital spending is being used to buy back shares ($3 billion by the end of 2000).

Sara Lee Corp. has raised dividends annually for twenty-four consecutive years. Dividend payments have been raised on average 12 percent a year (1983–2000).

### Annual Dividend Payment Per Share 1983–2000

Current yield on original 1983 investment 44%
Average annual dividend growth 12%
Total dividend growth 660%

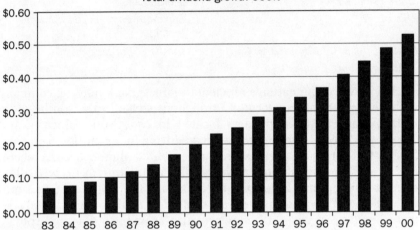

In 1983 one share of Sara Lee cost $1.20 and the dividend payment was $0.07 a share. By 2000 the dividend payment had risen to $0.53 a share; that is a 44 percent yield on the dollars invested in Sara Lee in 1983. The yield went from 5.8 percent to 44 percent over eighteen years.

### Annual Share Price 1983–2000

Average annual share price appreciation 18%
Total share price appreciation 1,980%

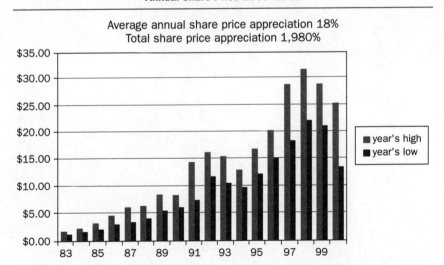

The share price of Sara Lee went from $1.20 in 1983 to $25 in 2000. The dollars invested in Sara Lee in 1983 appreciated 1,980 percent in eighteen years.

# WACHOVIA CORP.
## WB (NY)

*Share Price: $57*

*P/E: 14*

*Market Cap: $10 Billion (Large Cap)*

*Return on Share Equity: 16%*

*Yield: 4.2%*

*Dividend Payment per Share: $2.28*

*Industry: Banking*

Wachovia is the nation's nineteenth-largest bank holding company with nearly 800 offices located throughout states in the southeastern United States. Offices are also located in New York, Chicago, and Tokyo. Wachovia is in the process of acquiring Interstate/Johnson Lane (IJL), a full-service securities brokerage, which should become accretive to earnings in subsequent years. The acquisition of IJL will allow cross-selling opportunities; the IJL brokers could sell Wachovia's mutual funds and the bank's corporate customers could obtain IJL's investment banking services. Wachovia is also seeking to obtain corporate debt and equity underwriting capabilities, which the acquisition of IJL will provide.

Wachovia has raised its dividend every year for the last twenty-three years. The past eighteen years Wachovia has raised its dividend payment on average 12 percent a year.

### Annual Dividend Payment Per Share 1983–2000

Current yield on original 1983 investment 37%
Average annual dividend growth 12%
Total dividend growth 640%

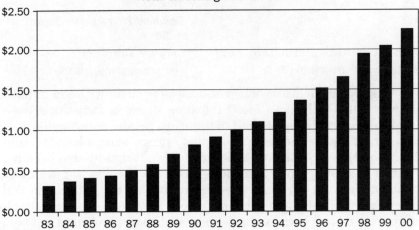

In 1983 one share of Wachovia cost $6.20 and the dividend payment was $0.31 a share. By 2000 the dividend payment had risen to $2.28 a share; that is a 37 percent yield on the dollars invested in Wachovia in 1983. The yield went from 5 percent to 37 percent over eighteen years.

### Annual Share Price 1983–2000

Average annual share price appreciation 15%
Total share price appreciation 1,110%

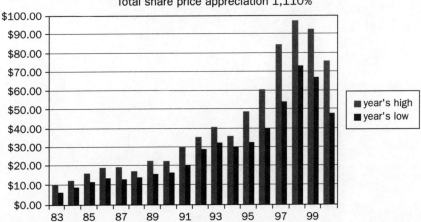

The share price of Wachovia went from $6.20 in 1983 to $75 in 2000. The dollars invested in Wachovia in 1983 appreciated 1,110 percent in eighteen years.

# WALGREEN CO.
## WAG (NY)

*Share Price: $41*

*P/E: 54*

*Market Cap: $38.4 Billion (Large Cap)*

*Return on Share Equity: 18%*

*Yield: 0.3%*

*Dividend Payment per Share: $0.14*

*Industry: Drugstore*

*Operating Margin: 7.1%*

Walgreen is the nation's largest drug store chain with $15 billion a year in sales. Walgreen's has 3,165 drug stores in forty-three states. Their pharmacies generate half of the sales, general merchandise is 23 percent of sales, and nonprescription drugs, cosmetics, toiletries, liquor, and beverages are the balance of sales. Walgreen's has been renovating its existing stores and adding new stores. Its has had twenty-six consecutive years of record sales and profits. As an aside, when Walgreen opened a new store in my neighborhood a few years back, the old drug store a block away from the new Walgreen store could not compete with the service, efficiency, and lower prices at Walgreen's. Walgreen is pursuing an aggressive expansion strategy. It is planning to operate 6,000 stores by the year 2010. Overseas expansion is untested.

Officers and directors own 1.8 percent of the stock. Walgreen has raised its dividends for twenty-five consecutive years. The past eighteen years the company has increased dividends on average 11 percent annually.

---

**Annual Dividend Payment Per Share 1983–2000**

---

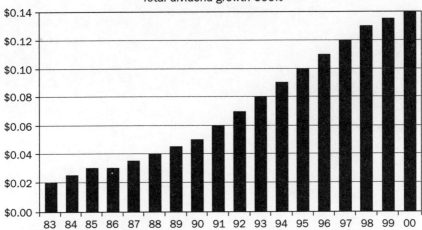

Current yield on original 1983 investment 11%
Average annual dividend growth 11%
Total dividend growth 600%

In 1983 one share of Walgreen cost $1.25 and the dividend payment was $0.02 a share. By 2000 the dividend payment had risen to $0.14 a share; that is an 11 percent yield on the dollars invested in Walgreen in 1983. The yield went from 1.6 percent to 11 percent over eighteen years.

---

**Annual Share Price 1983–2000**

---

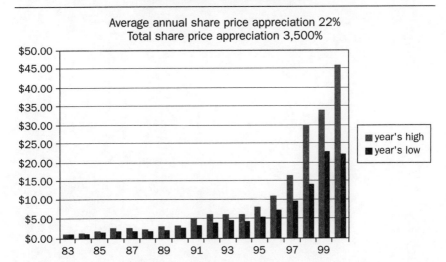

Average annual share price appreciation 22%
Total share price appreciation 3,500%

The share price of Walgreen went from $1.25 in 1983 to $45 in 2000. The dollars invested in Walgreen in 1983 appreciated 3,500 percent in eighteen years.

# The Mules

*High Initial Yield, but Slow Dividend Growth*

## AMERICAN WATER WORKS COMPANY, INC.
## AWK (NY)

| | |
|---|---|
| *Share Price: $27* | *Yield: 3.4%* |
| *P/E: 17* | *Dividend Payment per Share: $0.90* |
| *Market Cap: $2.4 Billion (Mid Cap)* | *Industry: Water Utility* |

American Water Works is the largest investor-owned water utility in the United States. It operates in twenty-three states and has been in business for forty-nine years as the American Water System.

The Ware family owns 20 percent of the outstanding common stock. Officers and directors own 22 percent of common shares. The company has been a slow-growing utility that has raised its dividend every year for the past twenty-five years. Growth may be picking up. American Water Works has become a leading consolidator in the water industry. Many smaller municipalities are finding it more cost efficient to turn over their water systems to American Water Works. In 1998 the company acquired nineteen smaller water systems. The company brings economies of scale to the water business by providing a full range of centralized support functions to its subsidiaries. Geographic diversification (American operates water facilities in twenty-three states) allows this company to hedge its exposure to the impact of regional weather and local water quality laws. There is also a need for water cleaning just about everywhere in the world, although American's expansion is all within the continental United States at this time.

Dividend growth of 9 percent a year is excellent for a utility company. Currently, its share price of $27 yields a 3.4 percent dividend.

---

**Annual Dividend Payment Per Share 1983–2000**

---

Current yield on original 1983 investment 18%
Average annual dividend growth 9%
Total dividend growth 400%

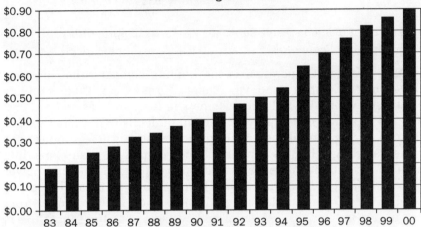

In 1983 one share of American Water Works cost $4.90 and the dividend payment was $0.18 a share. By 2000 the dividend payment had risen to $0.90 a share; that is an 18 percent yield on the dollars invested in American Water Works in 1983. The yield went from 4 percent to 18 percent over eighteen years.

---

**Annual Share Price 1983–2000**

---

Average annual share price appreciation 10%
Total share price appreciation 450%

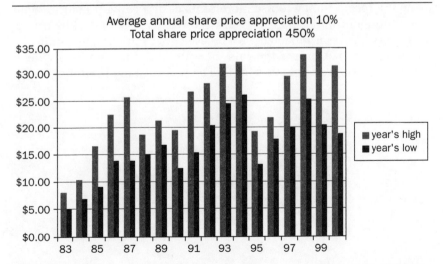

The share price of American Water Works went from $4.90 in 1983 to $27 in 2000. The dollars invested in American Water Works in 1983 appreciated 450 percent in eighteen years.

## DUKE ENERGY CORPORATION
## DUK (NY)

*Share Price: $85*
*P/E: 24*

*Market Cap: $32 Billion (Large Cap)*
*Return on Share Equity: 13%*

*Yield: 2.6%*
*Dividend Payment per Share:*
*$2.20*
*Industry: Electric Utility*

Duke Energy Corporation is the holding company that includes Duke Power Company and Pan Energy Corporation. Duke supplies electric power to two million customers in the Carolinas and has natural gas pipelines that supply 12 percent of the natural gas in the U.S. Duke is buying natural gas gathering and processing assets, along with some natural gas liquids pipelines. The company is also expanding pipeline operations in the Northeast. Duke is planning to build power plants in Maine, Texas, and Florida in preparation for deregulation and competition. Duke also has a significant portion of its revenues from non energy industrial subsidiaries and overseas operations that Duke is expanding.

Duke produces 37 percent of its electricity from three nuclear plants, and 56 percent from coal. Duke is a large-cap utility with a dividend payment that has a yield below its industry peers. Duke has raised its dividends annually for twenty-three of the past twenty-five years. Utilities are slow growers, as is their rate of dividend growth, 4 percent annually for Duke Energy (1983–2000). This company has made it a recent policy to use more of its cash for investment in plant and equipment rather than to aggressively increase its dividend payouts. This has been reflected in increased share prices. Duke must be the exception that proves the rule: in spite of not raising its dividend for the last two years, I have kept this company in my portfolio.

### Annual Dividend Payment Per Share 1983–2000

Current yield on original 1983 investment 20%
Average annual dividend growth 4%
Total dividend growth 90%

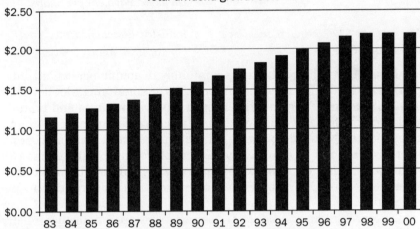

In 1983 one share of Duke Energy cost $11 and the dividend payment was $1.16 a share. By 2000 the dividend payment had risen to $2.20 a share; that is a 20 percent yield on the dollars invested in Duke Energy in 1983. The yield went from 10 percent to 20 percent over eighteen years.

### Annual Share Price 1983–2000

Average annual share price appreciation 12%
Total share price appreciation 720%

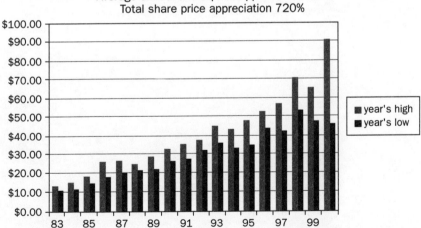

The share price of Duke Energy went from $11 in 1983 to $90 in 2000. The dollars invested in Duke Energy in 1983 appreciated 720 percent in eighteen years.

## EXXONMOBIL CORP.
## XOM (NY)

*Share Price: $87*

*P/E: 21*

*Market Cap: $306 Billion (Large Cap)*

*Return on Share Equity: 22%*

*Yield: 2.0%*

*Dividend Payment per Share: $1.78*

*Industry: Petroleum (Integrated)*

*Operating Margin: 16%*

Exxon Corp, the world's largest publicly owned integrated oil company, almost doubled its size through its merger with Mobil Oil in 1999. ExxonMobil is primarily engaged in exploration for and production of crude oil and natural gas; manufacturing of petroleum products; transportation and sale of crude oil, natural gas, and petroleum products. ExxonMobil is also involved in exploration for and mining of minerals in addition to oil. Oil prices usually ride a roller coaster of their own, and the share price of oil companies usually follows the wild ride.

ExxonMobil has raised its dividend on average 5 percent annually for the past eighteen years.

## Annual Dividend Payment Per Share 1983–2000

Current yield on original 1983 investment 25%
Average annual dividend growth 5%
Total dividend growth 130%

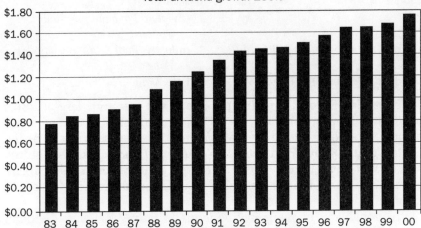

In 1983 one share of ExxonMobil cost $7 and the dividend payment was $0.78 a share. By 2000 the dividend payment had risen to $1.78 a share; that is a 25 percent yield on the dollars invested in ExxonMobil in 1983. The yield went from 10 percent to 25 percent over eighteen years.

## Annual Share Price 1983–2000

Average annual share price appreciation 16%
Total share price appreciation 1,260%

The share price of ExxonMobil went from $7 in 1983 to $95 in 2000. The dollars invested in ExxonMobil in 1983 appreciated 1,260 percent in eighteen years.

# NEW PLAN EXCEL REALTY TRUST
# NXL (NY)

*Share Price: $13*

*P/E: 10*

*Market Cap: $1.1 Billion (Mid Cap)*

*Dividends Declared to FFO: 80%*

*Yield: 12.4%*

*Dividend Payment per Share: $1.65*

*Industry: Real Estate Investment Trust*

*Book Value per Share: $15.25*

New Plan Excel Realty Trust is one of the countries largest REITs (real-estate investment trust). New Plan specializes in apartments and income producing shopping malls mainly in the Eastern half of the United States. New Plan leases to many national chains including Kmart, Wal-Mart, Winn-Dixie, Food Lion, and Krogers. The company owns almost 20 million square feet of retail space and over 8,000 apartment units.

Although the increase in dividends is only 7 percent, dividend yield starts out at a very high level. If revenues go up, the dividend increase will go up as REITs are required by law to pay out most of their profits in dividends to shareholders. This stock has performed poorly due to continued problems following the takeover of Excel by New Plan Realty. With an astronomical dividend payout of 12.4 percent and a share price below the book value of the hard assets of this company, this represents a way to invest in real estate and may be viewed as a fixed-income investment.

Officers and directors own about 8.5 percent of the outstanding shares.

## Annual Dividend Payment Per Share 1983–2000

Current yield on original 1983 investment 24%
Average annual dividend growth 7%
Total dividend growth 220%

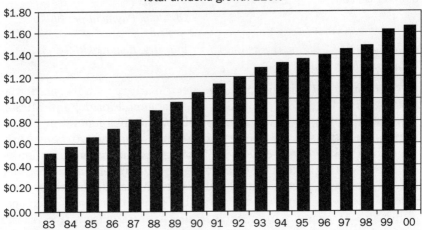

In 1983 one share of New Plan Excel Realty Trust cost $7 and the dividend payment was $0.51 a share. By 2000 the dividend payment had risen to $1.65 a share; that is a 24 percent yield on the dollars invested in New Plan Excel Realty in 1983. The yield went from 7 percent to 24 percent over eighteen years.

## Annual Share Price 1983–2000

Average annual share price appreciation 5%
Total share price appreciation 140%

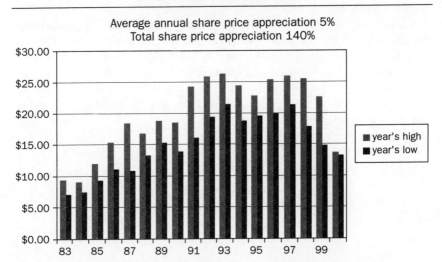

The share price of New Plan Excel Realty Trust went from $7 in 1983 to $17 in 2000. The dollars invested in New Plan Excel Realty in 1983 appreciated 140 percent in eighteen years.

## SOUTHERN COMPANY
## SO (NY)

*Share Price: $33*
*P/E: 17*

*Yield: 4.1%*
*Dividend Payment per Share:*
*$1.34*

*Market Cap: $20.2 Billion (Large Cap)*
*Return on Share Equity: 13%*

*Industry: Electric Utility*

The Southern Company is a large electric utility with its base in the southeastern United States, in Georgia, Alabama, Florida, and Mississippi. Southern is, however, aggressively expanding generating capacity into other parts of the country, including New England, New York, and California, giving Southern 9,500 megawatts of generation. Southern is one of the larger cap electric utility companies in the country and its goal is to increase marketable capacity to 20,000 megawatts. Seventy-five percent of Southern's electric generation comes from coal with about 17 percent from nuclear and 4 percent from hydro. The electric utility industry is undergoing deregulation. This is a state by state process, since these utilities have been regulated by the states they reside in. Throughout the 1990s utilities, under the threat of deregulation and competition, have been focusing on expanding their nonregulated businesses and generating low-cost electricity to stay competitive. Retail electricity markets will probably be open to competition in the next ten years. Southern has also expanded its utility operations overseas.

Like most electric utilities, Southern Company has a high initial dividend yield that is good for those needing immediate income. The growth of its dividend, however, is very slow, typical of utilities. Southern's goal is to raise annual share earnings 6–8 percent a year. Southern has not raised its dividend over the last two years while it has prepared to spin off Southern Energies, Inc., which will be a significant value to shareholders.

## Annual Dividend Payment Per Share 1983–2000

Current yield on original 1983 investment 19%
Average annual dividend growth 3%
Total dividend growth 50%

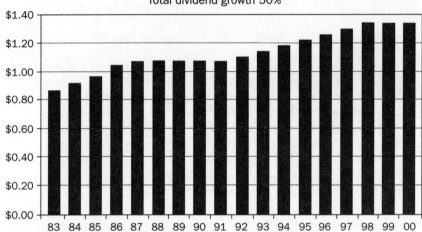

In 1983 one share of Southern cost $7 and the dividend payment was $0.87 a share. By 2000 the dividend payment had risen to $1.34 a share, that is a 19 percent yield on the dollars invested in Southern in 1983. The yield went from 12 percent to 19 percent over eighteen years

## Annual Share Price 1983–2000

Average annual share price appreciation 9%
Total share price appreciation 400%

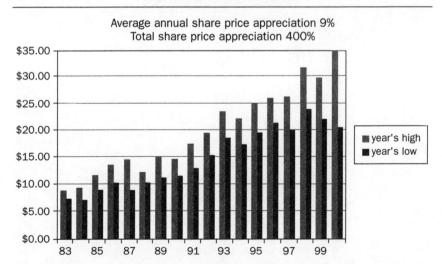

The share price of Southern went from $7 in 1983 to $35 in 2000. The dollars invested in Southern in 1983 appreciated 400 percent in eighteen years.

# TECO ENERGY, INC.
## TE (NY)

*Share Price: $32*

*P/E: 17*

*Market Cap: $3.7 Billion (Mid Cap)*

*Return on Share Equity: 14.5%*

*Yield: 4.2%*

*Dividend Payment per Share: $1.35*

*Industry: Electric Utility*

TECO Energy's main holding is Tampa Electric, which supplies electric power to over half a million customers in central Florida. Residential and commercial customer growth has climbed by more than 3 percent over the past year. The company gets more than a quarter of its earnings from unregulated businesses such as transport, coal mining, and independent power projects, which can earn higher profits than utility operations. Almost all of TECO's energy is produced by coal-fired plants. TECO has a large coal-mining operation and also produces methane gas from the coal fields. They also have a large, unregulated energy business here and overseas. The unregulated business should rise to around 35–40 percent of TECO's total business. TECO has accomplished this through expansion of independent power projects overseas, in countries such as Portugal and Guatemala.

TECO has raised dividends every year for the past forty-one years. This utility starts with a high dividend payment (4.1 percent) for those requiring income, but slow dividend growth (6 percent).

### Annual Dividend Payment Per Share 1983–2000

Current yield on original 1983 investment 26%
Average annual dividend growth 6%
Total dividend growth 170%

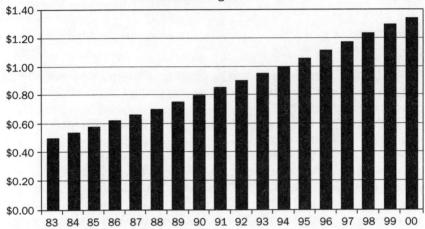

In 1983 one share of TECO cost $5.20 and the dividend payment was $0.50 a share. By 2000 the dividend payment had risen to $1.35 a share; that is a 26 percent yield on the dollars invested in TECO Energy in 1983. The yield went from 9 percent to 26 percent over eighteen years.

### Annual Share Price 1983–2000

Average annual share price appreciation 10%
Total share price appreciation 520%

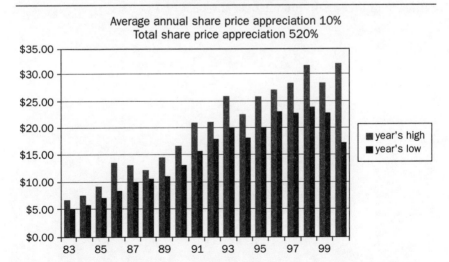

The share price of TECO went from $5.20 in 1983 to $32 in 2000. The dollars invested in TECO Energy in 1983 appreciated 520 percent in eighteen years.

# UTILICORP UNITED, INC.
## UCU (NY)

*Share Price: $29*                     *Yield: 4.1%*

*P/E: 14*                               *Dividend Payment per Share:*
                                        *$1.20*

*Market Cap: $2.4 Billion (Mid Cap)*    *Industry: Electric Utility*

*Return on Share Equity: 11%*

UtiliCorp is an energy-services provider that you may consider if you need income now and are not as concerned with growing dividends for the future.

UtiliCorp has three main divisions, providing both regulated and non regulated energy services. They provide electric services to many states, mainly in the Midwest, as well as Canada and New Zealand. This electricity is generated mainly from coal-fired plants with no exposure to nuclear energy. The Canadian component is mainly hydro-electric. The second division is a large independent supplier of natural gas known as Aquila Energy. The third division is Utilco Group, an operator of independent electric-generating projects. UtiliCorp's has a growing energy marketing business. This is a high-volume, low-margin business that UtiliCorp has managed to make profitable, where others have failed. UtiliCorp has raised dividends for forty-three consecutive years. The past eighteen years the company raised dividends at the average annual rate of 6 percent. Part of the slow rate of growth is due to the fact that the company has concentrated on growing the business rather than raising dividends over the past two years.

### Annual Dividend Payment Per Share 1983–2000

Current yield on original 1983 investment 26%
Average annual dividend growth 6%
Total dividend growth 200%

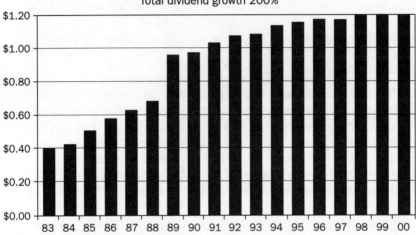

In 1983 one share of UtiliCorp cost $4.50 and the dividend payment was $0.40 a share. By 2000 the dividend payment had risen to $1.20 a share; that is a 26 percent yield on the dollars invested in UtiliCorp in 1983. The yield went from 9 percent to 26 percent over eighteen years.

### Annual Share Price 1983–2000

Average annual share price appreciation 11%
Total share price appreciation 540%

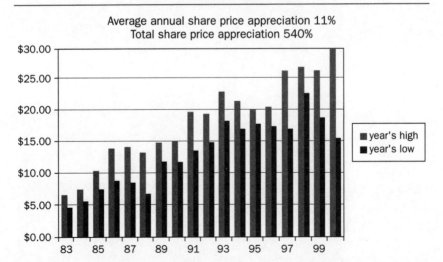

The share price of UtiliCorp went from $4.50 in 1983 to $29.00 in 2000. The dollars invested in UtiliCorp in 1983 appreciated 540 percent in 18 years.

## VERIZON COMMUNICATIONS
## VZ (NY)

*Share Price: $48*

*P/E: 13*

*Market Cap: $116.8 Billion (Large Cap)*

*Return on Share Equity: 41.5%*

*Yield: 3.2%*

*Dividend Payment per Share: $1.54*

*Industry: Telecommunication Services*

Verizon Communications was created by the merger of Bell Atlantic and GTE. The resulting company is the primary provider of local telecom services in the Mid-Atlantic region. (Bell Atlantic had merged with Nynex in 1997.) The combined companies have 100 million telephone access lines and 26 million wireless customers worldwide. Ninety-four percent of the company's switches are digital. This company is the second-largest telephone company in the U.S. and the country's wireless leader. Analysts are anticipating that this merger will be accretive to earnings and will bring cost synergies to the new company.

Verizon Communications has raised dividends on average 4 percent annually. The company has not raised dividends the last two years, presumably due to pressures from the merger and the need for telecoms to raise capital for making improvements on infrastructure, but a dividend rise is expected in 2001.

### Annual Dividend Payment Per Share 1983–2000

Current yield on original 1983 investment 19%
Average annual dividend growth 4%
Total dividend growth 110%

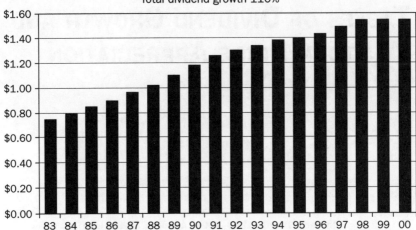

In 1983 one share of Bell Atlantic cost $8 and the dividend payment was $0.75 a share. By 2000 the dividend payment had risen to $1.54 a share; that is a 19 percent yield on the dollars invested in Bell Atlantic in 1983. The yield went from 10 percent to 19 percent over eighteen years.

### Annual Share Price 1983–2000

Average annual share price appreciation 13%
Total share price appreciation 740%

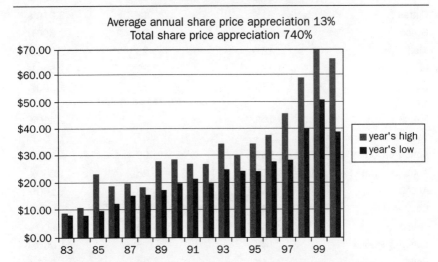

The share price of Bell Atlantic went from $8 in 1983 to $67 in 2000. The dollars invested in Bell Atlantic in 1983 appreciated 740 percent in eighteen years.

# Appendix 2

## Tables of Dividend Growth and Stock Price Appreciation

| Dividend Growth, 1983–2000 (Arranged high to low) | | | |
| --- | --- | --- | --- |
| | Average Annual Dividend Growth Rate | No. of Years Dividend Growth | Total Dividend Growth |
| Fannie Mae | 30% | 15 | 11,100% |
| Home Depot | 26% | 13 | 1,500%* |
| Wal-Mart Stores | 24% | 19 | 4,500% |
| Eaton Vance | 21% | 19 | 1,900%* |
| Cintas | 21% | 18 | 3,070% |
| Sysco | 19% | 24 | 2,300% |
| Medtronic | 18% | 23 | 1,800% |
| Philip Morris | 17% | 32 | 1,540% |
| Hewlett-Packard | 17% | 13 Not raised in 2000 | 1,500% |
| Merck | 16% | 17 | 1,410% |
| Tootsie Roll | 16% | 37 | 1,250% |
| Abbott Laboratories | 15% | 29 | 1,170% |
| Automatic Data Proc | 15% | 25 | 1,060% |
| AFLAC | 15% | 18 | 1,100% |
| Cooper Tire | 14% | 21 | 950% |
| Wrigley | 14% | 20 | 900% |
| Schering-Plough | 14% | 15 | 1,000% |
| Pall | 14% | 20 | 1,000% |

266

|  | Average Annual Dividend Growth Rate | No. of Years Dividend Growth | Total Dividend Growth |
|---|---|---|---|
| Con Agra Foods | 14% | 23 | 1,030% |
| State Street | 14% | 22 | 1,000% |
| Illinois Tool Works | 14% | 38 | 990% |
| Pitney Bowes | 14% | 17 | 940% |
| Albertson's | 13% | 28 | 850% |
|  |  | Not raised in 2000 |  |
| Wilmington Trust | 13% | 19 | 830% |
| Gillette | 13% | 23 | 830% |
| Johnson & Johnson | 13% | 38 | 790% |
| Avery Dennison | 13% | 25 | 800% |
| American International Group | 12% | 15 | 650% |
| Sara Lee | 12% | 24 | 660% |
| Hillenbrand Industries | 12% | 30 | 630% |
| Northern Trust | 12% | 15 | 620% |
| Wachovia | 12% | 23 | 640% |
| Pfizer | 12% | 33 | 620% |
| Walgreen | 11% | 25 | 600% |
| Heinz | 11% | 35 | 590% |
| PepsiCo | 11% | 29 | 520% |
| Coca-Cola | 11% | 38 | 520% |
| Clorox | 11% | 24 | 570% |
| Hershey Foods | 11% | 26 | 500% |
| Jefferson-Pilot | 11% | 33 | 530% |
| General Electric | 11% | 25 | 590% |
| Becton, Dickinson | 10% | 28 | 430% |
| PPG | 10% | 29 | 450% |
| Procter & Gamble | 9% | 47 | 360% |
| Colgate-Palmolive | 8% | 38 | 270% |

### Slow-Growing Dividends, With Immediate Income:

|  | Average Annual Dividend Growth Rate | No. of Years Dividend Growth | Total Dividend Growth |
|---|---|---|---|
| American Water Works | 9% | 25 | 400% |
| New Plan Excel Realty | 7% | 19 | 200% |

| | Average Annual Dividend Growth Rate | No. of Years Dividend Growth | Total Dividend Growth |
|---|---|---|---|
| Utilicorp | 6% | 43 | 200% |
| TECOEnergy | 6% | 41 | 220% |
| ExxonMobil | 5% | 18 | 130% |
| Duke Energy | 4% | 23 (Not raised 1999–2000) | 90% |
| Verizon | 4% | 18 | 140% |
| Southern Company | 3% | 9 (Not raised 1999–2000) | 50% |

*Home Depot started paying dividends in 1989 and Eaton Vance in 1985.

**Stock Price Appreciation, 1983–2000 (Arranged high to low)**

| | Average annual Stock Price Appreciation | Total Share Price Appreciation |
|---|---|---|
| Home Depot | 54% | 26,820% |
| Medtronic | 29% | 9,730% |
| AFLAC | 29% | 9,770% |
| Wal-Mart | 29% | 9,900% |
| State Street | 28% | 8,400% |
| Northern Trust | 27% | 7,260% |
| Eaton Vance | 26% | 3,820% |
| Tootsie Roll | 25% | 5,500% |
| Fannie Mae | 25% | 5,210% |
| Cintas | 25% | 5,490% |
| American International Group | 25% | 5,050% |
| Schering-Plough | 24% | 4,730% |
| Wrigley | 23% | 4,080% |
| PepsiCo | 23% | 3,980% |
| Becton, Dickinson | 23% | 1,520% |
| Merck | 23% | 4,170% |
| Pfizer | 22% | 3,560% |
| Gillette | 22% | 3,210% |
| Coca-Cola | 22% | 3,370% |
| Automatic Data Proc. | 22% | 3,350% |
| Walgreen | 22% | 3,500% |
| General Electric | 21% | 3,140% |

| | | |
|---|---|---|
| Illinois Tool Works | 21% | 2,780% |
| Sysco | 21% | 2,850% |
| Colgate-Palmolive | 20% | 2,710% |
| Clorox | 19% | 2,100% |
| Jefferson-Pilot | 19% | 2,010% |
| Abbott Laboratories | 19% | 2,140% |
| Philip Morris | 19% | 2,150% |
| Johnson & Johnson | 18% | 1,960% |
| Pitney Bowes | 18% | 1,980% |
| Avery Dennison | 18% | 1,710% |
| Sara Lee | 18% | 1,980% |
| Albertson's | 17% | 1,460% |
| Hershey Foods | 17% | 1,530% |
| Hewlett-Packard | 17% | 1,500% |
| ExxonMobil | 16% | 1,260% |
| Procter & Gamble | 16% | 1,380% |
| Wilmington Trust | 16% | 1,430% |
| Hillenbrand Industries | 15% | 1,080% |
| Wachovia | 15% | 1,110% |
| Heinz | 15% | 1,080% |
| Cooper Tire | 14% | 970% |
| PPG | 13% | 830% |
| TECO Energy | 13% | 606% |
| Verizon | 12% | 720% |
| Duke Energy | 12% | 720% |
| Con Agra Foods | 11% | 550% |
| UtiliCorp United | 11% | 540% |
| American Water Works | 10% | 450% |
| Pall | 9% | 400% |
| Southern Company | 9% | 400% |
| New Plan Excel Realty Trust | 5% | 140% |

# APPENDIX 3

## DIRECT STOCK PURCHASE PLANS

**AFLAC, Inc.**

1932 Wynnton Road
Columbus, GA 31999
www.aflac.com
800-235-2667

Plan features: Cash dividend, dividend reinvestment option,
optional cash purchase. Minimum initial purchase (non-
shareholder), $750; minimum optional cash purchase
(shareholder), $50; maximum optional cash purchase,
$120,000.
Plan Fees: Per-share commission on sales, varies.

**Becton, Dickinson and Co.**

One Becton Drive,
Franklin Lakes, NJ 07417
www.bd.com
800-955-4743

Plan features: Cash dividend, dividend reinvestment option,
optional cash purchase. Minimum initial purchase (non-
shareholder), $250; minimum optional cash purchase
(shareholder), $50; maximum optional cash purchase, none.
Plan Fees: Per-share commission on sales, $0.15. Sales fee, $15.

## Duke Energy Corp.

422 South Church Street
Charlotte, NC 28242
www.duke-energy.com
800-488-3853

Plan Features: Cash dividend, dividend reinvestment option, optional cash purchase. Minimum initial purchase (non-shareholder), $250; minimum optional cash purchase (shareholder), $25; maximum optional cash purchase (per year), $20,000.
Plan Fees: None.

## ExxonMobil Corp.

5959 Las Colinas Blvd.
Irving, TX 75039
www.exxon.com
800-252-1800

Plan Features: Cash dividend, dividend reinvestment option, optional cash purchase. Minimum initial purchase (non-shareholder), $250; minimum optional cash purchase (shareholder), $50; maximum optional cash purchase (per year), $200,000.
Plan Fees: Per-share commission, $0.10. Sales fee, $5.

## Fannie Mae

3900 Wisconsin Avenue NW
Washington, DC 20016
www.fanniemae.com
800-BUY-FANNIE

Plan Features: Cash dividend, dividend reinvestment option, optional cash purchase. Minimum initial purchase (non-shareholder), $250; minimum optional cash purchase (shareholder), $25; maximum optional cash purchase (per year), $250,000.
Plan Fees: Initial investment fee, $15. Per-share commission, $0.12. Sales fee, $15.

## General Electric Co.

3135 Easton Turnpike
Fairfield, CT 06431
www.ge.com
800-786-2543

Plan Features: Cash dividend, dividend reinvestment option,
optional cash purchase. Minimum initial purchase (non-
shareholder), $250; minimum optional cash purchase
(shareholder), $10; maximum optional cash purchase (per
year), $10,000.
Plan Fees: Initial investment fee, $7.50. Per-share commission,
$0.15. Sales fee, $10.

## Gillette Co.

Prudential Tower Building
Boston, MA 02199
www.gillette.com
888-218-2841

Plan Features: Cash dividend, dividend reinvestment option,
optional cash purchase. Minimum initial purchase (non-
shareholder), $1,000; minimum optional cash purchase
(shareholder), $100; maximum optional cash purchase (per
year), $120,000.
Plan Fees: Initial investment fee, $10. Per-share commission,
$0.15. Sales fee, $10.

## Hershey Foods Corp.

100 Crystal A Drive
PO Box 810
Hershey, PA 17033
www.hersheys.com
800-842-7629

Plan Features: Cash dividend, dividend reinvestment option,
optional cash purchase. Minimum initial purchase (non-
shareholder), $500; minimum optional cash purchase
(shareholder), $100; maximum optional cash purchase (per
month), $10,000.
Plan Fees: Per-share commission, $0.12. Sales fee, $15.

## Hillenbrand Industries, Inc.

700 State Route 46 East,
Batesville, IN 47006
www.hillenbrand.com
888-665-9611

Plan Features: Cash dividend, dividend reinvestment option, optional cash purchase. Minimum initial purchase (non-shareholder), $250; minimum optional cash purchase (shareholder), $100; maximum optional cash purchase (per year), $50,000.

Plan Fees: Per-share commission, $0.10. Sales fee, $10.

## Home Depot, Inc.

2727 Paces Ferry Road
Atlanta, GA 30339
www.homedepot.com
800-928-0380

Plan Features: Cash dividend, dividend reinvestment option, optional cash purchase. Minimum initial purchase (non-shareholder), $250; minimum optional cash purchase (shareholder), $25; maximum optional cash purchase (per year), $100,000.

Plan Fees: Initial investment fee, $5. Per-share commission, varies. Sales fee, $10 service charge.

## Merck & Co., Inc.

One Merck Drive
Whitehouse Station, NJ 08889
www.merck.com
800-831-8248

Plan Features: Cash dividend, dividend reinvestment option, optional cash purchase. Minimum initial purchase (non-shareholder), $350; minimum optional cash purchase (shareholder), $50; maximum optional cash purchase (per year), $50,000.

Plan Fees: Initial investment fee, $5. Per-share commission, $0.01. Sales fee, $5.

## Procter & Gamble Company

One Procter & Gamble Plaza
Cincinnati, OH 45202
www.pg.com
800-764-7483

Plan Features: Cash dividend, dividend reinvestment option, optional cash purchase. Minimum initial purchase (non-shareholder), $250; minimum optional cash purchase (shareholder), $100; maximum optional purchase (per year), $120,000.

Plan Fees: Enrollment fee, $5. Per-share commission, $0.04. Sales fee (check with investor relations).

## Southern Company

270 Peachtree Street
Atlanta, GA 30303
www.southernco.com
800-565-2577

Plan Features: Cash dividend, dividend reinvestment option, option cash purchase. Minimum initial purchase (non-shareholder), $250; minimum optional cash purchase (shareholder), $25; maximum optional purchase (per year), $150,000.

Plan Fees: Enrollment fee, $10. Per-share commission, $0.06. Sales fee (check with investor relations).

## UtiliCorp United, Inc.

20 West Ninth Street
Kansas City, MO 64105
www.utilicorp.com
800-884-5426

Plan Features: Cash dividend, dividend reinvestment option, optional cash purchases. Minimum initial purchase (non-shareholder), $250; minimum optional cash purchase (shareholder), $50; maximum optional purchase (per month), $10,000.

Plan Fees: Per-share commission, varies. Sales fee (check with investor relations).

## Wal-Mart Stores, Inc.

702 SW 8th Street
Bentonville, AR 72716
www.wal-mart.com
800-438-6278

Plan Features: Cash dividend, dividend reinvestment option,
optional cash purchase. Minimum initial purchase (non-
shareholder), $250; minimum optional cash purchase
(shareholder), $50; maximum optional purchase (per year),
$150,000.
Plan Fees: Initial investment fee, $20. Per-share commission,
$0.10. Sales fee, $20.

## Walgreen Co.

200 Wilmot Road
Deerfield, IL 60015
www.walgreens.com
800-286-9178

Plan Features: Cash dividend, dividend reinvestment option,
optional cash purchases. Minimum initial purchase (non-
shareholder), $50; minimum optional cash purchase
(shareholder), $50; maximum optional purchase (per quarter),
$5,000.
Plan Fees: Enrollment fee, $10. Per-share commission, $0.10. Sales
fee, $10.

## DRIP and DSP Resource Materials

Carlson, Charles. *Buying Stocks Without a Broker.* New York: McGraw Hill, 1992.

Carlson, Charles. *No-Load Stocks.* New York: McGraw Hill, 1995.

Gerlach, Douglas. *Investor's Web Guide.* New York: Macmillan Computer Publishing, 1997.

www.netstockdirect.com. This web site provides a list of companies offering DRIPs and DSPs. The site is updated daily.

www.dripcentral.com. This web site has a comprehensive list of DRIPs and DSPs.

www.dripinvestor.com/. This is the web site of Charles Carlson. You can order a complete list of no-load stocks offering DSPs.

http://mk.ml.org/noload/. This site has a list of no-load stocks (purchase shares directly from the company).

# INDEX

# INDEX

Abbott Laboratories (ABT), 89,
144–45, 154–55
Accounting principles, standardized,
86
Aciphex, 186
Aflac, Inc. (AFL), 140, 156–57
direct stock purchase plan, 270
Albertson's, Inc. (ABS), 216–17
American Express, 135
American Home Products, 83
American International Group (AIG),
140, 158–59
American Stock Exchange, 119
American Water Works Company,
Inc. (AWK), 250–51
Annual rates of change, in *Value
Line*, 77–78
Annual reports, 70, 86
Annuities, 53–64
buying at retirement, 63
common terms used, 54–55
defaults on, 61–62
deferred, 54, 55–56
definition of, 54
dividend growth versus, 63–64
fees, 60
immediate, 54, 55
indexed, 55, 58, 60
inflation and, 56–58, 60
IRAs and, 63
joint and survivor, 55
life, 54
life insurance and, 62–63
loss of inheritance, 59
mutual funds versus, 59–60
non-spouse beneficiary and, 63
opportunity costs and, 62
penalties, 56
pros and cons of, 58–63

rating services, 62
regulations, 61
security and, 61–62
straight, 54, 55, 59, 60
summary of, 64
taxes, 56–60
for term certain, 54, 55
variable, 54–59
history of, 56–57
indexed annuities versus, 58
inflation and, 60
Apple Computer, 129
Aquila Energy, 262
Archer Daniels Midland (ADM), 66
Aricept, 198
Armour, 142, 168
Asmanex, 200
Asset allocation, 11–12, 17–18
bonds and, 45–46, 52
strategy for, 90–92
AT&T, 130–31
Automatic Data Processing (ADP),
140–41, 160–61
Avery Dennison Corp. (AVY),
148–49, 162–63

Barber, Brad, 10
*Barron's*, 67
*Beardstown Ladies, The* (Witaker),
68
Bear market, 91
Becton, Dickinson & Company (BDX),
89, 218–19
direct stock purchase plan, 270
Bell Atlantic, 264
Bells Labs, 131
Beneficiaries
designated, 111
non-spouse, annuities and, 63